JUSTICE FOR PEOPLE ON THE MOVE

By executive order, the USA has adopted an immigration policy that looks remarkably similar to a Muslim ban, and there are new threats to deport long-settled residents, such as the so-called Dreamers. Our defunct refugee system has not dealt adequately with increased refugee flows, forcing desperate people to undertake increasingly risky measures in efforts to reach safe havens. Meanwhile increased migration flows over recent years appear to have contributed to a rise in right-wing populism, apparently driving phenomena such as Brexit and Trumpism. In this original and insightful book, Gillian Brock offers answers and tools that assist us in evaluating current migration policy and in helping to determine which policies may be permissible and which are normatively indefensible. She offers a comprehensive framework for responding to the many challenges that have recently emerged, and for delivering justice for people on the move along with those affected by migration.

GILLIAN BROCK is Professor of Philosophy at the University of Auckland, New Zealand. Her books include *Global Justice: A Cosmopolitan Account* (2009), *Debating Brain Drain* (with Michael Blake, 2015), and *Cosmopolitanism versus Non-Cosmopolitanism* (2013).

JUSTICE FOR PEOPLE ON THE MOVE

Migration in Challenging Times

GILLIAN BROCK

University of Auckland

CAMBRIDGE
UNIVERSITY PRESS

CAMBRIDGE
UNIVERSITY PRESS

University Printing House, Cambridge CB2 8BS, United Kingdom

One Liberty Plaza, 20th Floor, New York, NY 10006, USA

477 Williamstown Road, Port Melbourne, VIC 3207, Australia

314–321, 3rd Floor, Plot 3, Splendor Forum, Jasola District Centre, New Delhi – 110025, India

79 Anson Road, #06–04/06, Singapore 079906

Cambridge University Press is part of the University of Cambridge.

It furthers the University's mission by disseminating knowledge in the pursuit of education, learning, and research at the highest international levels of excellence.

www.cambridge.org
Information on this title: www.cambridge.org/9781108477734
DOI: 10.1017/9781108774581

© Gillian Brock 2020

First published 2020

Printed in the United Kingdom by TJ International Ltd. Padstow Cornwall

A catalogue record for this publication is available from the British Library.

Library of Congress Cataloging-in-Publication Data
NAMES: Brock, Gillian, author.
TITLE: Justice for people on the move : migration in challenging times / Gillian Brock.
DESCRIPTION: Cambridge, United Kingdom ; New York, NY : Cambridge University Press, 2020. | Includes bibliographical references and index.
IDENTIFIERS: LCCN 2019042187 (print) | LCCN 2019042188 (ebook) | ISBN 9781108477734 (hardback) | ISBN 9781108733007 (paperback) | ISBN 9781108774581 (epub)
SUBJECTS: LCSH: Emigration and immigration–Government policy–Moral and ethical aspects. | Social justice.
CLASSIFICATION: LCC JV6271 .B76 2020 (print) | LCC JV6271 (ebook) | DDC 325.01–dc23
LC record available at https://lccn.loc.gov/2019042187
LC ebook record available at https://lccn.loc.gov/2019042188

ISBN 978-1-108-47773-4 Hardback

Contents

Preface

Migration has dominated contemporary political discourse for some years. But around 2016, the situation escalated dramatically. Suddenly migration "crises" were erupting at the borders of European states. The large-scale exodus from Syria prompted a vast population of desperate people to undertake increasingly dangerous journeys. Migrants were literally washing up on European beaches. Keeping foreigners out became something of a global obsession among affluent states. Presidential candidate Donald Trump promised to build a wall and get Mexico to pay for it. He also promised to ban Muslims from entering the United States and to deport undocumented residents in the USA as never before. The successful campaign for Britain to leave the European Union invoked much fear concerning rising numbers of immigrants. Canada and New Zealand passed legislation aiming to restrict foreign ownership of property. Australia stepped up naval patrols, ensuring any potential unauthorized boat arrivals were turned back long before they reached the country's shores and holding so-called boat people in offshore detention centers in which mental illness and self-harm became common.

According to recent global Pew Research Centre studies, about 45 percent of people around the world believe migration levels to their country should be reduced.[1] Immigrants are a popular scapegoat for all manner of perceived ills, including job losses, increased terrorism threats, rising housing costs, and deteriorating provision of social services. Anti-migrant candidates riding this pro-restrictionist tide are being successfully elected to political office in surprisingly high numbers; alarmingly, even in places such as Brazil and Germany that had recently prided themselves on promoting inclusive, welcoming environments for migrants.

---

[1] Phillip Connor and Jens Manuel Krogstad, "Many worldwide oppose more migration – both into and out of their countries," *Pew Research Center*, December 10, 2018, available at: www.pewresearch.org/fact-tank/2018/12/10/many-worldwide-oppose-more-migration-both-into-and-out-of-their-countries/

I found these trends deeply disturbing. I recall the day on which I decided that, as a philosopher who cares deeply about matters of justice, I ought to write a book about what migration justice requires and, equally importantly, prohibits. It was late January 2017. President Trump had just issued his notorious executive order prohibiting Syrian refugees from entering the USA, and placing a travel ban on people from seven nations that have large Muslim majorities.

I have no illusion that this book will magically reverse popular anti-migrant sentiment. The readers I aim at reaching are anyhow different in two ways. I hope to engage those who are interested in questions of migration justice and in answers that can also help assess current policy. So, the book is for those who wish to engage in reflection about questions that underlie immigration debates, such as: May each state decide its immigration policy as it sees fit? Are there any robust normative constraints on the policies states may permissibly adopt? What responsibilities do we have in relation to migrants? In answering those kinds of questions, I aim to offer answers and tools that assist in evaluating current migration policy that can help us determine which policies may be permissible and which are normatively indefensible. (Spoiler alert: The Muslim ban enacted in January 2017 cannot be justified.) I do not imagine that all readers want to reflect on these concerns. However, there certainly are readers who are interested in asking such questions and in seeking robust answers. This book is for them.

I have discussed central arguments in this book with a great many esteemed colleagues. I have also presented very early drafts of chapters at various conferences, including the American Philosophical Association's Pacific Division Meetings (in 2017), the American Philosophical Association's Central Division Meetings (in 2018), and a workshop on immigration and feasibility at Australian National University (in 2018). For very helpful comments on this work, I am especially grateful to Arash Abizadeh, Christian Barry, Charles Beitz, Alexander Betts, Michael Blake, Joseph Carens, Paul Collier, Stephen Davies, Luara Ferracioli, Bob Goodin, Nicole Hassoun, Javier Hidalgo, Peter Higgins, Cindy Holder, Will Kymlicka, Holly Lawford-Smith, Matthew Lindauer, Matthew Lister, Colin Macleod, David Miller, Darrel Moellendorf, Margaret Moore, Colleen Murphy, Jennifer Nagel, Kieran Oberman, David Owen, Alexander Sager, Sarah Song, Nicholas Southwood, Christine Straehle, Ashwini Vasanthakumar, Didier Zuniga, and two anonymous referees for Cambridge University Press. I am also especially grateful to Hilary Gaskin, my editor at Cambridge University Press, for being so supportive of the project and for acting promptly and professionally at every point. Hal Churchman, Thomas Haynes, Dick Hill, Mathew Rohit, and other members of the Cambridge team also assisted greatly in the publication process. Stephen Davies, Nancy Fisher, and Anne Stubbings deserve special thanks for helpful conversations and supportive cheer in dark times.

CHAPTER I

New Migration Justice Challenges and How to Solve Them
An Overview

I Introduction

Our contemporary moment presents significant new justice challenges for people on the move. Anti-migrant sentiment has emerged in several ways. By executive order, the USA has adopted immigration policy that looks remarkably similar to a Muslim ban. There are new threats to deport long-settled residents, such as the so-called Dreamers. Our defunct refugee system has not dealt adequately with increased refugee flows, forcing desperate people to undertake increasingly risky measures in efforts to reach safe havens. Increased migration flows over recent years appear to have contributed to a rise in right-wing populism, apparently driving phenomena such as Brexit and Trumpism. In this book, I address such migration justice challenges. I offer a comprehensive framework that can assist in responding to these developments, offering the tools we need to understand what justice requires for people on the move.

Given that many of the phenomena I aim to address have presented themselves as challenges only in the last couple of years, there is little sustained philosophical work on my core problems, and less on how to bring them together into one unified, comprehensive framework for thinking about justice and migration issues that can be used to evaluate policy concerning migration.[1] While I focus on some highly prominent topics, the framework can be applied to many other kinds of migration

---

[1] There are, of course, important exceptions. For some significant examples aiming to offer reasonably comprehensive accounts see Joseph Carens, *The Ethics of Immigration* (Oxford: Oxford University Press, 2013), David Miller, *Strangers in Our Midst* (Cambridge, MA: Harvard University Press, 2016), and Sarah Song, *Immigration and Democracy* (New York: Oxford University Press, 2018). There are excellent extended treatments of particular issues, especially on the right to exclude. See, for instance, Christopher Heath Wellman and Phillip Cole, *Debating the Ethics of Immigration: Is There a Right to Exclude?* (New York: Oxford University Press, 2011); and Christopher Bertram, *Do States Have the Right to Exclude Immigrants?* (Cambridge: Polity, 2018). There is also much excellent work on refugees, as I briefly discuss in Chapter 6. However, my account differs from all of these in aiming to offer a comprehensive framework for evaluating a wide range of current issues concerning

I

issues. In the next section, I discuss a sample of the core problems that my analysis aims to address.

2   Some Core Issues This Work Aims to Tackle

There are several kinds of prominent cases that present new challenges worthy of further philosophical work. I start with the 2017 executive order to ban people from seven predominantly Muslim countries from entering the USA. This case shatters many common assumptions about what states may not permissibly do in the name of self-determination. For some years, a state's banning admission for people of particular religious groups has typically been taken as *clearly* morally wrong.[2] But events of 2017 have forced us to consider what compelling arguments are available to justify this assumption and, thereby, to meet this challenge to settled views about migration justice.

Lurking in the background of this case is a second obstacle, concerning the perception of increased security and terrorism threats associated with migration. How should one make sense of these alleged threats, especially in a "post-truth" environment, one in which different parties proffer their own so-called evidence, sometimes of dubious veracity, in favor of their preferred views? The threat of terrorism and security issues were part of the alleged justificatory narrative for the ban, along with the introduction of several measures, such as suspension of refugee admissions and new extreme vetting procedures for all who aim to arrive in the USA. Are there new security and terrorism threats that warrant more draconian screening arrangements? What should we make of rhetoric to suggest that the threats are worse than ever? Even if there are such threats, what measures may we adopt to protect ourselves that are both reasonably effective and consistent with the demands of justice?

A third challenge arises from recent research in the area of development, peace, and conflict studies that forces us to rethink how we should help refugees effectively.[3] How to treat refugees fairly has been a significant

migration and justice, with special attention to being able to address particular challenges that have arisen over very recent years.

[2] Carens, *Ethics of Immigration*, 174, and Miller, *Strangers in Our Midst*, 95.

[3] Some particularly important works I discuss include Alexander Betts and Paul Collier, *Refuge: Rethinking Refugee Policy in a Changing World* (New York: Oxford University Press, 2017); Elena Fiddian-Qasmiyeh, Gil Loescher, Katy Long, and Nando Sigona, "Introduction: Refugee and Forced Migration Studies in Transition." In Elena Fiddian-Qasmiyeh, Gil Loescher, Katy Long, and Nando Sigona (eds.), *The Oxford Handbook of Refugee and Forced Migration Studies* (Oxford: Oxford University Press, 2014); Michael Clemens, Cindy Huang, and Jimmy Graham, *The*

concern for some time now. Drawing on this new research, we should rethink common assumptions about how to assist. For instance, the analysis casts doubt on the assumption that increasing admission or resettlement targets presents constructive solutions for all refugee situations. Broadening consideration to include assisting internally displaced people, along with others in host and home countries affected by refugee flows, we will need to reconsider different sets of solutions to these complex issues and the role multiple agents can, and should, play in addressing refugee problems.

A fourth challenge arises from recent policy announcements to deport long-settled members of communities that are declared as unauthorized or illegal migrants, such as the Dreamers or those from the Windrush generation. The case of the Dreamers seems particularly poignant. These migrants were brought by their parents to the USA illegally, often while they were very young. The reversal of Obama era legislation that allowed Dreamers to remain, calls into question another position that seemed to reflect widely shared views about what justice requires for long-settled irregular migrants who arrived as children.

Several other apparent difficulties will be addressed, sometimes more briefly, throughout this work. For instance, one challenge seems to stem from new social science research, especially from psychology, that suggests increasing levels of immigration may be bad for robust democracy, harmonious communities, and civic accord.[4] Immigration has also been linked to several phenomena such as a rise in right-wing populism, nationalism, Brexit, Trumpism, and a decrease in support for institutions that support social and global justice projects, along with a rise in ethnocentrism. Are

Economic and Fiscal Effects of Granting Refugees Formal Labor Market Access (Washington, DC: Center for Global Development, October 2018); Michael Clemens, Cindy Huang, Jimmy Graham, and K. Gough, *Migration Is What You Make It: Seven Policy Decisions That Turned Challenges into Opportunities* (Washington, DC: Center for Global Development, 2018); C. Huang, S. Charles, L. Post, and K. Gough, *Tackling the Realities of Protracted Displacement: Case Studies on What's Working and Where We Can Do Better* (Washington, DC: The Center for Global Development and the International Rescue Committee, 2018); C. Huang, *Global Business and Refugee Crises: A Framework for Sustainable Engagement* (The Tent Foundation and the Center for Global Development, 2017).

[4] For some of these concerns see, for instance, Jonathan Haidt "When and why nationalism beats globalism," *The American Interest*, 12 (1) (2016) available at www.the-american-interest.com/2016/07/10/when-and-why-nationalism-beats-globalism/; Will Kymlicka, "Solidarity in diverse societies: beyond neoliberal multiculturalism and welfare chauvinism," *Comparative Migration Studies*, 3 (17) (2015): 1–19; and Keith Banting and Will Kymlicka (eds.), *The Strains of Commitment: The Political Sources of Solidarity in Diverse Societies* (Oxford: Oxford University Press, 2017).

increasing levels of immigration bad for social or global justice projects? A careful analysis of the evidence is warranted.

I aim to address such problems in this work. The foundations for the framework are built in Chapters 2 and 3. Subsequent chapters develop and apply parts of the framework to specific issues. I next give a very concise chapter-by-chapter overview of how the book unfolds.

3   An Overview of the Chapter Contents

In the next chapter, Chapter 2, I briefly review some salient history concerning human migration to place migration issues in some context. I also begin to develop my normative framework.

In considering what just arrangements for human beings involve, we should pay special attention to our human needs, protecting basic liberties, fair terms of cooperation, and relevant social and political support necessary to sustain justice in diverse communities. Given its neglect, I note the significance of needs, especially our moral agency needs, in discussing matters of justice. I note how practices for delivering on justice will develop in particular locations. People's located life plans deserve respect, but this is complicated by the located life plans of others, histories of injustice, and the right to continued occupation of territory. This last issue, involving rightful claims to occupy territory, is particularly pressing if anyone is to have a defensible right to exclude others, as many migration policies presuppose. How can any current occupants of territory justifiably prevent anyone from migrating into their space, given our knowledge of how most settlements came into being? Perhaps no one has the legitimate authority to exclude anyone from moving into particular places? What case can be made that states and the boundaries they vigilantly guard are justified?

We see how good administration, and so administrative units, will play an important part in securing justice, though the argument does not point in favor of these units taking any particular shape. The state can play a valuable role in delivering on justice, as one kind of permissible administrative unit, among others. As I argue, delivering on our lofty justice ambitions also requires attention to some quite practical details. For instance, competent administration is important for adequate planning associated with meeting needs, protecting basic liberties, securing fair terms of cooperation, along with promoting the relevant conditions necessary to sustain enduring cooperative communities.

In our contemporary world, states perform central administrative functions, though various configurations could do what is required. States currently exist within a state system, which is the main administrative structure governing the people of the world. So, it is worthwhile to consider whether our contemporary arrangements – our state system – is just and, if not, what modifications are required. That is the focus of Chapter 3.

Chapter 3 seeks a justification for states' claims to have rights to self-determination that entail the right to control admission to their territory. Today, we live in states that assume they have certain rights and that agents of the state may act in certain ways that privilege the interests of their citizens. Our current arrangements may seem natural to us, perhaps the way things have always been. But, in fact, they have not always been this way. And they might indeed change in the future. So, we have reason to inquire: What justification can be offered for the assumed default position encompassing the state system, along with state claims to self-determination and strong rights to control borders? And, importantly, what compelling justification can be offered to "outsiders," those who currently find themselves beyond those borders and who might like to cross them?

In seeking a justification, we discover that in order for states to have robust rights to self-determination within a state system, they will also have many responsibilities. So, while there is much talk about the rights of states to self-determination in migration justice discussions, when we understand how the justification for this right must go for it to be defensible, the argument also generates strong obligations. States have responsibilities to promote conditions that support self-determining, just communities. Recognition of this point is not only missing in many of the conversations about migration justice, but must be part of the justification for any compelling argument for the right to self-determination to have force, so its importance deserves highlighting. A state's ability to exercise political power legitimately depends on its respecting human rights adequately and cooperating in a host of transborder activities, programs, and institutions that have as their aim securing robust arrangements capable of effective human rights protection. So, as I develop these ideas, there are important human rights standards that constrain legitimate states' abilities to act. In addition, there are important contribution requirements that states must meet in order to exercise power legitimately. Performance on both of these dimensions affects whether or not we have a legitimate state system, along with whether there are adequate contingency arrangements in place to deal with important shortfalls. Contribution to the legitimacy of the state system is an especially underappreciated area that is also importantly relevant to whether states have robust rights to self-determination. And without such rights, states may not have the justified rights they think they do have concerning control over who enters and remains on their territory.

I consider some of the core elements brought into view by this justification for the right to self-determination within the state system. For instance, respect for human rights plays a key role in understanding all of these core notions. I consider which human rights and other important features of contemporary human rights practice play this important role.

Having defended the core theoretical elements needed over Chapters 2 and 3, I begin to address the contemporary challenges, applying key parts of the framework and developing others in subsequent chapters.

Chapter 4 spotlights migration policy that seeks to exclude by limiting those who practice certain religions from gaining admission to a territory. I focus attention by asking: What is wrong with a ban on Muslims? Is a ban on Muslims impermissible because it violates human rights? While some think it is difficult to make such arguments directly, I offer an argument that is grounded in core aspects of the practice of human rights. Drawing on core elements of the argument discussed in Chapter 3, concerning the conditions states must satisfy in order to exercise power legitimately, we see that there are important internal and contribution requirements that enacting a Muslim ban fails to meet.

As I argue, a legitimate state cannot embrace a migration policy that bans Muslims from being admitted without such policies undermining the state's claim to legitimacy. I show how such policies violate key legitimacy requirements, by failing to meet both internal and contribution criteria. For instance, I show why such policies have important repercussions for citizens, threatening a range of rights including the right to freedom of religion and non-discrimination. I also demonstrate why such policies clearly violate requirements central to conventions on the elimination of discrimination, hatred, and intolerance, which are all prohibited by essential internal legitimacy requirements. In addition, such policies violate core contribution requirements. As one example, Muslim bans fail to meet accountability standards, according to which states are accountable for human rights protection, both to internal and external stakeholders. Muslim bans fail to be accountable to peoples (both Muslim and non-Muslim) across the world, along with Muslims and non-Muslim residents within the country. Furthermore, agents of the state have responsibilities to protect and promote the necessary conditions for a legitimate state system. The right of a state to self-determination is conditional on its discharging its responsibilities to promote conditions that can support self-determining, just communities. Too many of these conditions would be violated by Muslim ban policies.

In Chapter 5 I consider the challenge presented by new threats to deport long-settled members of communities who do not formally enjoy the legal status of citizen, but rather are classed as "undocumented," "irregular," or "illegal" migrants. These include the Dreamers, the Windrush generation, and those with Temporary Protected Status who have had that status revoked under the Trump presidency. To assist our analysis, I differentiate between five kinds of cases that raise slightly different issues, even though there is some commonality. I show why deportation, or even threats of deportation, for the long-settled involve grave injustices on a par with violating some of our most basic human rights. Indeed, evicting long-settled members would undermine legitimacy in several ways. Such actions threaten states' rights to exercise power legitimately by undermining core internal, system, and contribution requirements. And I show why the arguments used in defense of community members' alleged rights to continued occupation would be undermined by such evictions. In such cases, states may not claim a justifiable right to continued occupation nor can they claim that such a right entitles them to evict long-settled members of the community residing on that territory.

Chapter 6 covers some reasonably new challenges associated with massive refugee populations. Contemporary discussion of refugees in the normative literature has so far focused predominantly on a small set of questions: Who qualifies as a refugee? Do high income states have obligations to admit refugees? If so, under what conditions, and how many are they obligated to admit? What grounds obligations toward refugees? While all of these questions are important, there has been a substantial lack of attention to a question that is more fundamental, and shapes the grounds and content of responsibilities in connection with refugees. The question that is ripe for more sustained analysis is: How can we help refugees in ways that are effective for all key stakeholders? Key stakeholders in refugee policy include refugees, internally displaced populations who have not yet crossed a border, those left behind in states of origin, and those states and their citizens that bear the burden of hosting large refugee populations. I explore options that aim to offer good solutions for host and home countries, for the roughly 10 percent of refugees who typically make it to high income countries and the approximately 90 percent who do not. While there is still some scope for resettlement policies to play a role, many local solutions closer to the source of the crisis are often available and preferable. These can take different forms, and some of this variety is explored. Many of these solutions may be described as providing incubator zones for development – they focus on meeting a wide range of current needs of the displaced populations (such as for autonomy, work, opportunity, and community) while also preparing that population for life after conflict ends. Addressing such needs in ways that promote the interests of many other stakeholders can yield effective courses of action worthy of our support.

As I argue, ideally, robust comprehensive solutions to the refugee crisis share several features, such as the following three: First, solutions should be able to accommodate the vast numbers of displaced people (at present over seventy million).[5] Second, solutions should also aim to take account of the current and longer term needs of the displaced populations, along with those of other stakeholders. Third, they should not undermine, and should ideally facilitate, post-conflict recovery (where refugees are fleeing violence). As I argue, particular kinds of development oriented proposals meet these criteria well. There is a good case to be made that we should support these proposals and that they can help us outline the contours of our responsibilities in connection with refugees.

As my analysis shows, the shape and content of our duties to large scale refugee populations is quite different from what much normative theorizing suggests. On the empowerment promoting model I explore, we should be supporting more beneficial policies, including (where appropriate in particular circumstances) supporting and subsidizing enterprises that generate jobs, ensuring favorable trading arrangements are available (such as tariff free access to high income country markets), supporting policy conducive to stabilizing post-conflict societies, such as assisting with education and training, and, of course, playing our part in any resettlement programs that are still needed to supplement the programs focusing on development and post-conflict recovery.

Armed with this analysis of why our current refugee regime is inadequate, we are in a good position to discuss how reforms are needed to secure the legitimacy of the state system. As I highlight, our current institutions are failing many refugees and internally displaced people. These institutions need to be dramatically reoriented. I argue for a number

---

[5] See the United Nations High Commissioner for Refugees (UNHCR) website for constantly changing figures (www.unhcr.org). For a recent report see BBC, "More than 70 million displaced worldwide, says UNHCR," June 19, 2019.

of reforms. For example, I argue that global migration governance institutions are necessary and need to incorporate certain key ingredients. We need to allow for relevant beneficial partnerships, such as making policy space for business and civil society actors to play important roles, along with state actors. We need to ensure that local partners who have innovative and effective ideas about how to assist in specific contexts can be included in relevant programs that the international community helps support. Other desirable institutional changes include managing our refugee processing more fairly, so that refugees may apply for asylum in processing centers that are more proximate to the high need areas. Refugees should be able to apply for asylum in embassies within the country or nearby border locations, in efforts to minimize the amount of hardship asylum seekers currently suffer.

So, in short, the three traditional approaches to addressing the plight of refugees (namely, voluntary repatriation, local settlement, and resettlement), must be expanded. Given the scale of the refugee problems, we need to supplement these with new approaches, especially as persisting human rights violations in countries of origin make repatriation options less likely and give us important reasons to consider broadening the option set that we are able to provide refugees. I discuss a range of reforms that would better safeguard the human rights of displaced people or those vulnerable to displacement. In the absence of good faith and credible efforts at making such changes, our current arrangements for assisting refugees cannot be regarded as adequate. A state system that offered these up as the ways for dealing with refugees could not be legitimate.

Chapter 7 focuses on justice for temporary labor migrants, which involves vast numbers of migrants in our contemporary world. In some countries, foreign nationals make up over 50 percent of the labor force, and frequently more than 80 percent in countries in the Middle East. Though I survey a range of relevant normative issues concerning temporary labor migration, I focus especially on new sources of concern. For instance, given the scale of temporary labor migration, there are market opportunities that private recruitment companies have been keen to seize. Recruitment companies have often operated in a context where they have been guilty of serious deception, fraud, abuse, and failures to protect migrants, with both destination and home countries failing to take responsibility for oversight.

Labor migration is often characterized as beneficial to the migrants, along with both sending and receiving countries. While this is, on balance, true in many cases, there is also evidence that such arrangements can be highly detrimental to the migrants, especially under conditions of extreme power disparities. While the logic of mutual advantage has a place in considering labor migration justice, especially considering the scale of global unemployment and vulnerable employment, there should be important constraints on such programs. The constraints include requirements to ensure good measures are in place that can offer reasonable human rights protections for migrant workers. They also include requirements to protect against creating certain kinds of highly detrimental effects for non-migrants. As we discuss which rights deserve protection, we also notice that there is some scope for migrants to trade off protection of certain rights in exchange for labor market access, if they so choose. I develop principles to help us navigate which rights are "tradable" and which deserve rigorous protection.

In Chapter 8, I discuss how to deal with alleged new terrorism and security threats posed by migration. Fears concerning terrorism and security seem to have significantly set back the prospects for migration justice recently. I discuss some of the problems associated with assessing the weight that should reasonably be placed on terrorism and security in a world of strongly divergent ideological viewpoints, partisan news outlets, and the phenomenon of fake news. While there is some threat level, key issues include deciding what measures would be effective in combating it, while being commensurate with that threat level and not ignoring the opportunity costs pursuing such policies might entail, especially ones that might better promote the goals of a strong and inclusive society capable of resilience to such threats. I also consider whether some risks can be further reduced without compromising our values, principles, and other important justice goals. There are important concerns that arise about the measures we should take to protect against the perceived threat when they violate other demands of justice. For instance, excessive public expenditure in one domain when further outcome gains are insignificant and other important basic rights remain unaddressed, is relevant to assessing how well justice is achieved in particular societies.

I analyze why security threats get to be so readily coupled with migration issues. Here we find some familiar dynamics along with some new developments. Politicians have often been successful in adopting such strategies as scapegoating and exclusionary constructions of national identity. New developments include changing demographics and structural changes that have resulted in limitations on long-time residents' upward mobility, which can promote conflict and resentment. These sentiments can be amplified and harnessed to promote an anti-immigrant ethos in which unwise policies can flourish.

While each legitimate state has the right to have its own conversation about how best to combat terrorism and to make policy decisions accordingly, there are justice constraints on how that dialogue may permissibly unfold. Making good decisions about public funding should start with an accurate assessment of risks, for instance. In general, excessive spending on shoring up some human rights where further important gains are unlikely to materialize, especially when other human rights are neglected or not yet sufficiently secure, is relevant to how we evaluate society's behavior against a justice standard. So, ineffective spending on the right to security, when rights to basic education, food, housing, and health care remain unfulfilled, would lack justification.

I also show why there are many obstacles to having a more informed conversation about these matters, such as the many interests that converge on perpetuating a fearful environment. For instance, politicians know that fear can make people pay attention, so playing up reasons to be fearful can get voters to favor the politicians who promise to address their fears, and can be helpful to their election prospects. In trying to understand why people are so afraid, we see that there are psychological, cultural, and economic components. Changing demographics, structural changes, the sense of being left behind, and no longer having genuine opportunities for upward mobility are some of the drivers of fear and a sense of resentment directed at immigrants. However, a more accurate assessment of immigrants' contributions in many of these environments reveals that such views are unwarranted. For instance, immigrants have often helped create, and can continue to create, robust and dynamic economies that drive prosperity for many, if properly managed with complementary policies, such as those that seek to distribute gains widely.

In Chapter 9, I cover a number of issues, including these two important questions: How open should states be to more migrants? What responsibilities do states and citizens have in connection with reducing migration injustices? I also address a number of key objections to my account of migration justice, core positions, and recommendations. I begin by recapping some of the main features that states rightfully exercising power in a legitimate state system need to incorporate. States have important obligations to support institutions that can exercise effective oversight and regulate migration matters in ways that align with the robust human rights practice for which I argue. Impressive international policy gains show that there is an emerging willingness to support such a practice. As evidence, I outline the groundbreaking initiative, *The Global Compact for Safe, Orderly and Regular Migration*, adopted by 85 percent of the world's states at the end of 2018.

While the *Compact* is a good start, in at least one area it fails to offer sufficient progressive guidance. I argue that a legitimate state system must include rights to a fair process for determining migrants' rights, especially concerning rights to admission and to remain. I also argue that this would generally lead to an opening of borders, but very important constraints on such opening would still remain, such as those that are relevant to respecting, protecting, and fulfilling the human rights of those already residing on the territory. My position might be characterized as a human rights oriented middle ground between the positions of those who argue for open borders and their critics.

I also consider several objections to some of my central positions and policy recommendations. One form of resistance can be anticipated to institutional governance changes for which I advocate, such as improvements to our refugee regime. Proponents might maintain that real people cannot be expected to support either the policies or the politicians who would be inclined to make the necessary modifications. I discuss reasons to be more hopeful, the scope for progressive and gradual change, along with other ways we can better implement justice in our imperfect world. In considering key objections, we must deal with one important complaint that seems to have surfaced a great deal in recent years. Has migration been bad for justice in communities? Here we consider challenges that suggest increased migration is responsible for such phenomena as a decrease in support for the welfare state and a general swing toward right-wing populism, as manifested in Brexit and Trumpism. I consider reasons to be skeptical about taking such views as hard constraints that limit what justice can require. I also show that many assumptions have been made in these arguments that are not warranted and that can be refuted as we reflect on salient histories, empirical evidence, and, indeed, our obligations under the newly adopted *Compact on Migration*.

In addition, while some of the ethnocentric dynamics concerning migrants triggering perceived threat levels may exist, these tendencies certainly can be, and have been, successfully managed. For instance, all nations contain citizens who migrated from some other place but whose credentials as a citizen are now beyond reproach. Who we consider to be part of our community is an entirely malleable feature of our lives, so we should be skeptical about some of the arguments that suggest migrants are necessarily a threat to justice within communities. Indeed, the work of many NGOs that aim to create inclusive communities deserves more prominence. I discuss some examples that warrant more attention.

In the final part of the chapter we return to the issue of whether our state system can currently be regarded as legitimate. As matters currently stand, the state system cannot yet pass a basic legitimacy test, but I also show that there are some important corrective mechanisms now in view. If these are suitably supplemented with further measures, especially ones that hold states to account for their actions and decisions, this constellation of arrangements might well significantly reduce migration injustices. I highlight the direction we must take if we aspire to a legitimate state system capable of supporting justice for people on the move.

CHAPTER 2

Migration, Justice, and Territory
Toward a Justificatory Framework

1 Introduction

In this chapter my key purposes are to situate migration in historical context and to lay some normative groundwork for orienting my account of justice for people on the move. I break these tasks into three important sections.

First, I provide some background to migration debates by highlighting common reasons human beings have been moving about the planet from our earliest days. I note some important migration moments. Our species, *Homo sapiens*, has always moved around. Understanding the history of human beings means understanding the history of human migration. Our identities as individuals and as nations are heavily connected to migrations. Like our ancestors, central reasons for migration involve the quest for new opportunities, scarcity of resources, environmental challenges, religious persecution, ethnic tensions, wars, or unstable post-conflict societies. I consider some important historical moments as illustrations.

Second, I begin to develop my framework for navigating issues of migration and justice by outlining four core important aspects of justice. In considering what just arrangements for human beings involve, we should pay special attention to our human needs, protecting basic liberties, fair terms of cooperation, and relevant social and political support necessary to sustain justice in diverse communities. I discuss the neglected notion of need, noting the special significance of moral agency needs and derivative needs. These play a central role in motivating human beings in key ways, are important to their felt sense of well-being, and are crucial for capacities to take responsibility.

We note how practices for delivering on justice will develop in particular locations. People's located life plans deserve respect, but what this entails must take account of the located life plans of others, histories of injustice, and the conditions necessary for rightful continued occupation of territory.

This last issue involving rightful claims to occupy territory is particularly important if anyone is to have a defensible right to exclude others, as many migration policies presuppose.

Third, noting this complicated state of affairs, I draw attention to the fact that delivering on our lofty justice ambitions also requires attention to some quite practical details. For instance, we see how good administration – and so, derivatively, administrative units – will play an important part in securing justice, though the argument does not point in favor of these units taking any particular shape. A case can be marshaled for the state's playing a valuable role in delivering on justice, as one kind of permissible administrative unit among others. However, states exist within a state system and unless the set of states do a sufficiently good job delivering on core requirements of justice, the system may lack justification. Can our state system be defended? That task is left for Chapter 3.

2   Migration and History: A Brief Account of Some Seminal Issues

Migration has been at the heart of world history from when our species, *Homo sapiens,* first emerged. At least 200,000 years ago we evolved in Africa as modern human beings.[1] We began migrating within Africa at least 70,000 years ago, developing languages, forms of social organization, symbolic behaviors and technological innovations, these being some of the features that characterize "culturally modern" human beings.[2] As a result of diseases and environmental challenges, early populations of *Homo sapiens* were small and largely nomadic. Single regions could not typically support large populations, so bands needed to migrate in search of new

---

[1] Those who argue that the date is around 200,000 years ago include Robin Dunbar, *The Human Story* (London: Faber and Faber, 2004); Steven Mithen, *The Prehistory of the Mind: A Search for the Origins of Art, Religion, and Science* (London: Thames and Hudson, 1996); and Chris Stringer, "The Origin and Dispersal of *Homo sapiens*: Our Current State of Knowledge," in P. Mellars, K. Boyle, O. Bar Yosef, and C. Stringer (eds.), *Rethinking the Human Revolution* (Cambridge: McDonald Institute for Archaeological Research, 2007), pp. 15–20. For new evidence that pushes this date back even further see J. J. Hublin, A. Ben-Ncer, et al., "New Fossils from Jebel Irhoud, Morocco and the Pan-African Origin of Homo sapiens," *Nature*, 546 (2017): 289–292. *Homo erectus* and *Homo sapiens* spread from the Rift Valley in Africa between about 1.5 million and 5,000 years ago. See, for instance, Khalid Koser, *International Migration: A Very Short Introduction* (Oxford: Oxford University Press, 2007); S. Wells, *The Journey of Man: A Genetic Odyssey* (New York: Random House, 2002).

[2] T. Clack, *Ancestral Roots: Modern Living and Human Evolution* (New York: Macmillan, 2009); R. G. Klein, *The Human Career* (Chicago: University of Chicago Press, 2009); and Wells, *The Journey of Man*. On technical innovation see Stephen Davies, "The Social Conditions for Sustainable Technological Innovation" in Berys Gaut and Mathew Kieran (eds.), *Creativity and Philosophy* (London: Routledge, 2018), pp. 251–269.

opportunities. Though they returned to particular sites, they did not appear to favor permanent settlement in particular locations at that time. Changing environmental conditions, including changes in climate, drove much migration. By 40,000 years ago, our species appears to have traveled across all habitable lands of Africa, Australia, Europe, and Asia.[3]

Settlements eventually became popular, though it is important to note that the descriptors of "settled" and "nomadic" suggest a rigid distinction that is somewhat misleading.[4] For instance, nomadic bands sometimes practiced transhumant migration, that is, moving between nearby but different climatic zones on a seasonal basis to take advantage of different food sources. However, as a broad generalization over the course of human history, people became more settled in particular locations.[5] Global warming and cultural developments, especially in new technologies that facilitated the domestication of plants, led to many communities becoming settled. During the Agricultural Revolution (roughly 14,000 to 3,500 BP), communities began inventing ways to farm that could then sustain much larger and denser populations than previous ways of life that were based on foraging, hunting, and fishing.[6] There were several disadvantages introduced as well. Human communities became vulnerable to crop failures. Diets were less varied, leading to vitamin deficiencies and other negative health outcomes.[7] In addition, social structures changed. Farming is reasonably labor intensive and can create inequalities in social groups.[8]

Settled communities developed new economic needs concerning farming, food storage, tool production, and the like.[9] New forms of social

[3] Chris Scarre (ed.), *The Human Past: World Prehistory and the Development of Human Societies* (London: Thames and Hudson, 2013), 3rd edition, especially chapters 3 and 4.
[4] Chris Scarre, "The World Transformed: From Foragers and Farmers to States and Empires" in Chris Scarre (ed.), *The Human Past*, pp. 176–199.
[5] Scarre, *The Human Past*.
[6] Jean-Pierre Bocquet-Appel, "When the World's Population Took Off: The Springboard of the Neolithic Demographic Transition," *Science*, 333 (July 29, 2011): 560–561.
[7] J. H. O'Keefe and L. Cordain, "Cardiovascular Disease Resulting from a Diet and Lifestyle at Odds with Our Paleolithic Genome: How to Become a 21st Century Hunter-Gatherer," *Mayo Clinic Proceedings (Review)*, 79 (1) (2004): 101–108; and D. C. Sands, C. E. Morris, E. A. Dratz, and A. Pilgeram, "Elevating Optimal Human Nutrition to a Central Goal of Plant Breeding and Production of Plant-Based Foods," *Plant Science (Review)*, 177 (2009): 377–389.
[8] S. Langlois, "Traditions: Social" in Neil J. Smelser and Paul B. Baltes (eds.), *International Encyclopedia of the Social & Behavioral Sciences* (Oxford: Pergamon, 2001), 15829–15833; D. E. Brown, *Hierarchy, History, and Human Nature: The Social Origins of Historical Consciousness* (Tucson: University of Arizona Press, 1988).
[9] Scarre, *The Human Past*.

differentiation emerged to meet these demands.[10] Farmers invested energy and resources in assets (such as wells, canals, grinding stones, and pottery) required to grow, harvest and store crops. These efforts meant they were reluctant to abandon such investments, even when natural disasters occurred.

Nomads interacted with settled communities on several levels. Sometimes mutually beneficial trade occurred. But relationships were also often tense, as conflict arose concerning who could rightfully access such resources as land and water. Settled groups also began competing violently with other settled groups, leading to organized warfare.[11] In this context, constructing city walls to mark off territory and control, became popular. These were useful ways of

> ... controlling the entry and exit of animals and people; channeling drinking water and sewage; and marking off and defending the city's space from outsiders. Even small nomadic and settled communities learned to erect temporary fences against predatory animals and to enclose their domesticated animals. But settled communities often erected permanent barriers against nomadic herding communities who might regard crops and water as food and drink for themselves and their animals. Fixed walls thus defined the limits of formal control by the city's king and gods.[12]

Leaving behind our prehistoric and ancient past and reflecting on a broader sweep of human history, we note that central reasons for migration involved the quest for new opportunities, scarcity of resources, environmental challenges, religious persecution, ethnic tensions, wars, or unstable post-conflict societies. Much of this history will be familiar to readers and does not need further discussion here for the core purposes of this book. For instance, many readers will be familiar with history involving religious persecution as a cause of migration, because almost all religions have sad stories here. However, I draw attention to a few key moments that place some of the contemporary discussion in its historical context.

Famine and extreme scarcity have always driven large-scale movements of people. A notable case is Irish migration caused by the potato famine of 1845–1849 (which resulted in the halving of its then population, if we total the number of deaths and the number who emigrated as a result of the famine).[13] While need has always been a key driver, so has greed,

---

[10] Steven Mithen, *After the Ice* (Cambridge: Harvard University Press, 2004); N. Roberts, *The Holocene: An Environmental History*, 2nd edition (Oxford, Blackwell, 1998); Scarre, "*The World Transformed*"; and Scarre, *The Human Past*.
[11] Ibid.   [12] Michael Fisher, *Migration: A World History* (OUP, 2014),14.
[13] David Ross, *Ireland: History of a Nation* (New Lanark: Geddes & Grosset, 2002).

ambition, and a desire for dominance. The era of European colonial empires exemplifies this well, especially as it initiated significant new global migrations.

> Almost all humans on earth either participated in or resisted this new Eurocentric world system. Wherever in the Americas, Asia, Africa, or Australia that Europeans established colonies, European immigrants and their rule, including their imported crops, diseases, weapons, products, and cultures, profoundly dislocated local communities, leading many to migrate away. But European traders, settlers, officers, and officials also attracted indigenous people to translate, guide, serve, fight for, and otherwise collaborate with them.[14]

Being forced to leave has been another dominant cause of migration. One of the most destructive and large-scale forced migrations resulting from European colonialism was the Atlantic slave trade, in which vast numbers of people were transported to the Americas and the Caribbean, about twelve million from west Africa alone.[15] European colonial rule also often dislocated many local populations, either through direct conquest or through its consequences. Colonialism or its legacy also resulted in further large forced migrations. Boundaries were often drawn on arbitrary geographic lines, not appreciating that colonies frequently cut across ethnic groups.[16] Newly constructed state boundaries sometimes also joined communities marked by considerable ethnic tensions into one state. Once granted independence, politicians from dominant groups often forced other groups to leave, such as happened in Myanmar, Fiji, Sri Lanka, Uganda, and Zimbabwe. And colonially conceived new nations created further large forced migrations, such as happened when part of India was partitioned to form Pakistan in 1947, which overnight forced approximately 15 million people to migrate, resulting in large-scale violence and disruption.[17]

Innovation and new technologies have always facilitated new migration opportunities. For instance, once new medicines like quinine for protection against malaria were developed, Europeans immigrated to sub-Saharan Africa, aiming to exploit valuable minerals and raw materials. The scale and speed with which European colonial powers claimed parts of Africa prompted European nations to regulate activity during the

---

[14] Fisher, *Migration*, 74.   [15] Koser, *International Migration*.
[16] Muriel E. Chamberlain, *The Scramble for Africa* (London: Longman, 1999).
[17] Yasmin Khan, *The Great Partition: The Making of India and Pakistan* (New Haven: Yale University Press, 2007).

1884–1885 meeting of the Congress of Berlin, dividing up the remaining 80 percent of Africa not yet under the rule of colonial powers to particular European states so long as they sent sufficient soldiers, settlers, or officials to occupy those territories.[18] At that time, and with hardly any exceptions, the whole world was carved up into colonizing countries and colonies.[19] New borders not only displaced many people but caused much conflict as well.[20] Governments began setting policies concerning who could enter territory, with state agents dedicated to enforcing those rules.[21]

Perceived advantages to a nation have also been a major factor driving large-scale migrations. For instance, Britain and France allowed migration from their former colonies to meet labor shortages following World War II.[22] The UK's Nationality Act of 1948 allowed the 800 million citizens of the Commonwealth to immigrate to Britain.[23] But this became more difficult in the 1960s after 1.5 million nonwhite immigrants had already settled in Britain. Some nations permitted laborers to work in their countries without the right to become citizens. Prominent examples include the United States' Bracero Program, which brought temporary workers from Mexico to the United States from 1942 to 1964 and the "Guest worker" (Gastarbeiter) program, which brought Turks to Germany in the 1960s and 1970s.

As we see from this brief historical survey, humans have ended up where they are through a mix of both questionable and quite understandable motivations. This will be relevant as we try to understand what justice for people on the move consists in. In drawing this section to a close, it is worth underscoring six important points.

First, human beings have moved around our planet for a variety of reasons. The search to meet subsistence needs has played a central role. The era of colonial expansion nicely illustrates that other motivations have also driven migrations, including greed, competition, a desire for dominance, and a desire to seek out new opportunities.

Second, though nomadic patterns still exist among many groups, the vast majority of the human population has gravitated toward patterns that are more accurately described as settlement.[24]

---

[18] Muriel E. Chamberlain, *The Scramble for Africa* .   [19] Fisher, *Migration*, 102.   [20] Ibid., 102.
[21] Ibid.
[22] Randall Hansen, *Citizenship and Immigration in Postwar Britain* (Oxford: Oxford University Press, 2000).
[23] Hansen, *Citizenship and Immigration in Postwar Britain*.
[24] This is not to deny that within settled communities there can also be large-scale frequent movement, for instance between rural and urban environments, as happens in China, where

Third, while there is much continuity with past patterns, current migration trends are different from those of many of our ancestors' in several important respects. For instance, new transportation options enable vast numbers of people to undertake rapid intercontinental migrations. These can, and have, altered the speed and volume of migration. More generally, various technologies have significantly changed the nature of settlement and migration opportunities. Advanced food-production techniques have driven massive urbanization, with more than half of the world's population currently living in cities, a stark contrast with previous historical periods.[25] Sophisticated methods for extracting energy have also facilitated widespread industrialization. In addition, our globalized economic system of production and consumption creates new labor demands and possibilities on an unprecedented scale.[26]

Fourth, our system of controlling state borders is relatively recent in the context of human history. The perceived need for control and standardized procedures for migration is only about 100 years old. Following a massive volume of migration resulting from World War I, the League of Nations convened a conference in 1920 to establish our current system, consisting of standardized passports and other official travel documents. The UN and other organizations continued this work.

Fifth, it is also worth drawing attention to some other trends that go in the opposite direction. While nations still limit much migration, the EU is a notable example of the opposite. Free migration within the EU allows about 500 million citizens of 28 member nations to travel freely within this zone.

Sixth, it is important to appreciate how views about migration have changed over time. For instance, at one time migrations were viewed as wholly positive for expanding empires and aspiring nations. Even in recent history, nations often sought to fill labor shortages by encouraging migration. Various patterns developed in response to such needs, including a high level of temporary and circular migration. As I discuss further in Chapter 5, appreciating this history also helps us understand why some of

approximately 260 million people live away from their official home, with about 160 million in the group of long-term rural-to-urban migrants.

[25] These days more than half the world lives in urban areas. See, for instance, UN News, "More than half the world's population now living in urban areas, UN survey finds" available here: https://news.un.org/en/story/2014/07/472752-more-half-worlds-population-now-living-urban-areas-un-survey-finds. [Last accessed December 12, 2018].

[26] Sophisticated communication technologies also allow us to stay in touch with family and friends, very easily reducing a sense of isolation, if we do decide to migrate away from home communities.

these patterns may still continue, even though they are now classed as illegal migrations. From the migrants' perspective they might not be doing anything terribly wrong, since their movement was, until recently, considered highly beneficial and encouraged by state actors.

The rest of this chapter and the next one lay some of the important normative groundwork that can orient our thinking in seeking justice for people on the move.

3   The Important Role of Needs and Location in an Account of Justice

In earlier work I have argued for an account of justice that emphasizes a prominent role for four core features, namely (i) being enabled to meet our needs, (ii) protection for our basic liberties, (iii) fair terms of cooperation, and (iv) social and political arrangements necessary for supporting these key features, (i)–(iii).[27] A full defense of these views can be found elsewhere.[28] However, as I believe recognition of core human needs is a neglected issue when we think about justice quite generally, including when we consider what justice requires for people on the move, it is worthwhile to consider the importance of needs in further detail, which I do briefly in this section.

Of the many needs human beings profess to have, which of them deserve our moral attention? My account of our normatively salient needs anchors in the importance of moral agency. Why moral agency? We want people to be able to take responsibility for their lives and actions. Indeed, much of the moral and legal domain presupposes that they can do so. But assuming people can be meaningfully held responsible is unfair unless they have access to the necessary conditions required for being moral agents. So, I believe tying the normatively salient needs to moral agency is a reasonably secure connection for appreciating why these needs ought to have normative force.

Which needs are particularly important in securing moral agency? On my account, there are five core basic needs, all derivable from considering the important preconditions for moral agency. To be a moral agent crucially involves having the capacities to deliberate about and make choices concerning particular courses of action, along with the ability to

---

[27] See, for instance, Gillian Brock, *Global Justice: A Cosmopolitan Account* (Oxford: Oxford University Press, 2009).

[28] See, for instance, Brock, *Global Justice*.

act on deliberations. So, as I argue, to be candidate moral agents, we must have enough (1) physical and psychological health, (2) security, (3) understanding, (4) autonomy, and (5) sufficiently decent social relations. These five core needs I identify as basic, in that they must be sufficiently well met in order for us to be able to function as moral agents. To underscore the connection with moral agency, here I call these "moral agency needs."

To give a very brief defense of the importance of these five needs, we might consider that a sufficient level of physical health is required in order to be physically capable of performing actions.[29] One also needs to be free of certain internal and external constraints that prohibit the actor from taking action. One needs to be free from debilitating fear, and one needs a reasonably secure space in which to act, with assurance that acting will not be blocked or come at a high price. These examples illustrate why we must be free from certain psychological impediments and have adequate security to be able to act, so why psychological health and security should be sufficiently well satisfied for successful action. In defense of the third listed need, understanding, consider how in order to deliberate and make choices at a level eligible for attracting moral agency, one needs to have sufficient understanding of what is involved in choosing certain courses of action, their implications, along with their meanings in social contexts. So, for the options among which one is choosing, one needs sufficient information, capacity to understand, and capacity to reflect on those options and their implications. In defending the fourth listed need, a certain amount of autonomy is also presupposed if we are to be able to deliberate and make choices successfully, along with being able to act on one's choices. And in defending the fifth need, suitably supportive people are necessary in learning how to develop all these capacities and accomplish all of these goals, especially those involved with the third need, understanding. For effective learning to take place (a necessary activity on the path toward understanding), we need a certain kind of environment in which positive feedback validates limited achievement, creating a sense of competence and self-efficacy, which is necessary for effective learning and doing. Decent social relations with at least some others are necessary for effective learning to take place. Such relationships can also be important to fulfilling other needs as well; this category connects importantly with psychological needs, such as for esteem, respect, recognition, connectedness, or intimacy.[30]

---

[29] For a much longer defense see Brock, *Global Justice*, chapter 3, especially 63–69.
[30] For more on these arguments see Brock, *Global Justice*, 63–71.

Meeting the moral agency needs generates many other needs or conditions that must also be satisfied, as I illustrate shortly. We might call these other needs "derivative needs" to mark important distinguishing features. Unlike the five core needs that are universal in virtue of the demands of moral agency, these derivative needs can vary depending on particular contexts and individual personalities. However, and second, having noted that derivative needs can take many forms, we should also note that there can be high regularities to them as well. I illustrate with central examples next.

(i)   *Economic needs.* A need for sufficient health minimally entails a need to subsist, which in turn frequently entails a way to support oneself in particular social and economic environments. So, we need to have skills necessary for participation in an economy, and the skills we need are contingent on particular economies in specific contexts. We learn to harpoon whales, hunt caribou, milk goats, weave flax, repair computers, or perform actuarial tasks, depending on the skills required to participate in particular environments, which reward certain activities and not others. So, while the category of economic needs might be widely shared, the form that meeting the need should take in particular contexts can vary greatly.[31]

(ii)   *The need for a reasonably large supportive network of personal relationships, often described as "community."* The need for decent social relations with at least some others can be fulfilled by a very small group of people – technically, just one person can fulfill this need, linked as it is in its origins to effective learning. The idea with the need for community, by contrast, is that the group is much larger and forms more of a social support system consisting of many relationships of *roughly* similarly oriented people. Not every human being professes to have such a need. However, it is one that seems to be widely reported from across diverse cultures.

The salience of such a need can be linked to multiple core needs, most obviously the need for decent social relations, but also the need for psychological health. In a commonly articulated form, a need for community can also fulfill other expressed needs, notably psychological needs such as a need for a sense of connectedness.

---

[31] While we can derive the importance of economic needs through the basic need for subsistence, it also connects importantly with other needs, notably psychological needs such as to feel productive. Some also derive a sense of meaning and value in fulfilling economic needs.

A supportive network of personal relationships also links up with people's need for security.

(iii) *Political self-determination.* Autonomy is a central driver of many further needs, including *political self-determination*. As the need for autonomy signals, we have central needs to be authors of our own lives, that is, to have some important sphere of control over key decisions about the shape of our lives. The need for some personal control blends into participation in processes that allow collective control over our common affairs as well. While we can derive the importance of the need for political self-determination from the need for autonomy, again this need connects importantly with others as well, notably, with several psychological ones, such as for recognition, connectedness, or esteem.

Economic, social support (or community), and political self-determination needs are three very important categories of needs that are highly salient to many people's well-being and their felt sense of fulfillment. Each connects in complex ways with agency needs. And each can have significant implications for dealing justly with migrants, as we see in later chapters. It is very important to appreciate, however, that like all claims, the force a claim of need should have in particular contexts must be weighed against the force of others' needs, along with many additional considerations, such as what the other core features of justice require.

Note that there is an important role for location to play in understanding how all our needs matter to responsibilities, especially in the case of derivative needs. As we have seen in understanding our economic needs, the particular ways in which we orient ourselves and plan to meet needs is importantly determined by place and context. People form plans around particular forms of life in specific places; in short, they form "located life plans."[32] After all, people live their lives in particular social and geographical settings, and these features strongly influence their plans for their lives. Their legitimate located life plans deserve respect. Realizing that these located life plans will often be very important to people, we have strong

---

[32] The term "located life plans" seems to have been introduced by Anna Stilz. See, for instance, Anna Stilz, "Occupancy Rights and the Wrong of Removal," *Philosophy and Public Affairs*, 41 (4) (2013): 324–356; Anna Stilz, "Territorial Rights and National Defense" in Cecile Fabre and Seth Lazar (eds.), *The Morality of Defense in War* (Oxford: Oxford University Press, 2014), pp. 203–228; and Anna Stilz, "Settlement, Expulsion and Return," *Politics, Philosophy and Economics*, 16 (4) (2017): 351–374. Margaret Moore also notes the importance of location in human beings' significant plans and projects. See, for instance, Margaret Moore, *A Political Theory of Territory* (Oxford: Oxford University Press, 2015).

reasons to accommodate these where possible. In these located life plans, groups of people tend to form settled patterns concerning how to meet needs. Practices develop about "how we do things around here." These practices and patterns can and often do change in response to a variety of key factors, such as environmental challenges, technological innovation, social change, or ethical pressures. But they can also be remarkably stable for long periods as well.

Settled patterns for meeting needs presuppose reasonably secure access to territory. As we have seen, settlements are a dominant way in which humans have organized themselves in our contemporary world. For settlers to continue to have access to the territory on which they have settled, there is a presupposition that they may rightfully continue to occupy particular spaces. After all, they may have invested labor and resources in securing ways to meet their economic needs, such as by building terraced rice fields, canals, irrigation pipes, aqueducts, bridges, dams, railroads, water purification systems, and other expensive assets relevant to the local land. And they may have invested in purpose-built spaces to meet their needs for self-determination, for instance by constructing buildings to express their religious, cultural, social, or political views. Under what conditions may settlers continue justly to occupy their settlements?

Settlers may be justified in continuing a way of life on a particular territory if their settlement arose without wrongdoing and they do not promote wrongdoing. Obviously, there is much packed into that short sentence, and here I can only gesture at some of the central points. Examples of settlements arising through wrongdoing include settlers driving out previous inhabitants of a territory to make space for themselves, thereby significantly jeopardizing other peoples' ways of life including their economic, social, and religious practices, or preventing others from meeting their core needs. Of course, the history of the world suggests few (if any) actual settlements are beyond moral reproach now. Many involve unsavory histories of exactly the prohibited kind. And prevailing current practices may wrongly prevent others from meeting their basic needs. Examples of the latter might include the ways in which their economies are structured, current trade policies, or contributions to climate change resulting in the disappearance of habitable land.

This very brief sketch of an account of justified continued occupation of territory should give us pause in thinking that any actual settlements are on firm moral ground now and that their settlement on particular territories is strongly justified "all the way down." In many cases there might well be a strong case for reparations based on this history and it could take the form of more generous migration policies, though other forms of reparations might be a better fit. So, how, if at all, can *any* settlements now be justified, especially in excluding others who wish to join the settlement? How can any current occupants of territory justifiably prevent anyone from migrating into their space? Perhaps no one has the legitimate authority to exclude anyone from moving into particular places? These are important questions that deserve robust answers. Over the next few chapters I provide a framework for showing the necessary conditions for such legitimate authority, beginning with the next section.[33]

4 Can Conventional Arrangements Be Justified? A Few Cheers for Administrative Structures

In our actual world of settlements, there are probably hardly any strong claims to just occupation of territory in virtue of pristine histories. And even if the history of how a particular group came to settle on specific territory were perfectly proper, the issue of whether current territory holders engage in wrongdoing, or practices that enable wrongdoing, would still be salient. There are, however, other considerations that are also relevant concerning whether or not people may permissibly continue to occupy territory. People cannot undo what has come before them. But they can take some responsibility for what happens under their watch; they can make reforms that better align with what justice requires here and now. They can make improvements, given the hand they are dealt.

Furthermore, we are typically born into communities in which people have made a life for themselves somewhere. That life will be characterized by some practices, including those that aim to meet needs or secure other

---

[33] There is also a further issue around how much territory we may justly occupy even if some occupation is justified. Importantly, the size (and other features) of justified occupation can change in response to relevant factors. To make the point, consider this thought experiment. There are two islands, which have abundant resources occupied by populations that enjoy living on their respective islands. Let us say that the two populations have justified rights to occupy their islands. Now imagine a volcano destroys one such that it is left uninhabitable. The terms on which occupants may rightfully occupy the remaining island have shifted. In particular, they may not rightfully occupy that territory and exclude the population whose island was destroyed. Such practices would clearly involve wrongdoing on my account. In particular, the size of the territory that continued occupation justifies would need to alter to these new circumstances. I believe such natural disasters can alter how much territory the original group may justly continue to occupy in the face of a population that is now in dire straits. We may be required to downsize our lifestyles or make certain relevant adjustments because of the important claims of others. So, for instance, we may be required to move to more sustainable lifestyles and economic practices, which might reasonably limit consumption options. Sharing space is an inevitable, necessary aspect of a successful human population that has radically increased in size.

aspects of justice, among other ambitions. These justice-oriented practices can create legitimate expectations for many who might come to depend on their continuation in some form. There will be expectations about interactions that take certain forms. In short, there will be some conventional arrangements about our ongoing lives in particular locations. Can those perhaps be justified? If so, might that give us a compelling answer to the question of a state's current right to occupy territory along with rightful authority to control entry onto their territory?

In defense of some version of conventional arrangements, we might start by noting that people have ended up where they are and cannot all be required to move without creating massive disruption and further injustice. Feeling settled and at home in the world is, for many people, an important part of human well-being. Though not a decisive consideration, it should be given some weight as we consider what justice can require of us, under our watch.[34] Here we are, living together unavoidably side by side, our fates intertwined, and this situation means we have a shared interest in promoting conditions in which we can continue to enjoy doing so. So, as I see it, we have strong reasons to pay attention to people's abilities to meet needs, protect basic liberties and promote fair terms of cooperation, along with the social and political arrangements that support such goals. All of these are key requirements if harmonious living is to prevail.[35] These are conditions that I have also highlighted as core to justice.[36]

---

[34] Is the need to feel settled and at home in the world a real need? What about the need for adventure? Humans have always been a curious lot that seek out new experiences and adventures. Which needs dominate particular psychological profiles is a highly individualized matter, though there may also be aspects to this related to age, gender, and ethnicity. Also, like all needs that are rightly to inform normative policy, they must be interpreted and understood through ethical constraints, balancing the weight this need should be accorded with other salient considerations. Note that I am not assuming settled communities must be homogenous. The facts of settled communities make this impossible. Different people have ended up where they are and so, at some level, their communities already overlap with, or include, diverse others.

One other point may be worth mentioning concerning settlement. The majority of those who want to migrate these days desire to join a more settled community rather than to join up with nomads. So, taking this core case of settled communities' rights to continued occupation is important in considering a framework for justice and migration.

[35] Notice that if we have a shared interest in promoting the necessary conditions for justice in our communities, this will include a shared interest in promoting willingness to contribute to maintaining those necessary conditions. This affects the norms we should engender about our obligations within and across communities.

[36] As I have been discussing, we have a shared interest in promoting the necessary conditions for justice in our communities and justice among them, since just arrangements are the most durable and so most likely to promote peaceful coexistence. It is important to appreciate also that the requirement to underwrite the social and political arrangements that can sustain justice includes

Settlements have almost always had administrative structures and for very good reasons: settlements would not be very good places to live without them. Administrative structures are important in our quest to secure justice. There is much to be said on behalf of settlements, along with suitable administrative structures, as potentially good vehicles for securing justice. Recall that justice requires attention to four particularly important aspects: protection for basic liberties, enabling people to meet needs, fair terms of cooperation, along with social and political arrangements that support these core elements. Securing such goals requires considerable thought and planning in setting up institutions, policies, and practices that can deliver on what justice requires. Administrative arrangements are important in planning to meet needs, protect basic liberties, coordinate actions productively, regulate our activities in ways designed to promote harmonious living, and so on. Consider some examples which illustrate the issues.

Meeting needs is a complex business that requires careful reflection about effective measures, institutional design, and resources necessary to match policies that can successfully enable people to meet needs. Take some of our basic needs such as for health or education.[37] Meeting health needs requires considerable analysis of what it takes to secure health, along with good planning to ensure the necessary goods and services are available for the target population. To do this competently requires adequate administrative support. Central to good health-care planning and service delivery is having a good projection of the target population for whom provisions should be made for a given time frame. Effective administrations can measure population size, make relevant projections, and match capacity to meet needs for the anticipated group resident on a territory.

Protecting basic liberties will similarly require reasonably accurate analysis of sources of threats to liberties, analysis of adequate ways to protect against these for the projected population, along with matching resources to support necessary goods and services. This will perhaps include the training of sufficient personnel who might effectively assist in reducing salient threats through preventive measures. This will also require institutions, trained staff, and resourcing to bring liberty violators to account, for instance through adequate enforcement measures.

---

requirements to promote respect, esteem, cooperation, mutuality, and so forth. So, for instance, as I argue in Chapter 4, Muslim bans would undermine the kind of ethos necessary to sustain harmonious living, living as we do side by side with all manner of difference.

[37] This is the common way in which our need for understanding gets articulated.

Even this cursory discussion of what is needed to secure adequate health and basic liberties protection will make salient the importance of good administration to achieving core components for justice. Administrative units and administrators with some authority to implement plans and enforce rules, are both important parts of the practical business of securing our lofty justice ambitions.

The administrative units that loom large in our world today are states embedded in a state system, and so these are the arrangements that need robust justification. States are effectively the gatekeepers for entry into settlements and they guard these powers. How, if at all, can this be defended? I consider this question in more detail in the next chapter. However, it is important to appreciate the underlying issues here. Whether or not we had states, it would be useful to have administrative units, so we might well have good reason to put some in place. And the borders of those units would be somewhat controlled, as they have been throughout history, though perhaps for more benign reasons; namely, to facilitate good planning in bringing about justice in particular communities.

A few points should be clarified before we leave this chapter, which largely deals with laying important groundwork.

First, note that so far, my argument is in defense of administrative structures of some kind, and centrally revolves around facilitating effective planning and delivery of what justice requires. Borders, or at any rate, administrative structures, facilitate justice under the right circumstances, because of practical matters, such as adequate planning to meet needs. It is a separate question whether administrative structures and border units should be more porous, in the sense of permitting more people to enter or remain. As I see it, a borderless world would not be one *most consistent* with justice. The right kinds of borders under the right kinds of conditions help us achieve justice. I return to these points in the final chapter because there is much more to discuss about what the right kinds of borders and conditions are. It is perfectly consistent with my argument so far that any and all persons who apply to move administrative units should be permitted to do so if the administrators are given sufficient notice of a desire to move, so they can take this into account in their planning to deliver on justice goals.

Second, members of settlements have a duty to support institutional schemes already in existence that are either delivering effectively on core components of justice or are credible prospects for doing this here and now. I believe this is required if we are to cooperate on fair terms. Unwillingness to play our part in supporting what justice requires is unfair.

Furthermore, I believe we have natural duties of justice that require all of us to support the maintenance or bringing into being of institutions that can secure justice. As I discuss in the next chapter, this gives us some reason to care about our existing administrative structures, how well they do in securing justice, and how big the gap might be if they fall short.

How can this duty to support institutions that can secure justice be defended? I think in several ways. For instance, it is an implication of living on fair terms of cooperation with others. Importantly also, it is pretty close to being a conclusion that can be derived from core moral and factual views. First, consider the factual aspect. As I have just been arguing, ensuring that persons are justly treated requires institutions that can deliver on the elements of justice (so those that can actually facilitate meeting needs, protect basic liberties, secure fair terms of cooperation and under-write these necessary conditions). Second, in defense of the normative views, we might note that all persons are entitled to equal respect and concern.[38] And this requires that we assist in ensuring that persons are justly treated, at least where we can do so with reasonable accommodations on our part. So, each of us has a significant but limited moral obligation to support institutions that can deliver on justice.[39]

So, we have obligations to support the institutional schemes we have when they have a good chance of securing the requirements of justice. What does this entail in our contemporary world? I believe the modern-day state system, with suitable modifications, has such prospects, and more so than other *current* contenders for the role. In the next chapter I show why the current arrangements that make up our state system are not justified on typical defenses for it. I also show that, with reasonable modifications, current arrangements can survive important justification tests. These modifications are quite important but are also reachable from where we are, despite significant challenges to our prospects for achieving them any time soon.

A third key point should be noted as we transition to trying to imple-ment justice in our actual world. In the next chapter and beyond we come to appreciate that the most pervasive public language in use today for capturing concerns about justice is the language of human rights. Human-rights doctrine has been highly successful in implementing many justice

---

[38] I have discussed what this Moral Equality Imperative rules in and out in several places, such as Gillian Brock (ed.), *Cosmopolitanism versus Non-cosmopolitanism: Critiques, Defenses, Reconceptualizations* (Oxford: Oxford University Press, 2013), 1–34.

[39] Allen Buchanan makes a similar argument. See Allen Buchanan, *Justice, Legitimacy, and Self-Determination: Moral Foundations for International Law* (Oxford: Oxford University Press, 2004).

gains over the last sixty years or so. The four central scaffolds for understanding justice can be translated into this language and I have shown the
details of this elsewhere.[40] There are significant advantages in using the
dominant discourse of human rights. It connects us with a highly sophisticated and advanced apparatus currently in use in the world today that has
significant purchase in international affairs. Insofar as there is a public
morality of world politics, human rights play an important role in constituting it. As we see in Chapter 3, human rights play a very important role
in the global normative order we currently inhabit. Our human rights
practice contains some important mechanisms that are aimed at securing
compliance and accountability for performance. If these work as intended,
they have a good chance of reducing injustice in our world today and
therefore deserve our support. They offer us some ready-made channels for
attempting to realize justice in our contemporary world.

5 Conclusions

In this chapter I reviewed some important history concerning migration
and covered some important normative groundwork for developing my
account of justice for people on the move.

As we saw in Section 2, our identities as individuals and as nations are
heavily influenced by migrations. Humans have always moved about,
whether in search of new opportunities or because of scarce resources,
environmental challenges, religious persecution, ethnic tensions, wars, and
so on. While current migration patterns show much continuity with those
of our ancestors, migration opportunities have also changed in response to
new technologies.

Section 3 began to develop my framework for navigating issues of
migration and justice by outlining four core important aspects of justice.
We saw that justice requires particular attention to enabling people to
meet needs, protecting their basic liberties, promoting fair terms of cooperation, and attending to the social and political arrangements that can
sustain these components of justice.

In addition, as I noted, here we are living side by side in diverse
communities. We have good reasons to nurture the conditions necessary
to sustain harmonious living among difference. Indeed, we have justice-
based reasons to give this important weighting. Promoting the social and

---

[40] See, for instance, Gillian Brock, "Needs and Global Justice," in Soran Reader (ed.), *The Philosophy
of Need* (Cambridge: Cambridge University Press, 2005), pp. 51–72, especially 70–72.

political arrangements that can underwrite justice, such as by promoting those that facilitate fair cooperation and protection for basic liberties, is therefore central to creating and sustaining just communities (or even those that can support good lives). We also noted how practices for delivering on justice will develop in particular locations. People's located life plans deserve respect, but this is complicated by the located life plans of others and histories of injustice, a theme that will be further discussed, and be especially pertinent in Chapter 5, in considering what justice requires for those migrants who have entered the territory in ways thought to be illegal.

In Section 4, I drew attention to the fact that delivering on lofty justice aspirations requires attention to some quite practical details. I argued that administrative units can be very important in facilitating justice. Administrative units are important to adequate planning associated with meeting needs, protecting basic liberties, securing fair terms of cooperation, along with promoting the relevant ethos necessary to sustain enduring cooperative communities. In our contemporary world, states perform central administrative functions, but various configurations could do what is required, including larger administrative units and smaller ones. States exist within a state system that is the main administrative structure governing the people of the world. So, it is worthwhile to consider whether our current arrangements – our state system – is just and, if not, what modifications are required. This we do in the next chapter.

As the review of some of our history highlights, it is important to note that the modern state system comes on to the scene reasonably late in the human story and might well one day evolve to something else that contains both larger and smaller administrative units, trends that we can already see developing. My justice framework can be relevantly applied to changing administrative configurations, but I believe the underlying core components of justice will remain enduring touchstones in any good analysis. So, in considering just arrangements for human beings, taking account of our human needs, along with protecting basic liberties, fair terms of cooperation, and relevant social and political support will all continue to be salient, even under different administrative regimes. Understanding these four scaffolds is therefore an important base as we judge how well administrative structures deliver on justice, both now and in the future.

CHAPTER 3

Self-Determination, Legitimacy, and the State System
A Normative Framework

1 Introduction

We find ourselves in a world of states. Many assumptions are made about this state system, for instance that this is a natural way to divide up the world and that agents of the state may act in certain ways that privilege the interests of their citizens in deciding whether to admit noncitizens. Our current arrangements may seem natural to us – perhaps the way things have always been. But they have not always been this way and they might change in the future. What robust justification can be offered for the assumed position that states have rights to self-determination, which include reasonably strong rights to control borders? What arguments can be offered to those who find themselves excluded by the state, along with those who fall within the state's borders?

This chapter seeks a justification for these default arrangements concerning robust rights to self-determination within a state system, one that is compelling to both insiders (those who are members of the state) and outsiders (those who are not).[1] In seeking a robust justification, we discover that in order for the state system to gain legitimacy, states have many responsibilities. While there is much talk about the rights of states to self-determination in migration discussions, when we understand how compelling arguments for this right proceed, they generate strong obligations as well, obligations that seem to be unappreciated. States have responsibilities to promote conditions that support self-determining, just communities. Discussion of these supplementary responsibilities is missing in many conversations about migration justice, but since fulfilling these obligations must be part of any robust justification for the right to self-determination, they deserve more prominence. As I show, a state's

---

[1] For an excellent argument concerning why justification is owed to both nonmembers and members of a state see Arash Abizadeh, "Democratic Theory and Border Coercion: No Right to Unilaterally Control Your Own Borders," *Political Theory*, 36 (1) (2008): 37–65.

legitimacy depends on its respecting human rights adequately and cooperating in a host of international activities and institutions that have as their aim securing credible arrangements capable of reasonably effective human rights protection. Without sufficient action and commitment on these and related goals, rights to self-determination within the state system cannot be justified.

We also need to consider carefully core elements brought in to view by this argument. I discuss the criteria states must meet to have a legitimate right to self-determination, identifying three distinct aspects to these requirements. Respect for human rights plays an important role in understanding all of these criteria. I consider which human rights play this important role. Charles Beitz has offered a compelling analysis of human rights. Drawing on Beitz's practice-based conception of human rights, we are able to apply several elements to our analysis of how states can come to have a legitimate right to self-determination within the state system. As we see, for states to enjoy this right they must respect their residents' human rights adequately (an internal requirement) and play an appropriate role in contributing to the legitimacy of the state system (a contribution requirement), such as by participating in international arrangements that can deliver on human rights protection. The state system can be justified if states are meeting internal and contribution requirements and there are robust institutional arrangements in place that can deal adequately with gaps between minimum requirements and actual state performance. Mechanisms to correct for relevant performance failures must also be part of the institutional structure, for a justified state system. In this chapter I argue for the basic framework and develop key parts. In later chapters I explore the details of some mechanisms needed to correct for legitimacy breaches. For instance, in Chapter 6 I discuss the mechanisms required to deal with failures in the case of refugees; and in Chapter 7 I discuss the arrangements needed to secure temporary migrants' human rights adequately.

2   In Search of a Justification for States' Rights to Self-Determination within the State System

Let us start with a description of what may seem natural to readers. Many readers will have the view that members of a state have a right to decide what is best for them. So, for instance, they might maintain that political leaders in the United States of America should privilege what is best for people living in the USA. Politicians in the United Kingdom should do what is good for their citizens. And similarly, those in each and every state have a right to decide what is best for them and to enact matching policy. So, to illustrate the idea, if Americans choose to adopt policy that puts Americans first in trade, that's their prerogative. If those in Britain decide British jobs should go exclusively to British workers, they are entitled to do so. If New Zealanders restrict foreigners from purchasing land, residential property, or farms, such actions are permissible. In short, every state has the right to adopt policy that concerns itself almost exclusively with the well-being of its citizens over others (a position often referred to as "compatriot favoritism").[2] After all, every state has the right to self-determination, such that its citizens are free to determine their economic, social, and political affairs.

What justification can be offered for this assumed natural default position? One version of a defense might be summarized roughly along these lines:

> *Premise 1*: States should have the right to decide what is in their citizens' interests and to make policies and laws on the basis of their perception of those interests and their own views of what is good for citizens.

> *Premise 2*: Everyone belongs to some state or other, so all persons have a government committed to advancing citizens' interests and respecting their human rights, ensuring the persons on their territory can enjoy relevant freedoms and opportunities characteristic of a good life in their home state.

> Conclusion: So, these arrangements are fair.

What are we to make of this argument? One major weakness is that *Premise 2* is patently false in our world. Sadly, all persons do not live in a state governed in such a way as to respect their human rights and advance their interests, assisting them to enjoy core freedoms and opportunities. Indeed, if they did, many people would not seek to migrate away from such situations. The cases of Syrian refugees fleeing civil war and those who seek to escape dire poverty in central African failed states are just two examples of such government failures to protect core interests and rights.

Because *Premise 2* is clearly false, this particular argument fails.[3] We will need to begin our justificatory exercise again.

---

[2] For more on this position see, for instance, Gillian Brock, "Liberal Nationalism versus Cosmopolitanism: Locating the Disputes," *Public Affairs Quarterly, 16,* 307–327, 2002. For good recent discussion of the issues suggesting the position is incoherent see Lea Ypi, "Cosmopolitanism without if and without but" in Gillian Brock (ed.), *Cosmopolitanism versus Non-cosmopolitanism: Critiques, Defenses, Reconceptualizations* (Oxford, Oxford University Press, 2013), pp. 75–91.

[3] We do not need to consider whether *Premise 1* is true, since the argument fails in virtue of *Premise 2* being false. However, as becomes clear in this chapter, I do not believe that *Premise 1* is plausible.

Before we do so, it is worth noting that there is a burden of proof issue. The justificatory challenge changes with our starting point and affects the assumptions about who has to make an argument to whom. So, we should not start from the assumption that states are justified natural units. Rather, the prior question is: How can we justify a world carved up into states (the state system)? The rights states have need justification and cannot just be assumed. And the justification needs to be made in terms that everyone, including and especially those excluded from the state can appreciate as compelling. We will need to adopt a perspective that is mutually accept-able to both insiders and outsiders.

What kinds of norms governing the relations among persons – among those both inside and outside of particular communities – can be justified from a common standpoint, from a standpoint that both insiders and outsiders can find compelling? Following John Rawls' ideas, I have explored a way to answer this question in developing an account of global justice.[4] One accessible way to get at the relevant perspective is to ask: If people did not know whether they would be insiders or outsiders of particular communities, what kind of justification for the state system might they find compelling? We might find such a view compelling if it were indeed true that all persons have a government committed to pro-tecting and promoting their interests and human rights, ensuring the persons on their territory can enjoy freedom and opportunities character-istic of justice, as the previously discussed premise, *Premise 2*, described. In the absence of such a state of affairs (with adequate supplementary provi-sions for failures), anyone substantially disadvantaged by such inter-national arrangements has no reason to find such a justification for the state system compelling. Nor would they have good reason to find the compatriot favoritism view that legitimate states presuppose as remotely justified either – privileging the interests of fellow members when others fail to have their basic human rights secured would remain undefended.

Notice what is required if we do want to pursue this argument strategy. We should cooperate in a host of cross-border activities, programs, initia-tives and institutions that have as their aim securing good arrangements

---

It is not true that all states should have the right to decide such matters. At best, only legitimate states should have such a power. Also, minimally, citizens should have a role in shaping views about what is in their interests, so minimally only those states that give citizens an opportunity to participate in governing should have such rights, thus excluding dictators or authoritarian rulers from such rights. In addition, there are obvious problems with the idea that only compatriots matter, as we see in the arguments of this chapter.

4 Gillian Brock, *Global Justice* – see especially chapter 3.

that can deliver on human rights and other aspects of justice. So, those in one state will have responsibilities to many outside of their borders to assist in projects that strengthen protection and promotion of human rights where these are not secure or are being violated (along with ensuring people have secure arrangements that can underwrite and deliver on other core aspects of justice). A justification along these lines will require that we fulfill many international responsibilities, as a requirement of enjoying self-determination and the *defensible* right to privilege our compatriots' interests.

We have arrived at one important result so far in considering these arguments. The justification for states' rights to self-determination reveals that states have some important duties. They need to work with others to make it possible that all persons, no matter where they are situated on the globe, can rightly enjoy the protections and opportunities that are assumed by the kind of position outlined in *Premise 2* in the argument above. So, states will have obligations to support institutional arrangements that can respect everyone's human rights, whether or not they are on the territory of the state. States that do not meet these obligations cannot have a robust right to self-determination, as they understand the claim. To ensure such a robust right, states must play a role in securing the necessary conditions for all persons to enjoy human rights. When states do not discharge their obligations by playing their required part, their own legitimacy is in jeopardy. This argument has significant implications, and these will be developed throughout this chapter, along with chapters to come.

3 Three Layers of Legitimacy Constraints

Recapping what we have seen so far, we have taken states' claims to the right to self-determination within the state system and traced what must be the case for that kind of claim to be defensible. When we analyze what must be the case for the claim to be justified, we find there are plenty of resources that can be assembled to powerful normative effect, such as the idea that the claim is conditional on meeting certain requirements. One implication of the arguments made so far is that performance on human rights is an important marker of legitimacy, of a state's legitimate claim to have a right to self-determination.[5] We need to know much more about

---

[5] As should be clear, I am offering a moralized conception of legitimacy: states are legitimate if they are morally justified in wielding political power. Political legitimacy requires that a minimum threshold normative standard of justice is achieved. Other authors who offer similar views include Allen Buchanan, especially in *Justice, Legitimacy, and Self-Determination*; Allen Buchanan and Robert Keohane, "The Legitimacy of Global Governance Institutions," *Ethics and International Affairs*, 20

how performance on human rights will be assessed, if it is to play this role. This is discussed in Sections 5 and 6.

Second, while there is much talk about the rights of states to self-determination in discussions of immigration, we need to supplement this discussion with state responsibilities to promote conditions which support self-determining, just communities because these responsibilities play an important role in any cogent defense for the right to self-determination.

Third, so far, we have seen that, at least in theory, the right to self-determination within a state system can be justified. But we have also noted that important provisions for state failures must be part of the institutional architecture if the justification is to be compelling. As I have highlighted, the international community has certain responsibilities to attend to gaps when states fall below a threshold of performance on human rights.

My central argument requires three sets of legitimacy conditions to be met. To bring these out more clearly, the argument may be summarized as set out in (1)–(4), with further implications developed thereafter:

(1)   States may enjoy a right to self-determination when legitimacy conditions are met.

(2)   To exercise power legitimately,[6] states must respect their own citizens' human rights. (Legitimacy condition 1, (LC1), *Internal Requirement*).

(3)   Exercising power legitimately is also conditional on being part of a legitimate state system (Legitimacy condition 2, (LC2), *System Requirement*).

(4)   The legitimacy of the state system requires states to participate in the cooperative project needed to sustain a justified state system. Individual states have some positive obligations that are generated in virtue of the legitimacy conditions on the state system (Legitimacy condition 3, (LC3), *Contribution Requirement*).

---

(4): 405–437; Nicole Hassoun, *Globalization and Global Justice* (Cambridge: Cambridge University Press, 2012); and Anna Stilz, "Why Do States Have Territorial Rights?" *International Theory*, 1 (2) (2009): 185–213. The idea of political legitimacy has a long history, which I cannot cover here given my primary goals. For more on this history and competing accounts see, for instance, Fabienne Peter, "Political Legitimacy" in Ed Zalta (ed.), *Stanford Encyclopedia of Philosophy* (Palo Alto: Stanford, 2016). Available online at http://plato.stanford.edu/

[6] When I use the phrase "exercising power legitimately" throughout this book I mean "exercising political power legitimately."

One key implication so far is that:

(5)   Failure to perform on (LC1), (LC2), or (LC3) undermines the case for robust rights to self-determination. So, when *particular* state governments fail to perform adequately on human rights or fail to do what the presuppositions of a justified state system require, the state's own claim to exercise power legitimately can be called into question. This can have far-reaching implications, including throwing into doubt whether a state has a defensible right to control borders (inter alia).

But there are other more wide-ranging implications as well, such as:

(6)   Sufficient failure on the part of states to meet internal requirements, (LC1), in the absence of corrective measures, undermines the legitimacy of the state system. Similarly, sufficient failure to meet contribution requirements, (LC3), in the absence of correction, can also undermine the legitimacy of the state system.

So,

(7)   The state system needs to incorporate legitimacy correction mechanisms for such cases. We may need a range of such mechanisms, some to cover internal breaches of type (LC1). We may need another set of measures for contribution breaches of type (LC3).

(8)   Failure to incorporate such corrective measures undermines the legitimacy of the state system.

(9)   This has implications for all states since they all rely on a legitimate state system for their own legitimacy. All states' legitimacy is undermined by failures discussed in (8).

This has many further implications such as:

(10) Under such conditions, the claim to self-determination may not shield states from those who undertake actions that would better align with a justified state system (such as when they act in ways that can better secure human rights that are under threat).

A few examples of actions of the kind described in (10) might include refugees entering a state unlawfully when the state system fails to make adequate arrangements for their protection, once their own state has failed them and other states have failed to provide assistance. It might also include the creation of sanctuary cities that can shield undocumented migrants from deportation by an authority lacking the required legitimacy to do so. These are some of the implications discussed in other chapters, especially Chapter 6, when we discuss the situation of refugees, Chapter 5 (on undocumented migrants), and Chapter 9 (when we cover our responsibilities in relation to reducing migration injustice).

Clearly, human rights play a key role in these arguments and, to progress the argument, we need to understand them better. We also need to get a firm grasp on the complex ideas concerning how individual states should support the goals that are the target of a legitimate state system. What should particular individual states do to play their part in this collective project? We also need to discuss the complex ideas associated with how the international community should aim to remedy legitimacy failures. When the actual performance of states is not adequate, there needs to be a set of provisions in place to remedy the problem, to hold that state accountable, or for picking up the slack when that state cannot, or does not, do what needs to be done. In short, we need corrective mechanisms. Different kinds of state failures need different measures. Charles Beitz offers a helpful practice-based analysis of human rights, along with a sophisticated account of responsibilities in relation to those rights, which can assist considerably with all these tasks. I discuss this account in Section 5. Before I pursue these tasks, I pause to acknowledge that at least two other prominent migration justice theorists have also made some arguments similar to the strategies I pursue here, though to my knowledge neither has combined the various legitimacy arguments into a three-layered account of legitimacy, nor do they develop the account in the ways I do in this book.

4   Some Fellow Travelers

Those who have made similar arguments often draw out the implications of these views for refugees. Joseph Carens's arguments might be the most well-known. In searching for justifications for the duty to admit refugees, Carens notes that we can find one in the "normative presuppositions of the modern state system."[7] He says:

> The modern state system organizes the world so that all of the inhabited land is divided up among (putatively) sovereign states who possess exclusive authority over what goes on within the territories they govern, including the right to control and limit entry to their territories. Almost all human beings are assigned to one, and normally only one, of these states at birth. Defenders of the state system argue that human beings are better off under

[7] Joseph Carens, *Ethics of Immigration*, 196.

this arrangement than they would be under any feasible alternative . . . Even if being assigned to a particular sovereign state works well for most people, it clearly does not work well for refugees. Their state has failed them, either deliberately or through its incapacity. Because the state system assigns people to states, states collectively have a responsibility to help those for whom this assignment is disastrous. The duty to admit refugees can thus be seen as an obligation that emerges from the responsibility to make some provision to correct for the foreseeable failures of a social institution. Every social institution will generate problems of one sort or another, but one of the responsibilities we have in constructing an institution is to anticipate the ways in which it might fail and to build in solutions for those failures. If people flee from the state of their birth (or citizenship) because it fails to provide them with a place where they can live safely, then other states have a duty to provide a safe haven. Thus, we can see that states have a duty to admit refugees that derives from their own claim to exercise power legitimately in a world divided into states.[8]

David Owen uses a similar strategy and draws out some of the implications that may be justified when legitimacy conditions are not met. He argues for an international refugee regime that is based on obligations "that arise as conditions of the political legitimacy of the international order of states considered as a global regime of governance."[9] States are coparticipants in a practice of governance. Human rights abuses pose legitimacy problems for the state and the international order of states. The global regime of governance should develop capabilities for addressing such situations. Different human rights abuses will require different kinds of responses, but a general issue likely to arise is that legitimacy repair mechanisms are required. A refugee regime might constitute one such repair mechanism. In his view, fair arrangements for hosting or resettling refugees must be reached, and it is plausible that different states will have different responsibilities allocated to them (perhaps tracking Gross Domestic Product or other salient measures of capacity to integrate refugees). When states are not fulfilling their obligations under a just refugee regime, the legitimacy of the state system is called into question. He says:

> This implies that, in the absence of urgent action to redress this condition, the unprotected refugees are not obligated to accept the authority of the normative regime of governance that is the international order of states. Rather they are free to act in ways that breach those norms to the extent

---

[8] Ibid.

[9] David Owen, "In Loco Civitatis: On the Normative Basis of the Institution of Refugeehood and Responsibilities for Refugees" in Sarah Fine and Lea Ypi (eds.), *Migration in Political Theory* (Oxford: Oxford University Press, 2016), pp. 269–289, p. 270.

that it is necessary for them to do so in order to protect themselves. They would, for example, be justified in ignoring legalities of entry into another state. The contrast with the liberal sovereignty view is stark.[10]

When refugee crises remain unattended and states refuse to play an effective role in addressing them, the standing of states' rights to control entry is called into question. Owen's argument paves the way for those who support mechanisms that circumvent state's laws to occupy strong moral ground. For instance, those who construct "underground railways" or people smuggling systems of certain kinds might plausibly claim that such actions are not only justified by the legitimacy failure of the global governance regime but mechanisms such as these are morally praiseworthy or even obligatory.

Though Carens and Owen have used arguments based on the normative presuppositions of the state system to good effect with refugees, I believe these kinds of arguments have much broader implications that can be brought to bear in several relevant debates including how to rethink global obligations and governance in a variety of domains. In this book I draw out important implications for migration justice.

Having acknowledged the important related arguments these other leading figures have made, I continue to develop the idea of three layers of legitimacy to fortify my own account.[11] As I noted previously, neither of these leading authors have developed a three-layered account of legitimacy and this novel argument requires further discussion to appreciate just how it works.[12] Our next task is to understand the ways in which human rights can play important roles in defining legitimacy in our contemporary world.

5   Charles Beitz's Account of Human Rights

As Charles Beitz explains in his ground-breaking work, *The Idea of Human Rights*, there is an important emergent political practice around human rights.[13] Understanding this practice is important to appreciating the role

---

[10] Owen, "In Loco Civitatis," 285.

[11] More recently I came across the work of another prominent theorist who also develops similar themes, though once again he does not develop a three-layered account of legitimacy as I do. For a very interesting and accessible argument see Christopher Bertram, *Do States Have the Right to Exclude Immigrants?* (Cambridge: Polity, 2018). He argues that states have no credible right to exclude, given that our current system of migration controls are not justifiable to everyone. This has far-reaching implications including that no one need obey current immigration rules.

[12] As I see their arguments, they make a case that, at best, involves parts of (LC2) and possibly parts of (LC3). My account is far more wide ranging, as will become evident below and in later chapters.

[13] Charles Beitz, *The Idea of Human Rights* (Oxford: Oxford University Press, 2009).

of human rights in constituting the public morality of world politics.[14] A practice-based conception differs from two dominant positions on human rights: the idea of human rights as entitlements that belong to people as a matter of human nature and that of the idea of human rights as objects of agreement among diverse peoples.[15] By contrast, Beitz does not suppose that human rights express or come from one single value or concept. Rather, there is a distinct normative practice that operates in our contemporary world and we need to understand it before we can appreciate human rights' distinctive role.

According to the practice of international human rights, states must treat their own people in certain minimally satisfactory ways. Failure to do so triggers international concern that can take various forms. At the limit, sufficiently grave failures can be grounds for international military intervention, with various courses of action also available far short of that. So, one important implication of this practice is that recognition of a state's legitimate authority, including its authority to control its borders, hangs on adequate human rights performance. We need to understand the practice to flesh this out, starting with its origins and central commitments, along with mechanisms available for its implementation.[16]

In order to understand our contemporary emerging practice of human rights, we must begin with its history. The modern international human

---

[14] Beitz, *The Idea of Human Rights*. There are many excellent accounts of human rights, which include at least some desirable features, even though I have chosen a different path for this project. As we see in later chapters (especially Chapters 7 and 9), a practice-based conception offers some excellent ready-made channels for ensuring states follow through on implementation commitments and are held accountable for their actions, so that we can make progress on reducing migration injustices in our contemporary world. For some other strong accounts of human rights, see for instance, James Griffin, *On Human Rights* (Oxford: Oxford University Press, 2008); James Nickel, *Making Sense of Human Rights* (Oxford: Oxford University Press, 2006); William Talbot, *Which Rights Should be Universal?* (Oxford: Oxford University Press, 2005); and Nicole Hassoun, "Human Rights and the Minimally Good Life," *Res Philosophica*, 90 (3) (2013): 413–438. One issue that some opponents of practice-based theories find puzzling is how the norms of an actually existing social practice can have normative authority for us. As I show in Chapter 9, making extensive use of the recently adopted compact on migration, we see how the normative authority can rest on the content of the obligations embedded in its treaties, along with the agreements' credibility, consensual nature, "collective ownership, joint implementation, follow-up and review," as in fact the document itself highlights. While the social practice could theoretically evolve in undesirable ways, there are enough central features embedded in the practice (including the UDHR and core treaties) such that the necessary critical tools are available from within the practice to block such developments.

[15] For some examples of natural rights accounts see Maurice Cranston, *What Are Human Rights?* (London: Bodley Head, 1973); James Griffin, *On Human Rights*; Richard Tuck, *Natural Rights Theories* (Cambridge: Cambridge University Press, 1978). For examples of agreement theorists, see Michael Ignatieff, *Human Rights as Politics and Idolatry* (Princeton, NJ: Princeton University Press, 2001); and Rex Martin, *A System of Rights* (Oxford: Clarendon Press, 1993).

[16] Beitz, *The Idea of Human Rights*, 13.

rights practice that Beitz is concerned to understand originates from the settlement of World War II and the adoption of key documents such as the Universal Declaration of Human Rights (UDHR) in 1948, which I discuss first.

5.1   UDHR

Recalling that disregard for human rights has led to barbarous acts, and concerned to recognize the inherent dignity of human beings, the UDHR calls on individuals, nations, organizations, "and every organ of society" to "promote respect for these rights and freedoms and by progressive measures, national and international, to secure their universal and effective recognition and observance."[17] The Articles include a list of rights that aims to protect core interests in "personal security and liberty, legal personality, freedom of expression and association, participation in the political process, economic and social security, and participation in cultural life."[18] Articles 28 and 29 outline some of our responsibilities, including calling on us to support a social and international order in which human rights "can be fully realized" and to acknowledge that "everyone has duties to the community in which alone the free and full development of his personality is possible."[19]

The original Human Rights Commission set itself three tasks: the promulgation of a declaration of human rights; drafting "a binding international convention"; and working out mechanisms for how the convention might be implemented. Enforcement was envisaged as occurring in two tiers. The idea was to have human rights incorporated into domestic law and states would be the primary agents responsible for bringing about human rights adherence in their states. The second tier was to deal with government failures. As explicitly mentioned in the charter (and attracting unanimous support from all member nations), government failure on human rights standards should be of international concern. A working group considered several possibilities as to the form international concern might take, including mandatory reporting, "petition and inquiry by special commissions or a special human rights court,"[20] and where violations had been found "public censure and 'extreme action involving

---

[17] Universal Declaration of Human Rights (UDHR) available for instance here: www.un.org/en/universal-declaration-human-rights/
[18] UDHR.   [19] UDHR.   [20] Beitz, *The Idea of Human Rights*, 24.

reprisals and the use of sanctions'."[21] The working group embraced a scheme that combined several elements such as periodic reporting, monitoring, and adjudication. However, the full commission took no action on these recommendations. Looking at how the practice operates today, we find several features represented. There are reporting and monitoring elements and there are some provisions for complaints.

In addition to the UDHR, there are two covenants, one on civil and political rights (ICCPR) and the other on economic, social and cultural rights (ICESCR). According to these documents, civil and political rights "could be implemented immediately" but economic and social rights should be realized progressively, with each state acting both individually and "through international assistance and co-operation, to the maximum of its available resources."[22]

The UDHR, ICCPR, and ICESCR constitute what is conventionally known as the International Bill of Rights. The International Bill of Rights and four additional key treaties are widely regarded as the core documents that make up international human rights doctrine. These four additional documents are the Convention on the Elimination of All Forms of Racial Discrimination (CERD, 1969), the Convention on the Elimination of All Forms of Discrimination Against Women (CEDAW, 1981), the Convention gainst Torture and Other Cruel, Inhuman or Degrading Treatment or Punishment (CAT, 1987), and the Convention on the Rights of the Child (CRC, 1990).

5.2 Doctrine

The rights in the declaration and core documents consist in protecting an assortment of human interests. There are different ways to sort these. One classification Beitz uses is from Rene Cassin and distinguishes four categories.[23] First, there are rights to liberty and personal security. These include rights to "life, liberty, and security of the person; prohibition of slavery, torture, cruel or degrading punishment; right to recognition as a legal person; equality before the law; no arbitrary arrest; presumption of innocence."[24] Second, there are rights in civil society. These include free movement within the state, protections for privacy, and equal rights for men and women concerning marriage. Third, there are rights in the polity. These include freedom of association, conscience, and religion, and rights to participate in government. And fourth, there are economic, social, and

[21] Ibid.   [22] Ibid., 25–26.   [23] Ibid., 27.   [24] Ibid.

cultural rights – including rights to adequate food, housing, and medical care; free elementary education; and just remuneration and the right to freely chosen employment.[25]

The four core conventions add more important human interests that must be protected. Interestingly, as Beitz observes, these can require immediate action:

> The Convention on the Elimination of All Forms of Racial Discrimination commits the parties not only to eliminate racial discrimination in law and the practices of public institutions but also to use state power to prohibit and punish the public expression of "ideas based on racial superiority or hatred" (art. 4(1)). More strikingly, the Convention on the Elimination of All Forms of Discrimination Against Women commits the parties to "modify the social and cultural patterns of conduct of men and women" so as to eliminate "prejudices and customary and all other practices which are based on the idea of the inferiority or the superiority of either of the sexes" (art 5.). Both conventions call on parties to eliminate discrimination "without delay": unlike portions of the Covenants, neither bears interpretation as establishing long-term policy goals or "manifesto rights" that do not require immediate action.[26]

Beitz notes that human rights are sometimes conceptualized as minimal requirements for a decent human life or fundamental protections against the most egregious kinds of power abuse.[27] While these descriptions may have captured ideas of earlier declarations of rights, neither straightforwardly applies to the human rights practice of the postwar enactments, since they include also protections against various social and economic dangers and aim to guarantee some participation in political and cultural life. According to Beitz, contemporary human rights doctrine cannot be viewed as aiming "to articulate protections of timeless significance; it speaks to what might be described broadly as the conditions of modern life."[28] The contemporary practice has its own history and function and should not be confused with rights as discussed in various theoretical traditions (such as natural rights or agreement theories of rights). For Beitz, human rights are a "distinct normative system constructed to play a certain special role in global political life."[29] On his practical conception, we take the doctrine and practice of human rights as the source materials for understanding and constructing a conception of human rights.

---

[25] Beitz notes that the covenants and common articles also include a fifth category of rights: Rights of peoples – "most importantly, self-determination and communal control over 'natural wealth and resources'." Ibid., 28.

[26] Ibid., 29.   [27] Ibid., 30.   [28] Ibid., 31.   [29] Ibid., 68.

5.3   Implementation

State failures to accord with human rights standards are grounds for international concern. How is international concern expressed? The framers had in mind a juridical paradigm as a model of implementation, in which human rights would become part of domestic law enforceable in domestic courts. For those rights not easily implementable into domestic law, the rights should be accepted as matters to be incorporated in state policy. The idea was that there would be international monitoring for compliance by auditing states' self-reports, with repercussions for states judged to have failed. Some of the framers had hoped an international judicial capacity, such as a human rights court, would be instituted, to deal with disagreements between monitors and states and assign any penalties that might be needed. However, this did not happen, and monitoring agencies were limited to consultation, reporting, and public censure. It was hoped that in due course more robust forms of accountability might be put in place to incentivize better domestic compliance.

Beitz notes that our current global practice is quite complex. In some parts a juridical paradigm is in force, for instance in the regional human rights systems that include human rights courts with legal coercive capacity to insist on compliance with rulings.[30] The European human rights court is a good example of this. Various types of agents participate in human rights practice, including UN human rights agencies that are tasked with monitoring and reporting, international organizations, and nongovernmental agents (including social movement organizations and business firms). Beitz presents an implementation typology that includes six different kinds of action, which he labels as (1) accountability, (2) inducement, (3) assistance, (4) domestic contestation and engagement, (5) compulsion, and (6) external adaptation.[31] I discuss each in turn very briefly to get a sense of the complex mechanisms available for implementation and enforcement.

Accountability
The UN has a system of extensive reporting and auditing processes. These activities of UN human rights agencies, established by the main human rights treaties, are close to a juridical paradigm even if they technically fall short of it. These treaty bodies review and audit regular reports that states are required to provide evidencing their compliance. Nongovernmental

[30] Ibid., 32.   [31] Ibid., 33.

organizations have an important role to play as independent sources of information that can also be used to judge compliance. Four of the treaties also allow for individual rights of complaint and some also have independent procedures of inquiry.[32] When noncompliance is found, each body's principal recourse is consultation with the noncompliant state to identify ways to end violations,[33] though sometimes findings are also published.

A skeptic might question whether these processes can accurately be described as affording accountability, robustly construed. In response, Beitz draws on widely accepted notions of accountability in which "agent B is accountable to agent A if three conditions obtain: (i) A can require B to give an account of its compliance with a set of expectations or standards; (ii) A is empowered to judge whether B has complied with the standards; and, typically, (iii) A may impose sanctions on B if not."[34] Each element is technically in place in these international human rights accountability arrangements described, even if there are noteworthy problems, such as that required reports are often incomplete or late. Also, the treaty bodies are often insufficiently well-resourced to audit reports properly, and they may have at their disposal only limited sanction options, such as "naming and shaming" through public reporting of violations.

Of course, there is a difference between describing a process accurately and judging how effective it is. While skeptics may doubt that these processes are effective, Beitz, writing in 2009, notes that there is not much systematic evidence concerning their efficacy.[35] However, since Beitz made that assessment in 2009, quite a large literature has developed on these topics, showing considerable success in some areas, failures in others, mixed results in yet others, and interesting discussions about how we should judge progress is a further prominent development, some of which I discuss in Chapter 9.[36] But at any rate, as Beitz notes, the mechanisms technically do meet all the accountability conditions, so describing these as accountability systems is not inaccurate. In fact, it is only the treaty monitoring systems that *require* states to publicly account for their conduct.[37] These formal treaty monitoring systems play an important role in

---

[32] Ibid., 34.   [33] Ibid.   [34] Ibid., 35.   [35] Ibid.

[36] For excellent discussions see, for instance, Sally Engle Merry, *The Seductions of Quantification: Measuring Human Rights, Gender Violence, and Sex Trafficking* (Chicago: University of Chicago, 2016); Thomas Risse, Stephen Ropp, and Kathryn Sikkink (eds.), *The Power of Human Rights: International Norms and Domestic Change* (Cambridge: Cambridge University Press, 2009); and Kathryn Sikkink, *Making Human Rights Work in the 21st Century* (Princeton, NJ: Princeton University Press, 2017).

[37] Beitz, *The Idea of Human Rights*, 34–35.

being accountable to external audiences showing the international community how particular states are performing in relation to international standards.

Inducement

There are also less structured ways to encourage compliance. These include national governments and international organizations employing policies that incentivize human rights oriented activity, such as through offers of access to economic, social, and cultural resources, diplomatic incentives, providing special treatment in economic matters or the attachment of conditions to bilateral assistance.[38] In the 1970s, the USA, Japan, and some European states incorporated the protection of human rights into their foreign policy.[39] Others followed and so incentives to encourage human rights compliance became common. International organizations adopted some similar policies, for instance, international financial institutions included human rights compliance in lending agreements. And the WTO has a similar capacity, though it is seldom used.

Assistance

For some states, what they lack are the capacities needed to deliver on human rights. As one example, they may be deficient in economic capacity and therefore unable to produce sufficient goods needed to satisfy human rights. Alternatively, they may lack institutional capacity in areas such as policing, public administration, election monitoring, or legal institutions and so, because of such failures, be unable to deter, compensate, or deal adequately with deprivations. In such cases, external assistance aimed at improving institutional capacity might help, and this might take multiple forms depending on particular deficiencies. Assistance to strengthen institutional capacities may be particularly effective.

Domestic Contestation and Engagement

The mere understanding that there is an unfulfilled human right might stimulate local actors to pressure governments to make relevant changes. Processes of domestic engagement are another increasingly important set

---

[38] Ibid., 36.

[39] As an example of how this worked, in the USA foreign assistance and arms sales were conditional on meeting human rights standards. It is worth noting that changes of government may bring a return to such policies.

of mechanisms for implementing human rights, though they are often overlooked.

Compulsion

Compulsion is one limiting case of international action aimed at protecting human rights. While compulsion certainly is an option, it is often reserved as a last resort for only grave circumstances. Forms of compulsion include economic sanctions or military intervention.

External Adaptation

In contrast to mechanisms that seek to influence the behavior of domestic agents, obstacles to a government's inability to deliver on human rights may be traced to the policies of multinational actors, states, or regimes. Examples include trade policy that undermines food security or intellectual property rules that dramatically increase costs of pharmaceutical products to make them unaffordable for low income countries. In such cases, encouraging the relevant external reforms can yield improved human rights performance. So, for instance, encouraging drug companies to reduce the cost of their products in low income countries might make human rights concerning health easier to fulfill.

As we have seen then from this survey of six options, there is considerable complexity in implementing global human rights in practice. While some elements in the repertoire are close to a juridical paradigm, many measures differ quite sharply from it. Some activities are mainly persuasive. Others aim to support, coordinate, or mobilize domestic political agents, while others still aim to forge or strengthen transnational coalitions.[40]

5.4   Human Rights as an Emergent Practice

The global human rights practice has

> ... a set of rules for the regulation of the behavior of a class of agents, a more-or-less widespread belief that these rules ought to be complied with, and some institutions, quasi-institutions, and informal processes for their propagation and implementation. It is a general characteristic of social practices that under appropriate circumstances agents regard the rules as providing reasons for action and grounds of criticism. They also tend to believe it would be advantageous to have social processes that encourage

---

[40] Ibid., 40–41.

compliance and discourage noncompliance by other agents. These elements are plainly present in the human rights system.[41]

In addition to human rights offering rules and standards, human rights also function as standards of aspiration, offering ideals that can guide desirable political change. Beitz proposes a two-level model of human rights that involves a division of labor between states as the primary bearers of responsibilities to respect and protect human rights, and the international community, which acts to underwrite responsibilities. Government's failure to discharge its first-level responsibilities can be grounds for "appropriately placed and capable 'second-level' agents outside the state" to take action in several ways.[42]

The obligation to assist when human rights failures require action can vary according to particular relationships. The different interests human rights protect can also give different reasons to take action that may differ in urgency and strength. Beitz describes many possible kinds of relationships between those who need assistance and those in a position to offer assistance that could entail different responsibilities. These include current harmful interaction, historical injustice, non-harmful exploitation, and political dependence. For Beitz, each of these relationships or patterns "evokes a different kind of reason for action."[43] Agents will have different responsibilities depending on their relationships. Appropriate remedies also require different capacities.[44]

So, putting this all together, Beitz notes that international concern is currently expressed in unsystematic ways, "primarily by means of various forms of political action carried out by whichever agents are capable and appropriately placed and have sufficient reason to act. These agents include states acting unilaterally and in combination, international organizations, and a variety of other actors."[45] So the character of relationships between the potential beneficiaries and agents, along with other actors in the noncompliant state, are all relevant to defining responsibilities.[46] In addition, what is needed to secure particular human rights, the importance of

---

[41] Ibid., 42.   [42] Ibid., 109.   [43] Ibid., 171.

[44] Ibid., 173. Like Beitz, I argue for a similar position. In particular, we see that the convergence of three particularly salient criteria often provide sufficient reasons for parties that contribute to, benefit from, and have capacity to fix deprivation, to take responsibility for remedying that deprivation. I discuss such issues in multiple places, including Gillian Brock and Michael Blake, *Debating Brain Drain: May Governments Restrict Emigration?* (Oxford: Oxford University Press, 2015).

[45] Ibid., 197.   [46] Ibid., 198.

the interests threatened and the kinds of violations in play also matter to how to express concern over state failures to protect human rights.[47]

6   Meeting the Legitimacy Conditions

Drawing on Beitz's useful practice-based conception of human rights, we are now well positioned to tackle issues concerning the legitimacy conditions previously introduced. The minimum criteria to meet the legitimacy conditions, (LC1), (LC2), and (LC3) all need separate coverage.

6.1   Judging (LC1): Internal Treatment

In assembling the criteria that are to make up the minimum threshold for judging whether internal treatment requirements have been met, we might separate these into the rights that must be implemented immediately as opposed to those that allow for more progressive realization. Beginning with the UDHR, Articles 1– 21 are in the first category of rights that must be implemented immediately.[48] Next, I go through the core articles more carefully making some additional remarks.

All of Articles 1–11 must be on the list for immediate implementation as, in many ways, they simply restate some of the motivating ethos for why one should endorse the human rights doctrine in the first place or they clarify some of the more basic rights to life, liberty, and security, in prohibiting slavery and torture, protecting due legal process and equality before the law. From Articles 12 onwards, we start to see due recognition of an important interest that needs protection, with important qualifications being introduced as to what the content of the right includes and excludes. So, for instance, privacy and reputation should be respected and we should be protected from any *arbitrary* interference with these under the law (Article 12). Articles 13 and 14 have important bearing on movement. They specify:

13 (1)   Everyone has the right to freedom of movement and residence within the borders of each state.

   (2)   Everyone has the right to leave any country, including his own, and to return to his country.

---

[47] Of course, various kinds of actions are available as well, ranging from the persuasive to the highly coercive.

[48] More accurately, perhaps, there must be strong evidence of showing good faith efforts at respecting these rights immediately.

14. (1) Everyone has the right to seek and enjoy in other countries asylum from persecution.

(2) This right may not be invoked in the case of prosecutions genuinely arising from non-political crimes or from acts contrary to the purposes and principles of the United Nations.

Freedom of movement within the state is an important freedom, both in its own right and because of the ways in which it facilitates the fulfillment of other rights. Note that Article 13 (1) explicitly only covers freedom of movement within the state, not the freedom to move to one's preferred country. In addition, Article 29 places some important limits on these freedoms of movement (as it does with all human rights), notably when limitations on freedom are needed to secure due recognition and respect for other rights and freedoms such as "just requirements of morality, public order and the general welfare in a democratic society." So, there are significant justifiable grounds for limiting freedom of movement within human rights practice, an issue to be discussed in Chapter 9. Human rights concerning freedom of movement and asylum are discussed further in later chapters; here we continue with the task of compiling the list of rights that can be used to judge whether states perform adequately on internal treatment requirements.

Article 15 concerns the right to a nationality; Article 16 rights to marry and protection for the family.[49] Article 17 defends the right to own property. Article 18 protects freedoms of thought, conscience, and religion. Article 19 safeguards freedom of expression. Article 20 concerns the right to freedom of association and peaceful assembly. Article 21 fortifies participation in government and equal access to the public services provided. By contrast, Article 22 does not seem to me to be a clear candidate for inclusion in the basic legitimacy package that requires *immediate* implementation. Article 22 includes the right to social security and "economic, social and cultural rights indispensable for his dignity and the free development of his personality." While *commitment* to the right might be

---

[49] Rights concerning the family are covered in several places in later chapters, such as those on undocumented migrants (Chapter 5), refugees (Chapter 6), and temporary labor migration (Chapter 7). For some excellent work on family rights see Luara Ferracioli, "International Migration and Human Rights" in Chris Brown and Robyn Eckersley (eds.), *The Oxford Handbook of International Political Theory* (Oxford: Oxford University Press, 2018), pp. 520–532; Luara Ferracioli, "Family Migration Schemes and Liberal Neutrality," *Journal of Moral Philosophy*, 13 (2016): 553–575; Matthew Lister, "The Rights of Families and Children at the Border" in Elizabeth Brake and Lucinda Ferguson (eds.), *Philosophical Foundations of Children's and Family Law* (Oxford: Oxford University Press, 2018), pp. 153–170; and Matthew Lister, "Immigration, Association, and the Family," *Law and Philosophy*, 29 (2010): 717–745.

expected immediately, fulfilling these rights may well require a level of resourcing not yet available to very low income countries, so even with the best will in the world they may not yet be able to achieve what they would like and may hope to in the future. Requiring efforts to implement these rights *progressively* rather than immediately seems more appropriate.

Article 23 acknowledges the right to work at freely chosen activities, "to just and favorable conditions of work and to protection against unemployment." While these may be good goals to realize and be fully part of a state's aspirations, Article 23 (3), which concerns institutional guarantees, cannot always be implemented immediately, for similar reasons to why Article 22 is difficult in this regard. But Article 23 (4), that "everyone has the right to form and to join trade unions for the protection of his interests," is different. Failure to implement this right involves an important violation of freedom of association as guaranteed by Article 20.[50] And Article 23 (2), that everyone has the right to equal pay for equal work, is also different and, as an implication of Article 7 concerning nondiscrimination, should be part of the immediate implementation requirements.

Insofar as Article 24 recognizes some space for rest and leisure, it should be included. However, the part of Article 24 that endorses "periodic holidays with pay" is quite specific and should be read as more aspirational (and so not part of the *requirements* for immediate implementation in judging internal legitimacy). Similarly, Article 25 has strong aspirational ambitions, including as it does unemployment security and provisions for "sickness, disability, widowhood, old age or other lack of livelihood in circumstances beyond his control" and is vulnerable to similar concerns about low income countries' abilities to implement institutional provisions fully for all the cases listed, at least immediately and in the forms articulated. Having said that, the state should orient itself to ensuring people are able to meet basic needs as an important core element of a just society, so this is one of those goals that should be highly prioritized; making good faith efforts toward this more general goal of ensuring basic needs are met should be part of the requirements for a legitimate state. Given the priority that should be given to enabling people to meet needs, the state should show considerable commitment to the part of Article 25 that states, "everyone has the right to a standard of living adequate for the health and well-being of himself and his family, including food, clothing, housing

---

[50] Despite frequent pleas from low income countries that recognition of such a right would undermine economic interests, this article protects other interests that are also important for developing countries.

and medical care and necessary social services," at least to the extent that it is able. Whether or not this orientation amounts to unemployment security or other *institutional guarantees* seems to be a further issue.

Helping to equip citizens to participate in economic, social, and political activities requires basic education, and so the parts of Article 26 that protect basic education rights should be part of the minimum. Insofar as there is no cost issue with Article 27's right to participate in the cultural life of a community, it can be implemented immediately. *Commitment* to Article 28 is something that legitimate states should be able to endorse straight away, namely in recognizing that: "Everyone is entitled to a social and international order in which the rights and freedoms set forth in this Declaration can be fully realized." Insofar as they are not yet able to play a substantial part in upholding any costly aspects, that might require progressive realization. However, if there are no costs, or these are born by other states, commitment to Article 28 should be included in legitimacy requirements as, in many ways, Article 28 captures commitments already discussed in the main legitimacy argument, which generates the three central legitimacy conditions (LC1)–(LC3), as I discussed in Section 3. Note that Article 28 points in the direction of the need for contribution requirements, to be discussed with legitimacy condition (LC3) in the next section.

Finally, endorsing Article 29 as a matter of principle is important, as everyone should realize that there are duties to the community and that fulfilling human rights will require important duties for agents whose cooperation is needed if rights are to be adequately respected, protected, and fulfilled.

Recall that our human rights practice recognizes other documents as important, along with the UDHR. These are the International Conventions on Civil and Political Liberties; Economic, Social and Cultural Rights; along with the conventions on the elimination of all forms of racial discrimination, discrimination against women, rights of the child, and the prohibition of cruel, inhuman, and degrading treatment. While some of the core ideas are already covered by the UDHR, they add important emphasis and content. For instance, Article 4 (1) from the Convention on All Forms of Racial Discrimination specifies that states must use their power to prohibit and punish the public expression of 'ideas based on racial superiority or hatred' (art. 4(1)). This is a core idea that plays an important role in judging state legitimacy, as we see in the next chapter. And I believe prohibitions on cruel, inhuman, and degrading treatment will play an important role in judging legitimacy as well, as we see in Chapter 5 when we discuss whether states may eject long-settled migrants who are not citizens.

6.2   The Contribution Requirement (LC3), and System Legitimacy (LC2)

Discussing the contribution requirement, (LC3), must proceed next, because we are unable to assess system legitimacy, (LC2), in its absence. More precisely, we cannot discuss (LC2) without having a good appreciation of both internal and contribution requirements – so both (LC1) and (LC3) – along with how to proceed in the face of failures on (LC1) and (LC3). I sketch some of the core relevant ideas here and develop others in later chapters.

Recall that the legitimacy of the state system requires participation in the cooperative project needed to create or sustain a justified state system. Individual states have important positive obligations to contribute to this project that are generated by virtue of the legitimacy conditions on the state system. So, what are we to require of states in making the necessary contributions? How are we to evaluate contributions?

Assessing contribution should ideally take account of several ways in which states facilitate protection for a range of human rights, both now and in the future. As a rough indication of what might be included as measures of minimum contributions to a legitimate state system, we might start by considering indicators that enjoy broad support and are widely used in the world today. Top of that list might be country contributions in the area of Overseas Development Assistance (ODA). An advantage of using ODA is that there is good empirical evidence that level of economic development has a positive impact on rights protection.[51] But there are also significant disadvantages in using ODA, since ODA counts only financial contributions and in a misleading way. ODA is an indicator of international aid flows but it includes some loans. Furthermore, financial contributions are just one way in which development may be facilitated, and there are many others that may prove more effective. In addition, there is also much criticism concerning how financial contributions can distort or undermine the main aim of assisting development, for instance, when it leads to undesirable dependencies.[52]

---

[51] For instance, Todd Landman, *Studying Human Rights* (London: Routledge, 2006), 102. See also Kathryn Sikkink, *Making Human Rights Work in the 21st Century*.

[52] For one prominent example see Dambisa Moyo, *Dead Aid* (New York: Farrar, Strauss and Ciroux, 2009).

Since better measures are available, I suggest we use these when evaluating relevant contributions. One highly prominent alternative is the Commitment to Development Index (CDI), published by the Center for Global Development. The CDI ranks countries in terms of the development friendliness of their policies. As researchers on this project note, performance in a number of domains, not just financial contributions, are all relevant when we consider how states are contributing positively to sustainable development.[53] And when we evaluate contributions to development, we should take a more holistic approach, as the CDI does.[54]

The CDI assesses states' contributions in seven domains, namely in aid, trade, investment, migration, environment, security, and technology. The idea is that aid is not just about how much is given, but rather the quality of the aid matters greatly, along with state's supplementary policies in other areas. So, for instance, it is all very well to give funding through loans or grants, but if trade or environmental policies thwart beneficial, pro-poor, sustainable development, the net effect of a state's activities may well be negative. The index takes account of the ways in which policies in all seven areas contribute to development, and considers a more comprehensive range of relevant factors.[55]

Given its more sophisticated, multi-dimensional nature, we might use this CDI as *one* rough proxy of state contribution to building the kinds of societies likely to sustain a robust human rights practice.[56] In addition to the CDI, there are other aspects of contribution that should also be explicitly mentioned as we develop the requirements states must meet to satisfy (LC3). Because these can have an enormously powerful and pervasive effect on human rights practice, they should act as important further constraints on permissible action by states. In general, we might describe these as a commitment to the animating ideas and practices governing

[53] For more details about the Commitment to Development Index, see the website at www.cgdev.org/commitment-development-index-2018

[54] For more on the holistic approach, see the website at www.cgdev.org/commitment-development-index-2018

[55] See, for instance, www.cgdev.org/cdi-methodology

[56] We could also use an index composed of various indices, which has the advantage of taking account of many aspects that sustain strong support for human rights. Here we might include data from a wide range of sources including the highly respected Freedom House data, along with data from the office of the High Commission for Human Rights, and the World Bank World Development Indicators. I cannot consider these other possibilities here, given the primary aims of this book.

human rights today, as we have explored these ideas in Section 5. These include:

A commitment to maintain an ethos conducive to respect for the practice of human rights, such as that everyone deserves to be treated with dignity and respect as a human being (*Ethos Requirement*).

A commitment to practices of accountability (*Accountability Requirement*).

A general commitment not to promote arrangements in which respect and protection for people's human rights is significantly worsened, ceteris paribus. So, in the absence of compelling countervailing reasons, states should reject policies in which protection for people's human rights deteriorates markedly, especially when such protections are reasonably secure (*Constraint Against Worsening*).

A general commitment to show appropriate international concern as required by the practice, to undertake action when one is the agent capable and appropriately placed to have sufficient reason to act (*Commitment To Action Under Relevant Circumstances*).

As I consider in later chapters, including the next one, some kinds of actions on the part of state actors are highly destructive because of the ways in which they undermine the ethos and purposes of the contemporary human rights practice, along with respect for it. No matter what other contributions are made, some kinds of actions undermine respect for human rights practice and its efficacy so greatly that in virtue of those actions alone, the threshold contribution that (LC3) requires cannot be met.[57]

Given the discussion so far on (LC1) and (LC3), is the state system justified? What is my verdict on (LC2)? We have a contender for a legitimate state system when there is sufficiently good performance on human rights such that they are respected, protected, and fulfilled, at a reasonably robust level. When compliance falls drastically below the internal legitimacy minimum conditions articulated under (LC1), international measures are in place to remedy the situation and international actors play their part in contributing to securing the core basic rights. In addition, states generally make sufficient positive contributions as required by (LC3), such that the state system is reasonably functional in delivering on human rights. And international measures are in place and reasonably effective for dealing with situations of sufficiently grave noncompliance by states.

---

[57] Perhaps another aspect of why these actions completely undermine the possibility of reaching relevant legitimacy thresholds is that they have a bearing on whether or not internal standards (LC1) are really achieved. We discuss such a case in the next chapter.

We have yet to discuss what international measures would remedy relevant failures, along with what is required for international actors to play their relevant parts. These arguments are developed in later chapters. However, we do not need that detailed assessment because, just considering (LC1) and (LC3), it is hard to escape the conclusion that, as a group, states currently radically fail to make sufficient contributions to protecting human rights, and so that the state system (as a whole) does not reach the legitimacy threshold required. I realize that is a rather confident and sweeping claim that requires a full consideration of current efforts on a number of dimensions, including what institutional arrangements are in place to make up important current shortfalls. I do need to say much more about all of this, including what measures are currently on offer to correct for relevant failures or would be necessary should failures occur, and this happens in later chapters, such as in chapters on refugees (Chapter 6), migrant workers (Chapter 7), undocumented migrants (Chapter 5), and when we discuss some innovative measures available for correction, inter alia (Chapter 9). The details about why our current state system cannot pass a basic legitimacy test will be discussed in these chapters. For instance, in Chapter 6 we see that there are currently large forced migrations taking place with at least 70 million people currently in this category. Given the scale of the problem, and the inadequate and outmoded governance regimes surrounding protections for this large population, the international community has been unable to offer adequate arrangements to secure the human rights of the majority of these forced migrants adequately. I also discuss other troubling situations, such as significant failures to protect the human rights of migrant workers adequately in Chapter 7. So, in order to make my general case we will draw on some of this rich detail that is still to come. I review the analysis again in Chapter 9, when we are in a better position to evaluate claims about the current level of legitimacy of our state system. More importantly, we will also be in a good position to see where corrective measures are necessary, and the shape they should take, once the detail is provided.

7   Some Problems

Individual state's performance varies greatly on whether they are meeting both internal and contribution requirements ((LC1) and (LC3) respectively). While individual states may pass the threshold on (LC1) and (LC3), without significantly improved performance on (LC2) (that is, a legitimate state system), all states suffer from legitimacy defects. So, we have two important "weakest link" problems related to this issue. One problem is that no state can be fully legitimate unless we have a legitimate state system. Second, given that no state can be legitimate unless we have a legitimate state system, and the probability of at least one state not reaching the legitimacy requirement is high, some might wonder why they should even aim to do what (LC1) and (LC3) require, because we are collectively going to fail, given that at least one state is bound to let us down.

I have at least two responses to these issues. One response is that we might differentiate between interim and full legitimacy. A state may achieve interim legitimacy when it meets (LC1), plays its rightful part in contributing to a legitimate state system (by meeting all its contribution requirements), including by contributing to correction mechanisms appropriately. Further needed improvements to make the state system legitimate require others to improve in ways that are not easily subject to the compliant state's control; for instance, we need cooperation from others in enforcing international agreements, initiatives, policies, and so forth, *on their territory*. There is no requirement for a compliant state to make up the shortfalls created by noncompliant states, as a *general* rule; however, they should demonstrate relevant commitment to trying to achieve a legitimate state system by, for instance, showing willingness to get other states to comply with their obligations by bringing any influence they have to bear on the problem.[58]

In my view some countries might plausibly currently meet the requirements for interim legitimacy. Norway, Sweden, and New Zealand might be plausible contenders. Others such as North Korea, Syria, and Burma fall quite a far way off the mark. Judging which states meet the interim legitimacy threshold is obviously another complex task, which I set aside for now in favor of the topics central to the themes of this book. In this book I draw attention to ways in which actions concerning migration can be relevant in judging whether a state is closer or further away from interim legitimacy. As we apply the analysis to issues of migration, we will see how this plays out. For instance, as I show in the next chapter, state actions on banning Muslim migrants is actually an important case study, as it brings to light several ways in which migration policies can undermine state legitimacy and take states quite far away from passing minimum interim legitimacy thresholds.

---

[58] Depending on other features of the relationships they have with those suffering unfulfilled human rights, they may also have particular further obligations.

Recall the second issue concerning how the weakest link problem might undercut the motivation to achieve thresholds as set by (LC1) and (LC3). If everyone believes we will, collectively, fall short of the required thresholds, might there be point in even trying to achieve them? My response to this issue is that we all have duties of justice to contribute to the bringing about and maintenance of just institutions, as I discussed in Chapter 2. Our contributions make a difference to others' willingness to contribute so we must play our proper role, even if there is some probability of our collective efforts falling short in a particular instance. These efforts are not useless as they serve an important signaling role from which further gains can build. Seeking to live with others on fair terms of cooperation – a basic requirement of justice – demands that we play our part.

Consider one further objection to my account of legitimacy as discussed so far, namely that it is too crude. Some might argue that legitimacy is not an all or nothing affair but rather it is domain-specific. A state might have it in one respect and not in another. In short, legitimacy may be unbundled.[59] As Andrew Altman and Christopher Wellman observe: "To qualify as legitimate, a state must satisfactorily protect the human rights of its constituents and adequately respect the human rights of everyone else."[60] They continue: "We believe that political legitimacy can be disaggregated and thus need not be treated like a single on/off switch, whereby states are entitled either to complete sovereignty or none at all."[61] So consider a state that is not treating outsiders well. It might still retain some legitimacy concerning certain domains, such as to authorize marriage licenses or enforce traffic rules. As an illustration, Nazi Germany's significant violation of the human rights of large numbers of foreigners and German nationals would surely disqualify that state from meeting requirements for legitimacy (on both internal and contribution grounds).[62] However, marriages conducted by justices of the peace during the Third Reich should still be considered legally binding. The state would also be legitimate in prohibiting rape and punishing rapists. Even states that had horrible records on human rights might still retain certain aspects of legitimacy, for instance to make some rules and enforce them on their populations.

---

[59] Andrew Altman and Christopher Wellman, *A Liberal Theory of International Justice* (Oxford: Oxford University Press, 2009). There is also the issue of degrees of legitimacy, which can help address such concerns. For the idea of degrees of legitimacy see, for instance, Hassoun, *Globalization and Global Justice* and Nicole Hassoun, *Extending Access to Essential Medicine: The Global Health Impact Project* (Oxford: Oxford University Press, forthcoming in 2020).
[60] Ibid., 148.   [61] Ibid., 151.   [62] Ibid., 152.

Even granting such points, the issues of controlling borders and access to territory does raise the very domain of legitimacy that is germane to the topics under discussion. A central domain of legitimacy at issue in migration concerns the right to control entry on to territory. When practices on the territory involve significant wrongdoing, the right to occupy territory is under threat, as discussed in Chapter 2 (and further discussed in later chapters, such as Chapter 5 on undocumented migrants). And therefore, the justified right to exclude is precisely in question, since state action concerning exclusion presupposes a defensible right to occupy the space claimed by the state. So, even if we concede the important issue of unbundling legitimacy, states that do not pass the relevant legitimacy tests would not be exercising power appropriately when they seek to exclude would-be migrants, under certain circumstances.

8   Conclusions

States have many important duties that are associated with their claims to have the right to self-determination, if that right is to be defensible. Importantly, we saw how a compelling justification for that right requires us to work with others to make it possible that all persons, no matter where they are situated on the globe, can rightly enjoy a range of protections and opportunities neatly captured by a commitment to the practice of human rights. I have shown that several layers of requirements must be met for states to have a defensible right to self-determination, including making relevant progress with regard to the human rights of their citizens and making sufficient contributions to the maintenance of a legitimate state system that can secure human rights for all. States that do not meet these criteria cannot defensibly claim a robust right to self-determination, as they understand the claim. I develop the framework and arguments sketched here in chapters to follow.

I have made the case that there is a way to justify a revised state system if it includes three layers of legitimacy requirements, governing how states should treat their members and how they should contribute to the treatment of others. I have also signaled that corrective measures will be necessary to close important gaps. If the state system is to be justified, it will have to include certain kinds of provisions and protections for when the social institutions produce results that are counter to their central normative justification. The normative presuppositions of the state system, guide us toward what states must cooperate in doing if they are to retain legitimacy and some kind of legitimate right to self-determination. They show us what needs work and where efforts might usefully be applied. The case for such corrective mechanisms is developed in subsequent chapters, as we discuss cases involving refugees (Chapter 6), migrant workers (Chapter 7), and undocumented residents (Chapter 5).

CHAPTER 4

Muslim Bans

1 Introduction

May a country enact a ban on Muslims being admitted to its territory? Donald Trump not only promised to enact such policy, on many accounts, including those of Supreme Court justices, he succeeded. How did this happen? Was it morally justified? Can we defensibly enact migration policy that discriminates on the basis of religion?

In this chapter I argue that those seeking to exercise power legitimately cannot implement such policies. On the contrary, as signaled in Chapter 3, certain actions concerning migration can undermine the legitimacy of the state and the state system. One example of this would be an immigration policy that placed a ban on Muslims being able to enter a state. We discuss this case in detail in this chapter. It is interesting to note that despite much rhetoric concerning Muslim bans on the campaign trail and continuing into the Trump presidency, the actual executive order that was upheld by the Supreme Court in 2018 tried to justify the action on different grounds, centering on security issues. In this chapter, we consider both the central view that Trump and his many supporters wanted to convert into policy, along with the actual policy that the Supreme Court upheld in its controversial 2018 judgment. As I discuss, there is very good evidence that the later policy versions based on security were mere window dressing to mask the real motivation, which centrally revolved around conveying an anti-Muslim message.

Here we focus on whether a legitimate state can claim that it has a robust right to self-determination and that this right includes the right to prohibit Muslims from entering its territory. I argue that a legitimate state cannot do this and that the argument fails on a number of grounds. One argument is that if the state is to exercise power legitimately it must meet certain requirements, such as internal and contribution requirements, (as specified by (LC1) and (LC3) discussed in the previous chapter).

As I argue, policies of banning Muslims violate internal requirements on legitimacy, along with contribution requirements. By failing to achieve internal legitimacy standards and failing to discharge contribution obligations, they also contribute to a state system that lacks legitimacy. States that fail to meet these internal and contribution conditions, and perform no remedial actions, bring the state system into disrepute and therefore not only fail to contribute to (LC2), but may make its achievement more unlikely. Such states cannot gain interim legitimacy.

As I discussed in Chapter 3, for a state to be able to claim it has a defensible right to self-determination, a right that involves robust control over admission policies, it must meet sufficient legitimacy criteria. For these legitimacy conditions to be met, the state claiming the right to self-determination must respect all the core elements of our human rights practice, especially the basic tenets of the central human rights doctrines. As I argue in Section 4, Muslim bans would violate many of these. For instance, such bans have promoted the violation of rights to freedom of religion, nondiscrimination, and bodily security. We also see how they involve important failures in obligations to address discrimination based on ideas of religious hatred and intolerance, and those based on racial hatred and superiority, all of which are core components of our human rights practice. As I also argue in that section, such policies fail to meet a number of contribution requirements, such as those concerning accountability and maintaining an ethos conducive to respect for the practice of human rights.

My main argument can be found in Section 4. Section 2 covers some important background necessary to understanding the actual policy governing travel restrictions on many Muslims. Section 3 situates the central issue about whether states may permissibly adopt admission policies that ban individuals from particular groups in recent philosophical discussion. We see that there is some divergence of opinion on the crucial issue. Some believe that exclusion based on race or religion should be taken as a fixed point in our moral universe that we can all agree is morally unjustified. Others believe such views are surprisingly difficult to defend.[1] If we take such exclusion as a fixed point that is morally indefensible, this recent case seems to present a new challenge to some reasonably settled ideas about migration justice and prompts us to search for compelling

---

[1] For some of these contrasting views see Joseph Carens, *Ethics of Immigration*; David Miller, *Strangers in Our Midst*; and Christopher Heath Wellman and Phillip Cole, *Debating the Ethics of Immigration*. I discuss the key issues below, especially in Section 3.

arguments in support of these assumptions. Using the normative views I have been developing, we are able to identify some new arguments that can assist in fortifying confidence that such exclusions are morally indefensible. And for those who claim it is difficult to find an argument for the impermissibility of policies prohibiting those of certain races or religions from being admitted to a country, the arguments I present should address the perceived difficulty. Section 5 takes stock and concludes.

2   Some Background

During the 2016 Presidential campaign, Donald Trump repeatedly made many anti-Muslim statements. Some examples include a 2015 press release in which he called for a "total and complete shutdown of Muslims entering the United States."[2] He advocated for a "watch list" for Muslims resident in the USA.[3] During an interview in March 2016 he said: "I think Islam hates us."[4] This kind of anti-Islamic animus was central to Trump's style of politics. Many of his advisors shared his anti-Muslim views. For instance, Michael Flynn, who was to become his National Security Advisor, compared Islam to a malignant cancer and tweeted that fearing Muslims was rational.[5] Others who made similarly anti-Muslim statements included the Attorney General, Jeff Sessions. It is difficult to see how President Trump's policies can really be separated from candidate Trump's statements, even though some maintain one ought to do so.[6]

Very soon after President Trump took office, various executive orders concerning prohibiting the movement of Muslims were issued. The first came into effect on January 27, 2017 with executive order 13769, "Protecting the Nation from Foreign Terrorist Entry into the United States" ostensibly, as the name suggests, to protect US residents from terrorist attacks. With this order, Trump placed a travel ban on people from seven nations who have large Muslim majorities, namely Iraq, Syria, Iran, Libya, Somalia, Sudan, and Yemen. The order also prohibited Syrian refugees from entering the USA. As a matter of fact, the number of Americans

---

[2] Jenna Johnson, "Trump calls for 'total and complete shutdown of Muslims entering the United States'," *Washington Post*, December 7, 2015.
[3] Anthony Zurcher, "What Trump team has said about Islam," *BBC*, February 7, 2017.   [4] Ibid.
[5] Ismat Sarah Mangla, "Islam is a 'malignant cancer': The hateful rhetoric of Trump's new national security adviser," *Quartz*, November 19, 2016.
[6] Chief Justice Roberts, Supreme Court Syllabus No. 17-965, "Trump, President of the United States, et al.," Argued April 5, 18–Decided June 26, 2018.

killed in terrorist attacks by citizens of one of those countries was zero between 1975 and 2015.[7] In the same forty-year period only three deaths were attributed to refugees, all from Cuba, and the events took place in the 1970s.[8] For some comparison about threat levels to bodily security, consider that about 33,000 people die each year in the USA from gun violence.[9] Painkillers, the leading cause of accidental death, kill about 22,000 per year.[10]

But perhaps intelligence suggested the situation was about to change dramatically? A report compiled by the US Department of Homeland Security Intelligence and Analysis unit concluded that people from those seven countries posed no increased terrorism risk and, in general, country of citizenship is an unreliable indicator of potential terrorist activity.[11] Various experts roundly condemned the travel ban on several fronts including pointing out that 85 percent of terrorist attacks on US soil are perpetrated by citizens or those who have lived in the USA for a long time, who had been radicalized within the nation's borders.[12] Experts also pointed out that the current vetting procedures were quite robust.[13] So there seemed to be a lack of convincing evidence for the alleged increased threat level that would warrant such draconian measures.

That executive order was challenged and replaced by a series of other travel executive orders. Proclamation No. 9645, issued in September 2017, constituted the policy that incorporated improvements from previous failed versions. It sought to place entry restrictions on citizens from eight states because of their perceived defective systems for managing or sharing information about their nationals. Preceding selection of these eight countries, the US Department of Homeland Security (DHS) had developed an

---

[7] Uri Friedman, "Where America's terrorists actually come from," *The Atlantic*, January 30, 2017, available at: www.theatlantic.com/international/archive/2017/01/trump-immigration-ban-terrorism/514361/

[8] Ibid.

[9] Mona Chalabi, "How bad is US gun violence? These charts show the scale of the problem," *The Guardian*, October 5, 2017, available at: www.theguardian.com/us-news/2017/oct/05/us-gun-violence-charts-data

[10] Roland Hughes, "Trump's America: Are things as bad as he says?" *BBC News*, February 9, 2017, available at: www.bbc.com/news/world-us-canada-38911708

[11] Ron Nixon, "People from 7 travel-ban nations pose no increased terror risk, report says," *New York Times*, February 25, 2017.

[12] Ibid.

[13] Brian Michael Jenkins, "Why a Travel Restriction Won't Stop Terrorism at Home," The RAND blog, Rand Corporation. If there is a problem here, it lies not with the vetting procedures but elsewhere: we cannot predict human behavior far into the future. But this is not a fixable problem nor one that we should fixate over; the scale of the threat must be kept in perspective, as we discuss at length in Chapter 8.

information and risk-assessment baseline and evaluated data for all foreign governments. It claimed to identify those with deficient arrangements and gave governments a fifty-day period in which to improve. After the fifty days, the Acting Secretary of Homeland Security declared that eight countries remained deficient and these were Chad, Iran, Iraq, Libya, North Korea, Syria, Venezuela, and Yemen. Because Iraq had a close cooperative relationship with the USA, the Acting Secretary recommended it be exempt. Somalia was subsequently included because it had special risk factors concerning a significant terrorist presence in the country. Trump then accepted these recommendations and issued the proclamation, citing the need to improve identity management and information sharing practices.

The proclamation does have some exemptions, such as for lawful permanent residents of the USA. It also allows case-by-case waivers in special circumstances, when an alien demonstrates that "(1) denying entry would cause undue hardship; (2) entry would not pose a threat to public safety; and (3) entry would be in the interests of the United States."[14] Examples cited of grounds that would be considered for an exemption include aliens seeking urgent medical attention, to reside with a close family member, or to pursue significant business obligations. The proclamation also requires assessment every 180 days as to whether restrictions should be changed in light of new information. After 180 days of being implemented, Chad was removed because it had apparently improved practices sufficiently.

It is important to note that even though the exemption system existed, very few exemptions were actually granted. A total of 2 waivers out of 6,555 eligible applicants were successful during the first month.[15] The proclamation was supposed to give guidance to consular offices concerning how to determine waivers, yet no guidance was issued. Quite the contrary, consular officials stated that they did not have discretion to grant waivers, and that the waiver process was "window dressing."[16]

---

[14] *Trump versus Hawaii*, 585 U.S. (2018), No. 17-965, decided June 26, 2018, 37.

[15] Even though the number increased to 430 during the first four months of implementation, compared with pre-proclamation numbers, this is a very tiny percentage of those likely to be seeking admission for medical treatment and the other permissible grounds mentioned (p. 4, Justice Beyer, dissenting opinion). Amici also identified many in each category who should be admitted, including strong cases from more than 1,000 parents or children of US citizens who sought and were denied permission to enter the USA (p. 4, Justice Beyer, dissenting opinion).

[16] J. Sotomayor, dissenting on *Trump versus Hawaii*, 585 U.S. (2018), No. 17-965.

Various plaintiffs challenged the proclamation. In one important instance, a case was brought by the State of Hawaii, the Muslim Association of Hawaii, and three individuals whose relatives were affected.[17] The grounds included that the proclamation violates requirements in US immigration law that "no person shall be discriminated against in the issuance of an immigrant visa because of a person's race, sex, nationality, place of birth or place of residence" and that it violates the First Amendment's Establishment Clause, which prohibits the government making laws that establish a particular official religion or unduly favor one religion over others.

However, in a controversial decision that garnered five votes in support and four against, the Supreme Court upheld the proclamation. Those who voted in favor emphasized that the President had the authority to issue the proclamation, that it was based on legitimate purposes concerning national security risks, and that it did not explicitly invoke religion. In addition, they argued that statements concerning religious animus made on the campaign were not significant in assessing the proclamation.

Justice Sotomayor dissented, citing compelling grounds that are worth careful review. In her preamble to her opinion she noted that the USA was built on a commitment to religious liberty and that the court's decision failed to safeguard that principle. As she continued, the proclamation:

> ... leaves undisturbed a policy first advertised openly and unequivocally as a "total and complete shutdown of Muslims entering the United States" because it now masquerades behind a façade of national-security concerns. But this repackaging does little to cleanse Presidential Proclamation No. 9645 of the appearance of discrimination that the President's words have created. Based on the evidence in the record, a reasonable observer would conclude that the Proclamation was motivated by anti-Muslim animus. That alone suffices to show that plaintiffs are likely to succeed on the merits of their Establishment Clause claim. The majority holds otherwise by ignoring the facts, misconstruing our legal precedent, and turning a blind eye to the pain and suffering the Proclamation inflicts upon countless families and individuals, many of whom are United States citizens. Because that troubling result runs contrary to the Constitution and our precedent, I dissent.[18]

By going through Trump's recent record, she marshals a case that Trump demonstrated a pattern of hostility toward those of Muslim faith. During his bid for the presidency, "then-candidate Donald Trump

---

[17] *Trump versus Hawaii*, 585 U.S. (2018), No. 17-965.   [18] Sotomayor, dissenting, 1.

pledged that, if elected, he would ban Muslims from entering the United States. Specifically, on December 7, 2015, he issued a formal statement 'calling for a total and complete shutdown of Muslims entering the United States'. That statement, which remained on his campaign website until May 2017 (several months into his Presidency),"[19] contained the following provocative claims:

> Donald J. Trump is calling for a total and complete shutdown of Muslims entering the United States until our country's representatives can figure out what is going on. According to Pew research, among others, there is great hatred towards Americans by large segments of the Muslim population. Most recently, a poll from the Center for Security Policy released data showing "25% of those polled agreed that violence against Americans here in the United States is justified as a part of a global jihad" and 51% of those polled "agreed that Muslims in America should have the choice of being governed according to Shariah." Shariah authorizes such atrocities as murder against nonbelievers who won't convert, beheadings and more unthinkable acts that pose great harm to Americans, especially women.[20]

He continued: "it is obvious to anybody the hatred is beyond comprehension. Where this hatred comes from and why we will have to determine. Until we are able to determine and understand the problem and the dangerous threat it poses, our country cannot be the victim of the horrendous attacks by people that believe only in Jihad, and have no sense of reason or respect for human life. If I win the election for President, we are going to Make America Great Again."[21]

Trump repeated these and similar statements throughout his campaign. In March 2016 he said: "Islam hates us ... [W]e can't allow people coming into this country who have this hatred of the United States."[22] He also repeatedly asserted that "[w]e're having problems with the Muslims, and we're having problems with Muslims coming into the country."[23] He called for surveillance of mosques.[24] Though he sometimes described his policy proposals differently, sometimes in terms of trying to stop the spread of radical Islamic terrorism to the West, especially as the campaign progressed, his other statements show that he still endorsed earlier views.

---

[19] Ibid., 4.   [20] Ibid., 4–5.   [21] Ibid., 5.

[22] Jenna Johnson and Abigail Hauslohner, "'I think Islam hates us': A timeline of Trump's comments about Islam and Muslims," *Washington Post*, May 20, 2017.

[23] Erwin Chemerinsky, *Constitutional Law: 2018 Case Supplement* (New York: Wolters Kluwer Law and Business, 2018), p. 33.

[24] Chemerinsky, *Constitutional Law*, p. 33.

He was asked in July 2016 whether he wished to retract his pledged Muslim ban. Trump responded that he wished to expand rather than retract the desired policy. He said, "I actually don't think it's a rollback. In fact, you could say it's an expansion."[25] He then explained that he used different terminology because "[p]eople were so upset when [he] used the word Muslim."[26]

Shortly before the election, Trump acknowledged that his proposed Muslim ban had morphed into a plan to introduce extreme vetting from certain areas of the world. Even shortly after the election, on December 21, 2016, President-elect Trump was asked about rethinking his stance on Muslim registries and bans. He replied: "You know my plans. All along, I've proven to be right."[27]

The window dressing interpretation gains further force when we consider other incriminating statements Trump made to advisors. According to one advisor, "[W]hen [Donald Trump] first announced it, he said 'Muslim ban.' He called me up. He said, 'Put a commission together. Show me the right way to do it legally'."[28] Others associated with the White House confirmed that there was similar continuity with the past statements. The Press Secretary emphasized that Trump was continuing to deliver on campaign promises. Trump confirmed the continuity himself at campaign rallies, saying that these subsequent executive orders were just watered down versions of the original idea, and were implemented at the request of lawyers. He echoed these sentiments on Twitter, saying that they were politically correct versions designed to achieve the same policy outcomes as his original travel ban recommendations.

In November, 2017, President Trump re-tweeted three videos, which purport to show actual events. They show Muslims engaging in acts of violence. They were called "Muslim Destroys a Statue of Virgin Mary!," "Islamist Mob Pushes Teenage Boy off Roof and Beats Him to Death!," and "Muslim Migrant Beats up Dutch Boy on Crutches!"[29] These videos came from a British political party that declares opposition to "all

---

[25] Jenna Johnson, "Donald Trump is expanding his Muslim ban, not rolling it back" *Washington Post*, July 24, 2016 available at: www.washingtonpost.com/news/post-politics/wp/2016/07/24/donald-trump-is-expanding-his-muslim-ban-not-rolling-it-back/?noredirect=on&utm_term=.29f2c77512f3

[26] Chemerinsky, *Constitutional Law*, p. 33.

[27] Katie Reilly, "Donald Trump on proposed Muslim ban: 'You know my plans'," *Time*, December 21, 2016.

[28] Sotomayor, dissenting, 6.

[29] Jon Henley, "Videos tweeted by Trump: Where are they from and what do they show?," *The Guardian*, November 30, 2017.

alien and destructive political and religious doctrines," which, in their view, includes Islam.[30]

Putting this kind of huge body of evidence together, Sotomayor argues that the proclamation was just a vehicle to enact anti-Muslim policies that were on sufficiently firm legal ground. Sotomayor argued that presented with the context and such openly available data, a reasonable observer would conclude that "the primary purpose of the Proclamation is to disfavor Islam and its adherents by excluding them from the country" and that the "Proclamation was driven by anti-Muslim animus, rather than by the Government's asserted national-security justifications."[31] Despite numerous opportunities to distance himself from his previous statements about Islam, Trump declined to do this. On the contrary he continued to make the same kind of remarks that a reasonable observer would interpret as constituting a continuing attack on Muslims. As Sotomayor says: "Ultimately what began as a policy explicitly 'calling for a total and complete shutdown of Muslims entering the United States' has since morphed into a 'Proclamation' putatively based on national security concerns. But this new window dressing cannot conceal an unassailable fact: the words of the President and his advisors create the strong perception that the Proclamation is contaminated by impermissible discriminatory animus against Islam and its followers."[32]

Sotomayor argues that given the enormous amount of evidence concerning anti-Muslim animus, it is not plausible to maintain that the Proclamation rests on legitimate grounds. Sotomayor also argued that there are already adequate schemes in place to protect national security interests. The proclamation fails to articulate any "credible national-security interest that would go unaddressed by the current statutory scheme absent the Proclamation."[33]

Furthermore, there are good reasons to believe that even if we take national security seriously, a ban on Muslims runs counter to those very interests. Several former national security officials from both political parties have made these arguments. Former national security officials submitted a brief advising that these proclamations "do not advance the national-security or foreign policy interests of the United States, and in fact do serious harm to those interests."[34] In addition, various friends of the

---

[30] Chris York, "Britain First denounced by every major Christian denomination in the UK," *The Huffington Post*, January 30, 2016.
[31] Sotomayor, dissenting, 11.   [32] Ibid., 13.   [33] Sotomayor, dissenting, 21.
[34] Sotomayor, dissenting, 22.

court argued that there are serious deleterious effects on not only national security, but also health care, the technology industry, higher education, and the overall economy.[35]

As Sotomayor astutely observes, "the Proclamation permits certain nationals from the countries named in the Proclamation to obtain non-immigrant visas, which undermines the Government's assertion that it does not already have the capacity and sufficient information to vet these individuals adequately."[36] This point is really important and rather strikes at the heart of the alleged justification for the policy. As she also notes, comparing the number of strong applications lodged with the number of waivers granted, there is robust evidence, she concludes, that the Proclamation's waiver system is nothing but a sham. She recounts several details of many worthy applications being denied waivers. Key public statements add to the evidence that the true motivations lie elsewhere. Frank Wuco led the multi-agency review and helped with the enforcement process. His public statements include that it was a great idea to "stop the visa application process into this country from Muslim nations in a blanket type of policy," "that Muslim populations 'living under other-than-Muslim rule' will 'necessarily' turn to violence," that "Islam prescribes 'violence and warfare against unbelievers' and that Muslims 'by-and-large resist assimilation'."[37] Such public statements are relevant to understanding the real motivations of the policies. Sotomayor concludes that the evidence clearly shows "the primary purpose and function of the Proclamation is to disfavor Islam by banning Muslims from entering our country."[38] All in all, on this plausible interpretation of the proclamation, the policy denies fundamental rights of religious liberty and violates rights to freedom of religion. It is rooted in dangerous stereotypes about particular group members' abilities to assimilate and desire to harm the USA.

Considering some of this background material, we might discern at least five different possibilities for grounding travel restrictions on certain types of people seeking to enter the USA:

(1) A ban on Muslims based on the view that Muslims are – or are disproportionately likely to be – terrorists or likely to be sympathetic to those who are.

(2) A ban on Muslims based on the idea that the religion promotes hatred of Americans and violence toward them.

---

[35] Sotomayor, dissenting, 22. [36] Ibid. [37] Sotomayor, dissenting, 18.
[38] Sotomayor, dissenting, 23.

(3)   A ban on those from Muslim majority nations based on alleged concerns about security.

(4)   Travel restrictions on those who present terrorist threats.

(5)   A ban on those who allegedly present elevated terrorist threats, but this is just window dressing for policies of types (1) and (2).

While in some form (4) may well be a candidate proposal for being morally permissible, none of the others are. (1)–(3) are all based on false views, as I discuss in Section 4.1. In many ways, (5) is even worse than (1) and (2), as it tries to obscure its true purposes and presents as the more acceptable (4). It attempts to disguise the anti-Muslim sentiment that lies at its heart. Before we get to my key arguments, I should first discuss an apparent challenge that all theorists who seek to argue for the impermissibility of religion or race-based exclusions in admission policies must confront.

3   Some Philosophical Context and a Challenge

Some readers may think it will be rather easy to argue that Muslim bans cannot be morally justified.[39] Indeed, some have taken it as a point of wide agreement that admission policies that exclude prospective migrants on the basis of race or religion are obviously wrong, and so much so that we can take this as a basic point of agreement in our moral universe, as we set out to tackle more contentious issues.

In Joseph Carens' prominent discussion of the defensible criteria a state may use to exclude in immigration policy, he starts off noting what he takes to be a fixed point for us to get our bearings, namely the moral impermissibility of excluding people on the basis of race, ethnicity, or religion. He takes that as "a starting point for reflection on the more contested issues."[40] Something similar is assumed by David Miller. For instance, when he discusses economic migrant admission policies, he says, "to take the most obvious case, racially selective admissions policies must

[39] As I discuss in this section, some might think: Surely we have various human rights that would be straightforwardly violated if we ban certain religions, such as perhaps the right to freedom of religion (Article 18) or nondiscrimination (Article 7)? However, the human rights declarations leave the issue at the heart of these debates as a matter for interpretation, according to many, including Christopher Wellman, as we discuss later in this chapter.

[40] Carens, *Ethics of Immigration*, 174. To be clear, it is not the case that Carens thinks no justification can be given for the moral indefensibility of such views (concerning exclusion on the basis of race, religion or ethnicity). Rather, Carens believes that the indefensibility of such views will be widely shared among his readers, such that he can take it as settled for the purposes of his project in *Ethics of Immigration*.

be ruled out."[41] Exclusion by race or national background is unjustifiable, "since these attributes cannot be linked (except by wholly spurious reasoning) to any goals that a democratic state might legitimately wish to pursue."[42]

While I agree with both these authors' assessments, given the high level of support for policies that would enact Muslim bans, it is worth considering the arguments that can be brought to bear as to why we should take policies of this kind as clearly off the normative table. A further reason to examine the case is that some philosophers argue that it is difficult to make such an argument. Christopher Wellman holds such a position. While he is drawn to the conclusion that there must be something wrong with a country's denying admission on the basis of race (religion and the like),[43] he confesses to finding it "surprisingly difficult to provide an entirely satisfying argument for this conclusion."[44]

Wellman considers arguments from those who have attempted to address this issue of why exclusion on the basis of race must be wrong, finding them all to be inadequate.[45] The argument Wellman finds most compelling is one presented by Michael Blake, namely that exclusion on racist grounds would be insulting to members of that racial group already present in the state. Race-based exclusions would treat some insiders like "second-class citizens."[46] While Wellman believes this is the best argument to date, he notes several defects with it in justifying both too little and too much. It justifies too little if there are no members from that racial group already within the state. Both Blake and Wellman note that hardly any states are entirely homogenous and so this concern may be more of a theoretical than a practical constraint. But the argument also proves too much, in Wellman's view. If a state, say Norway, decides to admit 100,000 people from one particular group, but decides not to admit any more from that group because of a concern that further admissions would potentially create social or political challenges, it is understandable that some of the 100,000 already admitted might well be insulted by this decision. However, Norway should be allowed to adopt such a policy, on Wellman's view, in virtue of their rights to self-determination. In the end Wellman remains unsure that there is a robust argument as to why distinguishing

---

[41] Miller, *Strangers in Our Midst*, 95.   [42] Ibid., 106.
[43] Henceforth, while discussing Wellman's argument in this chapter, I will just refer to race rather than all the categories that might be included in the list, such as religion and ethnicity.
[44] Christopher Heath Wellman and Phillip Cole, *Debating the Ethics of Immigration*, 144.
[45] Ibid.   [46] Ibid., 148.

among applicants on the basis of race would be wrong. He confesses that "I do not yet have a fully satisfactory justification for this conclusion."[47]

Wellman notes in a footnote a suggestion I made to him some time ago. He reports that "[i]n private correspondence, Gillian Brock has proposed (but not necessarily endorsed) a more forceful and straightforward way to press this case. She suggests that, if there is a human right not to be discriminated against on grounds of sex, race, etc. then a state would not be legitimate if its immigration policy discriminated against applicants on these grounds. Many will no doubt be drawn to this account, but for reasons I outline [those he discussed concerning the Norway case], I am not sure that there is a human right not to be discriminated against."[48] While I believe such strategies can be successfully applied to the case at hand, here I press a different kind of argument, one which draws on aspects of the human rights practice that I have been developing.[49]

So, how might we go about arguing that such policies are morally wrong using a human rights account? Using the framework I have developed in previous chapters, and drawing especially on our human rights practice, I make a case as to how we can defend the position, showing how such policies would violate core internal and contribution requirements for state legitimacy. Section 4.1 summarizes some key moves. Section 4.2 elaborates on the core claims in some detail.

4   What Is Wrong with Muslim Bans? Let Me Count Some of the Ways

4.1   A Summary of the Central Argument

May a legitimate state claim that it has a robust right to self-determination and that this right includes the right to prohibit Muslims from entering its territory? I argue that a legitimate state may not do this, and that the argument fails on a number of grounds.

(1)   If the state is to exercise power legitimately, it will have to meet certain internal and contribution requirements, as specified by (LC1), (LC2), and (LC3).

---

[47] Ibid., 150.   [48] Ibid., 154.

[49] Interestingly, the Norway case, as Wellman describes it, is one that does not mention religion at all but rather country of origin. So, the use of "Pakistani" rather than "Muslim" thus obscures some of the issues I am trying to bring into focus. But the example is still relevant for illustrating the general issues.

(2) Muslim ban policies would fail to meet internal requirements (LC1).

(3) Such policies fail to meet contribution requirements (LC3).

(4) By failing to meet internal and contribution requirements, states also contribute to a state system that lacks legitimacy, so requirements for a legitimate state system (LC2) are not met.

(5) States that fail to meet (LC1) and (LC3), and perform no remedial actions, bring the state system into disrepute and therefore not only fail to contribute to (LC2), but may make its achievement more unlikely. Such states cannot gain interim legitimacy.

In Section 4.2.1 I show why there are internal failures. Section 4.2.2 demonstrates why contribution requirements would not be met.

4.2 Why Legitimacy Requirements Are Not Met

4.2.1 Internal Requirement Failures

A ban on Muslims entering a country would violate some of the core treaties and commitments that are central to human rights practice. In order to show why, I briefly discuss how to view a key underlying issue. Scholars are divided on whether the form of fear and hatred toward Muslims is a form of racism, religious intolerance, xenophobia, or something else, though the first two explanations seem to be the most dominant and I cover these two separately next.[50]

Assuming the root issue involves an expression of intolerance and fear of the Muslim religion, there are a number of core elements of our practice that the Muslim ban would violate. Indeed, combating religious intolerance and discrimination has been one of the top priorities of our international human rights regime since its founding. Genuine freedom to practice one's religion has been one of the most fundamental and internationally accepted human rights.[51] All major human rights treaties include clauses concerning prohibitions of discrimination on grounds of religion – for instance, UDHR (Articles 18 and 2 (1)) and the International Covenant on Civil and Political Rights (Articles 2, 4, 18, 20,

---

[50] For some of those who believe it is a form of racism or overlaps with it see D. Frost, "Islamophobia: Examining Causal Links between the Media and 'Race Hate' from 'Below,'" *International Journal of Sociology and Social Policy*, 28 (11/12) (2008): 564–578; Nathan Lean, *The Islamophobia Industry: How the Right Manufactures Fear of Muslims* (Pluto, 2012); S. Poynting and V. Mason, "The Resistible Rise of Islamophobia: Anti-Muslim Racism in the UK and Australia Before 11 September 2001," *Journal of Sociology*, 43 (2007): 61–86.

[51] Christian Walter, "Religion or Belief, Freedom of, International Protection," *Oxford Public International Law*, Max Planck Encyclopedia of International Law, 2008.

26 and 27). And further resolutions and declarations have indicated that there are a number of important responsibilities for state parties in regard to eliminating hatred and intolerance based on religion. For instance, Article 4 of the 1981 Declaration on the Elimination of All Forms of Intolerance and of Discrimination Based on Religion or Belief, which has the force of customary international law, requires states to "take all appropriate measures to combat intolerance on the grounds of religion or other beliefs in this matter" (Article 4 (2)), that "states should also take effective measures to prevent and eliminate discrimination on the grounds of religion" (Article 4 (1)). And the 1997 declaration adopted by the General Assembly on the Elimination of all Forms of Intolerance and Discrimination Based on Religion (55/97), enjoins state parties to "take all necessary action to combat hatred, intolerance and acts of violence, intimidation and coercion motivated by intolerance based on religion."[52] Furthermore, it urges states to "promote and encourage through the educational system, and by other means, understanding, tolerance and respect in matters relating to freedom of religion."[53] And it notes that "the exercise of tolerance and non-discrimination by all actors in society is necessary for the full realization of the aims of the Declaration."[54] Further resolutions adopted by the General Assembly in 2000 reaffirm the call for all governments to take "all appropriate measures in compliance with their international obligations ... to counter intolerance and related violence based on religion," "to take all appropriate measures" to combat religious hatred and intolerance, and to further commit to encouraging "understanding, tolerance and respect" in regard to religions.[55]

As signaled, some scholars are of the view that the kind of fear and hatred toward Muslims exemplified by policies that deny admission to Muslims is a form of racism, or it importantly overlaps with racist views. In this case there are further core elements of our human rights practice that are relevant to showing why there would be important internal failures. One example would be that such a ban would constitute a violation of the Convention on the Elimination of All Forms of Racial Discrimination. This convention "commits the parties not only to eliminate racial discrimination in law and the practices of public institutions but also to use state power to prohibit and punish the public expression of 'ideas based on

---

[52] *Elimination of All Forms of Intolerance and Discrimination Based on Religion*, Resolution 1997/18, and the accompanying declaration of the same name, Article (3(c)). Available at: http://hrlibrary .umn.edu/UN/1997/Reso18.html
[53] Ibid., Article 3(g).   [54] Ibid., Article 9.
[55] Resolution adopted on December 4, 2000. Fifty-fifth session, agenda item 114b.

racial superiority or hatred'."[56] So here we see that states have important duties to attend to public expression of ideas based on ideas of racial hatred; they have duties to attend to behavior and cultural patterns that perpetuate the spread of notions such as racial inferiority, or that some races are fitting targets of hatred or derision. The convention calls on parties to eliminate such discriminatory views without delay.

Drawing on some of the material introduced in Section 2, we see a clear pattern of state agents failing to prohibit and punish the public expression of ideas designed to perpetuate fear of Muslims. Indeed, we see a pattern that such agents were intimately involved in the public expression of exactly such ideas. Recall that Trump called for a "total and complete shutdown on Muslims entering the US," and this statement remained on his website for several months into his presidency. In that same long statement, he also claimed that "there is great hatred towards Americans by large segments of the Muslim population," suggesting that many believed violence towards Americans to be justified as part of a global jihad. He also added that Shariah law authorizes "beheadings and more unthinkable acts that pose great harm to Americans." The conclusions he draws are that the country cannot allow itself to be attacked "by people who believe only in Jihad, and have no sense of reason or respect for human life."[57]

These are public expressions by agents of the state that are designed to spread an anti-Muslim ethos (irrespective of whether the root concern is based on race or religion). They include ideas that aim to make Muslims fitting targets of fear and hatred. They are also based on a sense that Muslim ways of life are to be reviled and are inferior. Someone might wonder, nevertheless, whether they are true and, if true, worthy of public expression. The short answer is that, like all very general claims about a major religion with millions of followers, there will be diversity of opinion about what the religion's core tenets are. It is likely that some will advocate for an interpretation of the religion that, in their view, is committed to certain kinds of positions that promote violence. Others will have a very different view and believe that those who advocate for such violence are not following the central ideas espoused by the religion. After all, the Ku Klux Klan (KKK) based its views on an idiosyncratic interpretation of Christianity. We should not infer that beliefs held by the KKK are

---

[56] Charles Beitz, *The Idea of Human Rights*, 29. Convention on the Elimination of All Forms of Racial Discrimination. Available at: www.ohchr.org/en/professionalinterest/pages/cerd.aspx

[57] Trump website during his presidential campaign and for at least six months into his presidency.

representative of what many Christians believe, even if they were widely shared by Christians residing in the south of the United States about sixty years ago.

So, how representative are the claims Trump makes concerning what the majority of Muslims hold to be true? In answering this question, I draw on comprehensive studies conducted by the Pew Research Centre. This choice of research source is especially important because Trump repeatedly uses alleged research from this center in support of his views. Drawing on their research, we get some important data that run quite contrary to Trump's preferred narrative. For instance, the overwhelming majority of Muslims want to live peacefully with others and do not support violent causes.[58] In general, Muslims living in all countries are as concerned about the threat of Islamic extremism as citizens of Western countries are.[59] Muslims around the world mostly say that suicide bombings and other kinds of violence against civilians perpetrated in the name of Islam are "rarely or never justified."[60] Only 1 percent say that such attacks are often justified.[61] Most of those from countries with large Muslim populations are negatively disposed toward ISIS.[62] In fact, relatively few say that they view ISIS favorably.[63]

Trump and his associates continued the public expression of anti-Muslim positions (based on false claims about Muslim sentiments) well into his presidency. Trump's most revealing communications were often made on Twitter and at rallies for his supporters. At rallies he often admitted that many of his policies were just cleaned up versions to make lawyers happy. Instead of disavowing previous claims, he fostered the impression that he held exactly the same views. And his own instructions to advisors, to show him the right way to construct anti-Muslim policy so that it would be legally valid, confirm the continuity. Further public anti-Muslim moments came with the re-tweeting of fake videos designed to spread antagonism toward, and fear of, Muslims. All of these public statements and actions were clearly designed to promote a culture in which Islam was disfavored, to intensify fear and hatred of Islam. The conventions and resolutions discussed earlier in this section clearly articulate state agents' responsibilities in regard to punishing the expression of such ideas. Leaders clearly failed to punish the expression of ideas based on

---

[58] Michael Lipka, "Muslims and Islam: Key findings in the US and around the world," *Pew Research Center*, August 9, 2017. Available at: www/pewresearch.org/author/mlipka/8
[59] Ibid., 10.
[60] Ibid., 9. For instance, 92 percent in Indonesia hold such a view and 91 percent in Iraq.
[61] Ibid., 10.   [62] Ibid., 8.   [63] Ibid., 8.

misinformation and ideas designed to spread antagonism, fear, and intolerance among religions or races. Rather to the contrary, leaders were centrally involved in spreading them. In these ways, Trump and his associates failed to discharge their duties.

Such failures, though important, are just one of the core features of our human rights practice. We can supplement the case with several further failures concerning other core human rights, as I discuss next. I make a case that there are important failures concerning rights to equal protection under the law, freedom of conscience, freedom of religion, freedom to practice religion freely with others, freedom of association, and freedom of education, among others.

One might think that Muslim ban type policies clearly violate core human rights from the UDHR, namely the right to freedom of religion (Article 18) or nondiscrimination (Article 7). However, someone might object that while states clearly have rights to respect and protect these rights for *citizens*, their responsibilities in connection with nonresidents are subject to varying interpretation, including that states need not respect foreigners' rights in these areas.[64] Even if we concede this point, a case can be made that *citizens'* rights are affected by policies concerning foreigners. Insofar as Islam becomes a disfavored religion and a climate of anti-Muslim sentiment flourishes, citizens who are Muslim might well find their rights under threat, even if the migration policy targets are nonresidents. They may increasingly experience discrimination in the workplace, schools, and the public sphere more generally. They might increasingly become targets of hate crimes, as those with anti-Muslim views feel emboldened to express these in violent ways. And, as Americans can attest, all of these effects transpired, as I discuss next.

American Muslims' freedom of religion was substantially affected. Their rights to practice their religion freely came under threat as mosques and other Muslim identified centers were subject to more arson, desecration, and other forms of destruction.[65] For instance, by mid-March 2017, attacks of various kinds (including arson, violence, aggression, or threats of violence against Muslim identified buildings), had already doubled from the previous year. In 2017, 50 percent of Muslim Americans reported that they have recently found it more difficult to be Muslim in America, with

---

[64] Perhaps this is the thought that motivates Wellman's rejection of a human rights based strategy.

[65] Michelle Chen, "Donald Trump's rise has coincided with an explosion of hate groups," *The Nation*, March 24, 2017. Also "FBI: Spike in US hate crimes for third year in a row," *BBC*, November 13, 2018.

almost half reporting that they had "experienced at least one incident of discrimination in the past 12 months."[66]

A similar trend of increased attacks against synagogues, Jewish cemeteries, and other Jewish identified buildings was also apparent, along with targeting other minority religions.[67] Indeed, attacks on *visible minorities of all kinds*, not just religious minorities, was also reported shortly into the Trump presidency, as those with discriminatory views felt vindicated in expressing them more freely and violently, just as their President did. Disturbingly, some of these incidents took place in schools and were perpetrated by children.[68]

More generally, hate crimes that target minorities have increased over 2016 and 2017, and continuing into 2018.[69] The number of so-called Hate Groups that target religious minorities has also risen since Trump took office.[70] Hate groups are organizations that "through the statements of their leaders or their activities, follow practices or beliefs which malign or attack a class of people, usually for the latter's immutable characteristics."[71] And there have been some very public attempts to reassert the power of the right, such as in the case of the "Unite the Right" rally in Charlottesville, in August 2017. Angry white men marched through Charlottesville carrying flaming torches reminiscent of similar rallies conducted by the KKK, shouting slogans aimed at asserting their racial superiority. Activities in Charlottesville were clearly aimed at asserting dominance in putting minorities "in their place."[72] According to many commentators and experts, "Trump has created an atmosphere in which white nationalists have become emboldened. Indeed, they now believe they have the support of the American president."[73]

This kind of evidence suggests that the rights of citizens have been substantially affected. While some of the clearest cases of rights violations are the right to freedom of religion and the right to nondiscrimination,

---

[66] Michael Lipka, "Muslims and Islam," 11.

[67] Rachael Revesz, "US Islamophobia: Threats and acts of vandalism against mosques double so far in 2017," *The Independent*, March 15, 2017.

[68] Clark Mindock, "Number of hate crimes surges in year of Trump's election," *The Independent*, November 14, 2017; Sam Levin, "Legitimized in their hatred: A weekend of violence in Trump's America," *The Guardian*, May 31, 2017.

[69] Manu Bhagavan, "Minority Report: Illiberalism, Intolerance, and the Threat to International Society," *Raisina Files*, January 2018, 42–43.

[70] Corey Barnett, "Hate groups targeting religious minorities on the rise in the US," February 24. Based on research done by the Southern Poverty Law Center.

[71] Ibid.   [72] Bhagavan "Minority Report," 42.

[73] Ibid. See footnote 5 of that article for much more such evidence.

several other rights have also been increasingly violated or come under threat including Articles 1, 2, 3, 7, 18, 20, 26, and 28, concerning, for example, rights to equal protection under the law, freedom of conscience, freedom to practice religion freely with others, freedom of association, freedom of education, and so forth.

4.2.2 Contribution Failures

Muslim bans also constitute a failure to do one's part to sustain a legitimate state system, one conducive to supporting human rights. So, contribution requirements would fail to be met as well. In this section I show how.

Recall that in Chapter 3, I drew attention to several requirements that states must meet in order to contribute appropriately to a justified state system, one capable of sustaining a robust human rights practice. I noted that these principles embody the most basic commitments to the animating ideas and practices governing human rights today. These include: (i) A commitment to maintain an ethos conducive to respect for the practice of human rights, such as that everyone deserves to be treated with dignity and respect as a human being (*Ethos Requirement*); (ii) a commitment to practices of accountability (*Accountability Requirement*); (iii) a general commitment not to promote arrangements in which respect and protection for people's human rights is significantly worsened, ceteris paribus (*Constraint Against Worsening*); (iv) a general commitment to show appropriate international concern as required by the practice, to undertake action when one is the agent capable and appropriately placed to have sufficient reason to act (*Commitment To Action Under Relevant Circumstances*). Muslim bans violate all of these. As only one bad failure on a contribution requirement is sufficient to show that important legitimacy standards have not been met, we need only show how Muslim bans fall short in one case. In this case I believe Muslim bans fail on all grounds, though here I concentrate on cases (i) and (ii) in some detail, making only a few brief remarks concerning (iii) and (iv).

Failing to Meet the Ethos Requirement: Muslim bans would violate the spirit and ethos of human rights documents, which aim to treat each human being as an individual who has dignity and whose interests deserve consideration. The ban would fail to uphold the animating ideas of human rights. Every person deserves equal respect and deserves to have their application to be admitted to a country given genuine and proper consideration. Banning people by religion, race, or country of origin fails this minimal test of treating each person as an individual whose claims deserve fair consideration, in attending closely to the reasons why that person seeks to be admitted and their particular personal characteristics. A critic might claim that the waiver system takes account of these concerns and does consider individual cases on their merits. However, in earlier sections we have also seen why the waiver system is a sham, designed to deflect such concerns, but in practice operates as an effective way to block almost all cases being granted exemptions or waivers without the proper consideration required.

That the ban failed crucially in this idea of treating each person's claim as worthy of consideration can be seen by examining approval data carefully; hardly any waivers were granted, even though many highly worthy applications were received. For instance, thousands of applications were received from close family members to visit or reside with their parents or children, and almost all of them were declined.[74]

In addition, failure to uphold core duties associated with the conventions and resolutions canvased in Section 4.2 on eliminating religious and racial hatred, intolerance, and discrimination, spreads a message that it is acceptable for other governments to do likewise. It fails to contribute to a practice of compliance with human rights. Rather, to the contrary, it undermines such practices of compliance.

Failure to Meet Accountability Requirements: A Muslim ban would also violate some of the norms embedded in our practices of accountability, which require accountability to both internal and external audiences, for performance on human rights. In particular, such policy cannot be adequately justified to the international community, which includes many other nations that have large Muslim populations. That it fails to meet such accountability standards can be seen by some of the comments that Muslims both within America and around the world made in the wake of the ban. Iran's Foreign Affairs Ministry, along with the Supreme Leader Ayatollah Khamenei, said of Trump's order that it was not only counter-productive in trying to combat extremism, but was also insulting to the Islamic world. Reciprocal measures were imposed on Americans wishing to

---

[74] Jeremy Stahl, "The Waiver process Is fraud," *Slate*, June 15, 2018 available at https://slate.com/news-and-politics/2018/06/trump-travel-ban-waiver-process-is-a-sham-two-consular-officers-say.html. Also Sima Alizadeh, "The 'Waiver' Camouflage, a closed door policy for travel ban countries" blog post, *Think immigration* website, available at https://slate.com/news-and-politics/2018/06/trump-travel-ban-waiver-process-is-a-sham-two-consular-officers-say.html

enter Iran.[75] Many from the Shia community in Iraq condemned the ban, also calling for the removal of US citizens from Iraq, and this was echoed by the Iraqi parliament.[76] A great many people of Muslim faith from around the world echoed similar sentiments.[77]

Especially notable is world reaction, which roundly condemned the ban, from Western leaders. The UK Prime Minister's Office issued a statement indicating that it did not agree with the approach, while Foreign Secretary, Boris Johnson, condemned the approach as "divisive and wrong." Many other British politicians also spoke out against the ban, including the Mayor of London Sadiq Khan and the Leader of the Labour Party, Jeremy Corbyn.[78] And 1.6 million people signed a petition to stop a state visit of Trump to the UK on grounds that his discriminatory and misogynistic proclivities, along with his vulgarity, should disqualify him from such a visit.[79] France and Canada not only spoke out against the ban but also called on the USA to recognize its duties to receive refugees fleeing oppression and war.[80] And a long list of others joined in the condemnation, including many from Germany, Ireland, Sweden, and the Netherlands. The level of condemnation and protest both domestically and around the world from religious and political leaders, US diplomats, human rights groups, scholars, experts, think tanks, and academics, along with members of the business community among many others, was indeed very high, showing that in the eyes of many, such policy could not meet a robust accountability test.

---

[75] Ralph Ellis, Sara Mazloumsaki, and Artemis Moshtaghian, "Iran to take 'reciprocal measures' after Trump's immigration order," *CNN*, January 29, 2017; Iran Ministry of Foreign Affairs, "Statement of the Ministry of Foreign Affairs of the Islamic Republic of Iran," January 28, 2017. 436947.

[76] "Trump executive order banning refugees," *BBC* (January 29, 2017); Charlie Brinkhurt-Cuff, Martin Chulov, and Saeed Kamali Dehhan, "Muslim-majority countries show anger at Trump travel ban," *The Guardian*, January 30, 2017.

[77] Only the world's most repressive Muslim regimes did not join in the condemnation of the ban or offered support, notably Syrian President Bashar al-Assad and Foreign Minister Sheikh Abdullah bin Zayed Al Nahyan from the United Arab Emirates. See "UAE says Trump travel ban an internal affair, most Muslims unaffected," *Reuters*, February 1, 2017; and "Assad says Trump travel ban targets terrorists, not Syrian people," *Reuters*, February 19, 2017. Many of these countries go to great lengths to stay on side with the USA for a number of economic and strategic reasons. And others have a strong interest in maintaining that such policy decisions are within the rightful domain of sovereign nations because of their own poor record on human rights.

[78] "Theresa May finally passes judgment on Donald Trump's immigration ban," *The Independent*, January 29, 2107; *BBC News*, "Calls to stop President's state visit to the UK," January 29, 2017.

[79] "Trump executive order: Million sign petition to stop UK visit," *BBC News*, January 30, 2017.

[80] "Trump's refugee and travel suspension: World reacts," *BBC News*, January 28, 2017; Amanda Erickson, "Here's how the world is responding to Trump's ban on refugees, travelers from 7 Muslim nations," *The Washington Post*, January 29, 2017.

This kind of evidence shows that Muslim ban policies would fail to meet accountability standards to the international community, along with accountability standards that internal stakeholders demand.

The Constraint Against Worsening and the Commitment To Action Requirements: Drawing on material I introduced in Section 4.2.1, we saw how such policies set the tone and create the environment for further rights violations, as those with hateful views are emboldened to express them more directly and in violent ways. There I argued that protection for citizens' human rights deteriorated markedly during Trump's ascendancy and following Trump's taking office. Rights to equal protection under the law, freedom of conscience, freedom to practice religion freely with others, freedom of association, nondiscrimination, and so forth, all suffered important setbacks.

Muslim ban type policies also provide exactly the kind of ammunition extremists seek in promoting violence against Christians, Americans, and "Westerners," more generally. This hardly promotes the kinds of attitudes and dispositions we need for a robust human rights practice to flourish. Reflecting on the kinds of considerations reviewed in Section 4.2, Muslim ban type policies show why they cannot assist us in going in the right direction of a legitimate state system. On the contrary, they take us further away from realizing such objectives. Given the deterioration in human rights protections documented in Section 4.2.1, we see how Muslim bans not only violate the Constraint Against Worsening, but also the requirement to take appropriate action under relevant circumstances. State actors are clearly the agents capable and appropriately placed to have sufficient reason to act in this case – they can refrain from the policy choices they have made. Indeed, they are obligated to do so, as I have been arguing.

5   Conclusions

In this chapter I argued that a legitimate state may not embrace a migration policy that bans Muslims from being admitted, without such very policies undermining a state's claim to legitimacy. I have argued that such policies violate core legitimacy requirements, namely internal and contribution criteria. For instance, we saw how adopting such policies have had important spillover effects for citizens, threatening a range of rights including the right to freedom of religion and nondiscrimination. In addition, I argued that such policies demonstrate important failures to discharge obligations concerning eliminating discrimination based on ideas of racial hatred and superiority. We also saw how such policies violate core contribution requirements, such as failures to uphold the animating ideas of human rights and failures to meet accountability standards for human rights protection, to both internal and external stakeholders, and both Muslims and non-Muslims. More briefly, I also showed how such policies fail to meet other contribution requirements, such as constraints against worsening and requirements to take appropriate action in relevant circumstances. Furthermore, as we have seen, states – or rather agents of the state – have responsibilities to protect and promote the necessary conditions for a legitimate state system. State agents have important responsibilities in connection with our human rights practice, for instance to foster dispositions and attitudes that can sustain robust human rights practice. The international human rights regime includes a set of important responsibilities for state parties. By signing up to these agreements, states have agreed to act in accordance with them. Leaders therefore inherit important responsibilities in connection with the international obligations states have signed up to. State agents dramatically failed in their duties by enacting Muslim ban policies.

Clearly, then, Muslim ban type policies are not justified on my account. But we still might wonder how security should matter in just migration policy. After all, we do have rights to security. Is the right to security in tension with other rights and justice considerations? As I argue in Chapter 8, there is a place for concern with security. However, a number of relevant factors affect the weighting it should have relative to a host of other important considerations.[81] A just society will aim to get the balance right.

---

[81] Of course, rights to security should include protection from standard threats. But as we see in Chapter 8, terrorist activities are not standard threats; they are very remote possibilities. This is relevant to the weighting terrorism deserves, given evidence of risks and competing considerations, as I argue in Chapter 8.

CHAPTER 5

Irregular Migration

1 Introduction

In this chapter I consider the challenge presented by new threats to deport long-settled members of communities who are classed as irregular, undocumented, or illegal. By "long-settled," I have in mind people who have been on a territory for at least five years. May legitimate states permissibly eject such residents? By contrast, do legitimate states have an obligation to adjust the migration status of such residents so they are legally entitled to remain as permanent residents? In this chapter we see why legitimate states may not eject such members and should regularize their status in certain important kinds of cases.

I begin by discussing five different types of cases that involve large numbers of people and for whom threats of deportation are currently causing much distress. The five cases raise different issues and it is important to track some of those details. The cases I discuss are (1) those involving the Windrush generation, (2) holders of a status called Temporary Protected Status (TPS), (3) children brought illegally to a state at a young age (such as the so-called Dreamers), often by desperate parents seeking better lives for those children, (4) migrants who arrived without legal permissions at a time when there was tacit approval for their entry, and (5) cases that we might describe as migration in response to an illegitimate state system. The details of all five types are considered in Section 2. Reflecting on these five cases brings to light several relevant features – sometimes quite different – that are useful in our analysis of why it would be wrong to eject such long-settled members of communities, and why legitimate states have an obligation to offer options for adjusting the status of such members, so they have the legal right to remain permanently on the state's territory. Given this obligation, it follows that plans to eject such members are impermissible and constitute wrongdoing.

In contrast to Joseph Carens, who leans heavily on an account of social membership to explain why irregular migrants have justified claims to remain after a certain amount of time has elapsed, I believe such grounding is not a firm basis on which to rest the case. Ideas about social membership can promote unhealthy societal dynamics that run counter to the very kinds of inclusive communities we ought to promote. To make my case, I draw on other salient notions that I believe to be more robust.

Reviewing earlier arguments concerning justified occupation, we are reminded that the case for citizens rightfully remaining on their territory relies on important conditions. When long-settled migrants are to be evicted, one might plausibly challenge whether those conditions are met. One important condition in play is that citizens' continued occupation is defensible only if their practices do not perpetrate wrongdoing. I show why evicting these long-settled members would constitute wrongdoing. I show why deportation, or even threats of deportation, for the long-settled involve grave injustices on a par with violating some of their most basic human rights. Significant weight should be placed on people's located life plans. I show what this entails, and how it stacks up against other normatively salient considerations.

In addition, by reviewing the three layers of legitimacy requirements introduced in Chapter 3, namely, internal, system, and contribution conditions, we see that such evictions would involve important failures. By ejecting long-settled residents, those states would be failing to meet internal requirements, such as prohibitions against cruel and unusual punishment, to respect the right to a family life, or to abide by conventions on the rights of the child. These sorts of failures to uphold basic human rights on their territory renders those states that engage in such actions as unable to exercise power legitimately. There would be an important failure of internal requirements. A similar conclusion holds concerning contribution failures. In addition, we see that there are other failures that such actions would exhibit. There would also be significant failures to respect important located life plans and failures to appreciate the grave harm and suffering evictions cause, especially considering that regularizing status in the five cases causes no undue harm.

Putting all these considerations together, long-settled members of a community should have a right to remain. Legitimate states may not evict such members and, to the contrary, states have obligations to allow them to remain as permanent residents. We begin to discuss what irregular migrants, along with others, may defensibly do in response to state failures to recognize the right to remain in the five kinds of cases. Further discussion concerning obligations to reduce migration injustices continues in Chapter 9.

The structure of this chapter is as follows. In Section 2 I describe the five cases in more detail and analyze some of the features that make ejection in such cases wrong. In Section 3 I consider Carens's arguments for obligations to regularize status and discuss why I find the grounding idea of social belonging problematic. Section 4 covers a detailed discussion of why it would be wrong not to offer pathways to regularization for long-settled migrants. Several considerations are relevant. People who have settled into ways of life, and are then forced to uproot, frequently experience the rupture as involving considerable hardship and suffering, for them and those with whom they have formed significant relationships. People's located life plans deserve respect under certain conditions, especially when those plans cause no undue hardship to others, as I argue in Section 4.2. In Section 4.3, I argue that after a reasonable period of time has elapsed, people described in cases (1)–(5) have a right not to be kept in limbo but deserve to be recognized as a member of the society in which they have been participating. Furthermore, as I argue in Section 4.4, evicting long-settled members threatens a state's right to exercise power legitimately by failing to meet core internal, system, and contribution requirements. In Section 4.5, I show how such actions also undermine the argument settlers may press concerning rightful continued occupation. Section 5 considers whether there are strong countervailing reasons to block my central arguments concerning the obligation to regularize status and shows why common objections do not succeed. Section 6 concludes.

2   Five Different Cases

We begin with five different kinds of cases of so-called illegal immigration in order to explore salient issues that the various cases bring into view.

2.1   The Windrush Generation

The Windrush generation refers to a group of people who came to the United Kingdom between 1948 and 1971 from the Caribbean.[1] The British Nationality Act of 1948 decreed that citizens of Commonwealth countries were also citizens of the UK. Members of the British Empire –

---

[1] The term "Windrush" derives from the ship the MV *Empire Windrush*, which arrived in Tilbury Docks, Essex on June 22, 1948.

British citizens according to the Act – were encouraged to come to Britain and help rebuild a nation recovering from World War II, a war in which many had fought on behalf of the British. A large number of vacancies were advertised in efforts to fill post-war labor shortages and many embarked on their journeys in response to such advertisements. Exact figures of how many are included in the Windrush generation are difficult to clarify, as many of those who arrived were traveling on their parents' passports and so never had their own separate travel documents recorded. This particular wave of immigration ceased with the passage of the 1971 Immigration Act, which meant that a British passport-holder born overseas was permitted to settle in the UK only if they had a parent or grandparent born in the UK and had a work permit.

The UK Home Office did not keep records of those granted permission to remain and issued no paperwork. In 2010, the government of the day destroyed the landing cards that had been completed by the Windrush generation. This makes it quite difficult for those who are part of that cohort to prove that they were residing in Britain legally.

Changes to immigration law in 2012 brought the general problem to light. These changes required presentation of formal residency or citizenship documentation for several purposes, such as in order to work legally, access treatment through the National Health Service, or to rent a property. Those who lacked such documents were informed that they now needed evidence concerning permission to continue working and living in the United Kingdom. It was only at this point that many from the Windrush generation first became aware that there was any issue concerning their status as British permanent residents. For instance, some were informed that they could no longer be employed, had their driving licenses withdrawn, or were refused access to health-care benefits.

The initial government response was fairly bureaucratic, and amounted to a strict enforcement of these new laws. Many lost their jobs, were denied urgent health-care treatment, had their driving licenses or other benefits withdrawn, were threatened with deportation (and, in sixty-three cases, were deported, probably wrongly), along with other ham-fisted attempts to enforce the letter of the law.[2] However, due to a high level of public concern and media attention, the Home Secretary at the time, Amber Rudd, apologized for the way the Windrush generation had been treated

---

[2] "Windrush: Sixty-three people may have been wrongly removed," *BBC News*, May 15, 2018, available at: www.bbc.com/news/uk-politics-44131136

and eventually created a task force to help applicants with appropriate documentation.

There are several factors that make this an easy case, in my view. The original migrants were entitled, invited, and encouraged to come to Britain. Their presence was highly beneficial to Britain and much welcomed. They presented all the relevant documentation that was required at the time. If there were inaccurate records kept about arriving migrants and their children, this was entirely the government's fault. And if records were destroyed in the Home Office, again, this can hardly be blamed on the Windrush generation. The government apology and subsequent efforts at assistance seem to be some recognition of their strongly justified claim to remain.

2.2   Temporary Protected Status in the USA

TPS is a visa category that confers legal residency in the USA. It is granted to those from countries affected by natural disasters and armed conflicts, for whom remaining in countries of origin would be exceedingly challenging. It allows those granted the status to live and work in the USA for limited periods. In 2017, there were about 320,000 people who were residing legally in the USA on such status, mainly from ten countries including El Salvador, Honduras, Haiti, Syria, Nicaragua, and South Sudan.[3]

There is a problem with those who have been granted TPS status for a long period, such as ten years or more, and who have recently been informed that they are now scheduled for expulsion. Some on this status have been in the USA since the 1990s, so at least a couple of decades. However, the Trump administration has decided not to renew the TPS legal residency status of hundreds of thousands of people. For instance, 200,000 El Salvadoreans are scheduled for expulsion.[4] The case of El

---

[3] D' Vera Cohn and Jeffrey Passel, "More than 100 000 Haitian and Central American immigrants face decision on their status in the U.S.," *Pew Research Center* (November 8, 2017). Available at: www.pewresearch.org/fact-tank/2017/11/08/more-than-100000-haitian-and-central-american-immigrants-face-decision-on-their-status-in-the-u-s/

[4] This proclamation was issued on January 8, 2018. It was declared that the Temporary Protected Status of 262 500 El Salvadorans to live and work in the USA would be terminated. This group was admitted after a 2001 earthquake created a humanitarian crisis. Heather Timmons, "Questions US officials couldn't answer about ending 'temporary protected status' for 200 000 people" *Quartz,* January 9, 2018, available at: https://qz.com/1174581/tps-trump-and-dhss-decision-on-el-salvador-immigrants/

Salvador is particularly draconian. The typical Salvadorean person in the USA has been in the country for twenty-one years,[5] and 192,000 of their children were born in the USA.[6] Ninety percent have jobs. Thirty-three percent own homes. In short, many of these people are now strongly integrated into US society.[7]

El Salvador will have difficulty integrating 200,000 new arrivals into its economy; that number is the equivalent of a sudden 3 percent population increase.[8] About 40 percent of El Salvadoreans are underemployed and two-thirds work in the informal sector.[9] More worrying, El Salvador is still one of the most violent countries in the world. Returning migrants are easy targets for crime, especially extortion by some of the most ruthless gangs in existence, including the notorious MS-13. Even if deported, many of the deportees will urgently seek ways to leave, joining the many who already leave the country every day.

Some of those on TPS status are eligible to apply for permanent residency, in virtue of having had children born in the USA, but the process is onerous and requires the parents of such children to leave the USA while the application is considered (so for a period of between three and ten years). For these sorts of reasons, many will simply decide to remain in the USA illegally, even if they lose their jobs and homes. But theirs will be a precarious existence. This group is easier to locate and deport than other undocumented migrants, given TPS visa requirements to supply regular updates on residency addresses.

The effects on both the USA and El Salvador are predicted to be immense.[10] For some of the jobs El Salvadoreans currently hold, it will not be easy to find Americans willing to replace them. This is especially the case with jobs that are lower paid, involving lower skill levels, such as is apparently the case for certain plumbing and heating jobs.[11] Predictions about losses that can be expected in light of revoking TPS from Hondurans, Haitians, and El Salvadoreans include shrinking GDP by

---

[5] "A fearful welcome: How will El Salvador cope with deportees from America?" *The Economist*, January 2018.

[6] Ibid.   [7] Ibid.

[8] Also, there are some logistical details that have not been fully worked out. The number of scheduled deportation flights coupled with aircraft capacity will mean that the USA will actually only be able to send back around 56,000 per year ("A fearful welcome," *The Economist*, January 2018).

[9] "A fearful welcome," *The Economist*, January 2018.

[10] Amanda Baron, Jose Magana-Salgado, with Tom K. Wong, "Economic contributions by Salvadorean, Honduran and Haitian TPS Holders," *Policy Report*, April 2017.

[11] Ibid.

$45.2 billion, deportation costs of $3.1 billion, and US employers will have to absorb turnover costs of about $1 billion.[12] For these sorts of reasons, Amanda Baron and Jose Magana, make the case that "it is in the national interest for DHS to renew TPS for El Salvador, Honduras, and Haiti."[13]

What are we to make of this decision to revoke TPS status for those who are long-settled in the USA? While TPS is by definition supposed to be a limited-residency status, by continuously renewing it for so long, those on these visas might form reasonable expectations about how their lives would continue. Up until 2017, there was no indication that their ability to remain legally in the USA was about to be terminated. Rather to the contrary, they were given the impression that their continued residence was causing no concern. As discussed in Chapter 2, people form located life plans, and these are weighty considerations in evaluating what it is reasonable to do after an extended period of time. Furthermore, by letting them stay for so long, the USA facilitated the development of a network of relationships that are mutually beneficial to both US citizens and to residents with TPS standing, thereby affecting a range of other people's located life plans. Some US citizens, such as employers, have made extensive plans based on the presence of these residents, expanding their businesses, developing their workforce, making important investments, and so on. The US citizens have an important interest that is not being factored in properly as well. The located life plans of US citizens, while perhaps less dramatically affected, are also relevant to whether states act permissibly when they evict long-settled residents.

Some of the salient issues as to why ejection would be wrong in the case of long-settled holders of TPS visas include the following considerations. They were legally permitted onto the territory. They were allowed to remain for a reasonably long period and given an understanding about how their lives would go forward. They formed reasonable located life plans, working, living, and participating in communities, much like other residents. Their presence caused no undue hardship but rather made positive contributions to the USA. In addition, in many cases, such as that of El Salvador, significant weight should also be given to the fact that the situation prompting the original humanitarian concern warranting

---

[12] Ibid.   [13] Ibid.

initial entry has not resolved sufficiently to provide a credible environment in which basic human rights of repatriated citizens will be protected.

Ejection is even more unjust for those who have American children who only know America as home. Separating members of mixed status families would typically constitute a grave harm and, as I discuss further below, constitutes a very important form of wrongdoing that violates core requirements for the state's legitimacy, such as the rights of the child and rights to a family life. While those who have US citizen children over twenty-one can apply to have their children remain in the USA, there are lengthy wait times before these applications will be considered, and furthermore parents would have to leave for an extended period of time anyhow while the application is processed. Separating families for years on end, especially those involving young children, seems a particularly cruel form of punishment, and would be a violation of another core human rights requirement for states to exercise power legitimately (as specified by for instance Article 5, UDHR).

2.3 Children Arriving Illegally at a Young Age, Having Been Brought by Parents

While the first two cases involve legal entry that was either encouraged or permitted, in this class of cases the original entry was not legally sanctioned. However, clearly, children being brought by adults who arrive illegally cannot be held accountable for such actions. And if they arrive at a very young age and have grown up in the USA, knowing no other place as home, their ejection would typically be especially cruel, imposing significant hardship and distress on those ejected. To destroy their status in their adopted society would, in such cases, be a harsh form of punishment, on a par with torture. Banishing people from a territory used to be a form of severe punishment for grave crimes. Yet in these cases, it is not clear what serious crime these children have committed that would warrant such treatment. If any crimes were committed, these were not committed by the children. Rather, these children are innocent. It is also noteworthy that many are making important contributions to their adopted societies, contributing their skills and labor to the well-being of US citizens, such as by serving in the military.

Ejection would also involve important violations of core requirements on which the legitimacy of state action depends. In some cases, it might violate the children's rights to a family life. In typical cases, inflicting this punishment on the children would be a violation of Article 5 and core tenets of the Convention Against Torture and Other Cruel, Inhuman, or Degrading Treatment. So, such actions would involve important violations of internal legitimacy requirements, a theme I continue to discuss in Section 4.4. The legitimacy of the state's exercise of power would therefore be under threat, given these important violations.

2.4   Illegal Migration at a Time When There Was Widespread Tacit Approval for Such Flows

Some undocumented migrants came at a time when understandings and expectations about enforcement were very different, such as in the early 1990s. Their presence was highly beneficial to US citizens, and many engaged in mutually advantageous interactions.[14] Are the circumstances surrounding these waves of immigration more like being tacitly invited onto the territory? Let us consider in more detail why that question might be raised and why a positive answer to it may be appropriate.

When large waves of immigrants arrived illegally in the early 1990s, very lax enforcement policies suggested such migrants were not doing anything particularly bad.[15] Citizens were aware of the presence of large populations of undocumented migrants eager to work for low wages. The fact that citizens frequently employed these migrants and that their labor was highly valued may well have given the further impression to the migrants that there was no intention of ejecting them. A reasonable interpretation of these kinds of facts may have been that such migrants had been given a certain understanding that their presence was welcome and immigration laws would not be enforced in their kinds of cases, so long as they remained in the shadows and stayed out of trouble. There are many laws on the books that are not enforced, so immigrants' understanding may have seemed reasonable.

Reflecting on views about similar earlier patterns adds to the strength of their case. As we saw in Chapter 2, migration was regarded as welcome and of high benefit to aspiring and dominant nations. Colonizing nations often found it useful to encourage settlers to occupy territory or fill labor shortages. Even highly established states often welcomed and encouraged

---

[14] This wave of immigration helped grow the US economy considerably. See, for instance, data at the Migration Policy Institute website, available at: www.migrationpolicy.org/article/immigration-united-states-new-economic-social-political-landscapes-legislative-reform

[15] See, for instance, data at the Migration Policy Institute website, available at: www.migrationpolicy .org/article/immigration-united-states-new-economic-social-political-landscapes-legislative-reform

a steady flow of migrants. For instance, looking at recent history we can see there were regular patterns of high circular migration between Mexico and the US. Mexicans would travel back and forth regularly in response to a variety of factors, including seasonal labor demands. This history is relevant to assessing what to make of migration, now deemed illegal, even though it follows the same patterns that were formerly legal and encouraged. Ruling regimes may have changed their views about welcoming seasonal migration, but from the migrants' perspectives, attitudes may be more difficult to shift. Indeed, from their vantage point, they may not think of themselves as doing anything terribly wrong if they are simply following these once legal and welcomed patterns. And it may be difficult to change attitudes about the morality of such lawbreaking, if it follows patterns that were, until recently, legal and welcomed.

2.5   Migration in Response to State System Failures

Another category of cases of illegal migration worth considering results from failures of our state system to make adequate provisions for those who are victims of large-scale human rights violations. We might describe these movements as direct responses to a state system that has not made adequate provisions for intolerable states of affairs in which human rights are massively violated or under significant threat. As I discuss in Chapter 6, many refugees are exactly in this position. Many fleeing persecution judge that being legally recognized as a refugee entitled to resettlement may well prove to be very challenging, and there is a high chance of their being sent back to a situation they consider untenable. So, in response to this assessment, they may decide to enter (or remain on) a territory illegally. Many fleeing dire circumstances around the world might well believe this to be their only available option.

In trying to assess what to make of these cases, we might note similar problems concerning justified responses to injustice are not new. Desperate people have often undertaken perilous journeys to enter countries illegally, in efforts to escape injustice. Consider how people fleeing persecution from Russia or Nazi Germany were justified in attempting to cross borders illegally, for instance, by hiring people smugglers to transport them to safety across borders, especially as the international community was unable or unwilling to stop their suffering. Crossing borders illegally under such circumstances was clearly a justified response. In such cases the migrants' actions are a form of self-defense in a world that has become a threat to their survival. So, similar cases of crossing borders in efforts to seek safety can be justified today, given that the international community fails to make provisions for similar victims trying to escape a failed state system.

3   The Passage of Time and Why It Matters

In four of the five cases introduced in Section 2, the passage of time is one of the factors that makes eviction morally problematic. Why does the passage of time matter to the strength of one's claim to remain? For Joseph Carens, the core grounding concept is the idea of social membership. The key ingredients for being a social member are residence and time. For Carens, the term "social membership" "evokes the sense that being a member of a society involves a dense network of relationships and associations."[16] The ideas of "residence and time are proxies for richer, deeper forms of connection but that we have both practical and principled reasons not to go beyond these proxies, at least under most circumstances."[17] Indeed, "simply living in a state over time is sufficient to make one a member of society and to ground claims to legal rights and ultimately to citizenship."[18] For Carens, the key period is five years. Why five years as the target length for a right to stay? His answer is that "one is too short and ten too long given common European understandings of the ways in which people normally settle into the societies where they live."[19]

Carens uses the notion of social belonging as a core idea in making his case. I appreciate that this may be an effective way for him to argue his case because it will resonate well with some people, especially considering the long history of such appeals to social belonging in transcending class difference. Nevertheless, I believe it may be unwise to rest the normative case on these grounds. One reason is that it gives people the sense that you *should* feel that you belong somewhere. It has normative implications about how one ought to feel, perhaps even that one is entitled to feel that one belongs somewhere, and that this sense of comfort should be secure. This can set up unhelpful dynamics, such as an unhealthy attachment to keeping one's community as a comfortable space in which we can all enjoy an "effortless and secure sense of belonging."[20] What is the danger? As communities become larger and more diverse, they inevitably must include more people who may present as different from original community

---

[16] Joseph Carens, *Ethics of Immigration*   [17] Ibid., 165.   [18] Ibid., 168.   [19] Ibid., 114.
[20] Avishai Margalit and Joseph Raz, "National Self-Determination," *Journal of Philosophy*, 87 (9) (1990): 439–461.

members. Some begin to feel that they are strangers in a strange land and that they do not belong anymore. It may not take much for them to feel the attraction of populist leaders who claim to be able to restore life to when there was a sense of "effortless and secure belonging" when, for instance, their group flourished before the arrival of so many "foreigners."[21] So, one of the downsides of all this social membership and belonging discourse is that it can make people feel that something is fundamentally wrong if they do not experience themselves as enjoying a sense of belonging and comfort with others perceived as making up a large section of the population in their community.[22]

In addition, the notion of belonging sets up an unnecessary tension between those who belong and those who do not, between insiders and outsiders. This sense of "us" and "them" is often at the heart of other migration related injustices, as we see in later chapters. Furthermore, the idea of belonging can invoke assumptions about what it is to belong to a certain group, that rely on fictitious accounts of who the group is and what it takes to be a "proper" member of it. In reality, "we are more like strangers who are thrown together, locked in a room or on a bus, united by nothing other than shared circumstances."[23]

I believe the passage of time does matter but not for the kinds of reasons Carens emphasizes.[24] People settle into ways of life that can then become

---

[21] To be clear, I do not think the felt need to belong must take this shape. I think desires to feel accepted, understood, recognized, and valued, which lie at the heart of the felt need to belong, can be met in many ways. Unfortunately, too often these desires take the undesirable form I document in this section.

[22] For more on this phenomenon see, for instance, Arlie Hochschild, *Strangers in their own Land: Anger and Mourning on the American Right* (New York: The New Press, 2016).

[23] Banting and Kymlicka, "*Introduction: The Political Sources of Solidarity in Diverse Societies.*" Here they are describing Jacob Levy's views as articulated in chapter 4 of that volume, "Against Fraternity."

[24] In addition, while I believe many irregular migrants also make important contributions to their host societies, I am reluctant to ground their claim to remain solely on this basis, for several reasons. Here I discuss some reasons to worry about Sarah Song's excellent treatment of the issues (chapter 10, *Immigration and Democracy*). As she has recently so well argued, a fair play argument can be marshaled in virtue of irregular migrants' extensive contributions to the flourishing of their host societies (in addition to Carensian style arguments in virtue of social membership). They are owed the benefit of citizenship in virtue of contributions over a sustained period of time. I think this fair play argument has some force, but I wonder whether it has enough to work for all irregular migrants. First, there might be some people whose contribution to their adopted society might appear questionable, and so it might thereby follow that their case is not strong. Second, others may challenge whether undocumented migrants' contributions are sufficiently great to merit the benefit of citizenship, especially in virtue of the unconsented nature of their arrival. All in all, while I recognize there are some strengths to this position, along with some potential weaknesses, I explore a different argument here. For more on Song's position see *Immigration and Democracy*, especially chapter 10.

immensely important to their wellbeing and sense of purpose in life. Uprooting them from those settled ways of life can cause extensive hardship and harm to those who become separated, both to the ejected migrant and to those who remain in the country doing the ejecting. Their located life plans deserve respect. So, while Carens connects with these ideas through his notion of social belonging, I think we can get to the core ideas by different paths that are on firmer normative foundations, ones that will be more in accordance with my cosmopolitan conception of migration justice.[25]

Several central arguments of this kind are developed in Section 4. People have settled into ways of life and uprooting them would typically cause considerable hardship and disproportionate harm to them and those with whom they have formed significant relationships. Their claim to remain is frequently compelling. This becomes clear when we consider the hardship such policies cause mixed status families. We explore this line of argument in Section 4.1. In Section 4.2 I marshal an argument centered on the importance of respect for located life plans under certain conditions. In Section 4.3 I show that the right not to be kept in limbo applies to our core cases. Section 4.4 shows how evicting the long-settled would undermine legitimacy in several ways. I argue that evicting long-settled members threatens a state's right to exercise power legitimately by undermining core internal, system, and contributions requirements. In Section 4.5 we review arguments used to justify continued occupation and how they place limits on what occupants may do now. Evicting long-settled members triggers the constraining conditions, so that such actions would be

---

[25] Curiously, I do not think that Carens needs to appeal to social belonging to make his own case. In fact, the details of his case rely more on what it is to live a typical human life that is going well, rather than a notion of social belonging, as such. These passages are illustrative. He says, for instance: "There is something deeply wrong in forcing people to leave a place where they have lived for a long time. Most people form their deepest human connections where they live. It becomes home. Even if someone has arrived only as an adult, it seems cruel and inhumane to uproot a person who has spent fifteen or twenty years as a contributing member of her society in the name of enforcing immigration restrictions. The harm done to her is entirely out of proportion to the wrong of unauthorized entry and settlement." (Carens, *The Ethics of Immigration*, 149).

And also this:

"Ten years is a long time in a human life. In ten years, connections grow: to spouses and partners, sons and daughters, friends and neighbours and fellow-workers, people we love and people we hate. Experiences accumulate: birthdays and braces, tones of voice and senses of humor, public parks and corner stores, the shape of the streets and the way the sun shines through the leaves, the smell of flowers and the sounds of local accents, the look of the stars and the taste of the air – all that gives life its purpose and texture. We sink deep roots over ten years, and these roots matter even if we were not authorized to plant ourselves in the first place." (Ibid., 150).

In these accounts what matters is living a full and meaningful life rather than social belonging. These kinds of reasons converge with the factors that I also believe to be salient.

impermissible, if continued occupation is to be justified. Rather, to enjoy continued rightful occupation, states have an obligation to offer a pathway to regularize the status of such members so that they have the legal right to remain permanently on the state's territory, should they so wish.

4   Why Would It Be Wrong Not to Regularize Status after a Period of Time?

4.1   Mixed Status Families

Let us start the analysis with a relatively easy case that actually involves huge numbers of people, namely mixed status families.[26] The state must respect certain basic rights of citizens – such as the right to a family life, the right to form and maintain certain kinds of intimate relationships – and that means the state must respect certain rights of citizens even when it has other goals it might like to pursue.[27] Rights to a family life typically involve that family members reside in close proximity, at least in the case of close relatives, such as a spouse or young children. If children are to develop and thrive, they typically need access to their parents and secure access to membership in societies that provide them with their options for located life plans. Citizens have the right to bring in "outsiders," or allow noncitizens to remain, when they are in this intimate core group. So, family ties can sometimes constitute good reasons for blocking deportation.

   To think that all long-settled families will just go back to some country they left a long time ago involves a fantasy.[28] On the contrary, there is a

---

[26] The number of people living in mixed status families in the USA is currently very large; 9.6 million adults are in such families with 5.9 million children who are US citizens. While many of these unauthorized immigrants are eligible for a green card, they would have to leave the country to adjust their status and endure a long wait period (three to ten years) before reentry would be permitted. For more on such facts, see for instance, "The Facts on Immigration Today: 2017 Edition," *Center for American Progress website*, available at: www.americanprogress.org/issues/immigration/reports/2017/04/20/430736/facts-immigration-today-2017-edition

[27] For a similar argument see Matthew Lister, "*The Rights of Families and Children at the Border*," chapter 7, pp. 153–170. For more excellent work on family rights see Luara Ferracioli, "Family Migration Schemes and Liberal Neutrality," *Journal of Moral Philosophy*, 13 (2016): 553–575; Luara Ferracioli, "International Migration and Human Rights" in Chris Brown and Robyn Eckersley (eds.), *The Oxford Handbook of International Political Theory* (Oxford: Oxford University Press, 2018), pp. 520–532; and Matthew Lister, "Immigration, Association, and the Family," *Law and Philosophy*, 29 (2010): 717–745.

[28] As Rep. Luis Gutierrez (D-Ill) said, "The White House is peddling a fantasy where hundreds of thousands of people who have established their lives, families, and businesses in the US for decades will leave or can be rounded up and deported. Turning immigrants living and working in the US

high probability that many of those families will see remaining illegally as their only real option, especially if family members who are lawful residents remain. The policy has the undesirable effect of turning participating, long-settled residents in our communities into law-breakers, for no good reason. In addition, the rights of US-born children can be significantly under threat, if parents feel that they need to minimize interactions with state authorities. They may fail to seek necessary health care or education for those children, concerned that their own status will be brought to light and thereby increase the risk of deportation.

4.2   Respect for Located Life Plans

What about other ways in which eviction might be wrong that are not connected with mixed status families? Here I discuss the weight of located life plans.

Recall that there is an important role for location to play in understanding how we make our way in the world, and so the nature of our responsibilities. As I argued in Chapter 3 when examining our economic needs, for instance, the particular ways in which we orient ourselves and plan to meet subsistence needs are importantly determined by place and context. People develop plans around particular forms of life in specific places and orient their lives toward these.

Social contexts matter greatly in the development and implementation of these life plans. In particular social settings, we might have learned a new language, learned skills that are useful in certain contexts and not others, formed relationships with community members, and built up considerable human and social capital in a particular environment that is not transferable. Economic skills rewarded by a particular economic context may be of low value in others. More generally, how one develops and implements one's life plans typically involves considerable investment of oneself and one's resources. Ceteris paribus, legitimate, located life plans deserve respect.

Leaving contexts in which one is long-settled may involve starting over, which is typically experienced as highly challenging for those who have lived large segments of their lives in the places they now consider to be home. While we should expect to have to adjust our located life plans in

---

into undocumented immigrants defies logic, even for this president" cited in Ryan Devereaux, "Ignoring violence in El Salvador, Trump ends years of special protective status for immigrants" *The Intercept*, available here: https://theintercept.com/2018/01/08/el-salvador-immigration-tps-trump/

response to relevant factors, such as technological and social changes, there is a difference between being uprooted and making adjustments while core fundamentals remain in place and under supportive conditions. While some thrive on change, many find change that is too rapid and that is coupled with decreased support distressing. For many who are ejected from their familiar surroundings to an environment in which they have not lived at all (or not for a very long time), that kind of change is likely to be experienced as disorienting and arduous. Removing long-settled migrants whose presence on the territory poses no threat to safety, especially when the country to which they would be deported is not in a position to respect, protect, or fulfill basic human rights and assist with necessary adjustments to legitimate life plans, would be morally wrong.

4.3 The Right Not to Be Kept in Limbo and the Need to Feel Settled

In addition, as I discuss in Chapter 6, it cannot be reasonable to expect people to live in a state of high uncertainty about territory of residence indefinitely. I believe we have a right not to be kept in limbo in these matters after a certain period has elapsed. Cases of illegal entrants who have settled for long periods would all have a strong claim in virtue of this further consideration to have their status regularized.

A position introduced in Chapter 2 might also play a supporting role here. People often express a need to feel settled. This can connect importantly with needs concerning security or with deep psychological needs, such as to feel recognized as a person who has standing in the community, to make sense of one's life, or for order in one's life. Being left in limbo and in a state of high uncertainty often takes people further away from meeting such important needs. While the weight all our needs claims should have must be evaluated in contexts where other needs and justice considerations also play a role, it can be the case that there is no strong countervailing reason not to allow people who are long-settled to remain (especially when significant hardship is inflicted on them by eviction, and there are benign or positive effects on others in a settled community). And there are important moral considerations in play that suggest we ought to consider the well-being of such members in determining what fairness for this group requires.

4.4 Performance on Internal, System, and Contribution Requirements

Recall also that for states to exercise power legitimately, a number of conditions must be met. These were described earlier as internal, system, and contribution requirements. Deporting these long-settled residents is relevant to meeting all three sets of conditions, as I show in this section.

To remind the reader of some key points, in Chapter 3 I argued that a state's ability to exercise power legitimately is conditional on its respecting adequate human rights protections. These protections apply in a range of areas, but apply especially to how people are treated who are on the state's territory (*Internal Requirements*). As I also argued, the legitimacy of individual states is further conditional on their being part of a legitimate state system (*System Requirements*). The legitimacy of the state system requires states to participate in the cooperative project needed to sustain a justified state system. Individual states have some positive obligations to make certain important contributions to that system and to refrain from acting in certain ways (*Contribution Requirements*). When governments fail to perform adequately in meeting these requirements, the state's own claim to exercise power legitimately can be called into question.

As I argue in this section, a state which expelled long-settled residents would violate internal and contribution requirements. It would therefore contribute to undermining system requirements as well. So, far from having rights to eject under such circumstances, such actions would undermine the legitimacy of the state that undertook such actions.

Let us consider how these legitimacy requirements would be violated. In some cases, states would be separating mixed status families, and so would be violating conventions on the rights of the child. We also have a right to a family life and, in many cases where there are mixed status families involved, ejection would violate this right. These would all be straightforward violations of core requirements on the legitimacy of state actions. Rights to a family life are a core feature of UDHR (e.g. Article 16). And respecting such core aspects of the Convention on the Rights of the Child would have a similar standing.

Moving away from what you might think of as some easy cases, in all five categories I introduced, uprooting the long-settled, who are effectively being banished, counts as a violation of Article 5 of the UDHR, that no one shall be subjected to torture or to cruel, inhuman, or degrading treatment or punishment. As I noted earlier, banishment is a harsh and cruel punishment that was reserved for serious crimes. In all the cases discussed here, it is not always clear that *any* crimes were committed by those being punished. This is obvious in the case of the Dreamers and Windrush generation. One might also challenge whether the harshness of treatment is merited, given the absence of wrongdoing on the part of those being banished. A case can also be made that ejecting the long-settled in these cases violates Article 9 of the UDHR that no one should be subjected to arbitrary exile. And such ejections might also contravene the requirement that everyone be given a fair hearing (Article 10, UDHR). So, these violations are sufficient to conclude that internal legitimacy requirements would not be met.

Even more importantly perhaps, the eviction of long-settled members also fails to meet contribution requirements. Recall that in Chapter 3 I drew attention to several requirements that states must meet in order to contribute appropriately to a justified state system, one capable of sustaining a robust human rights practice. In general, we might describe these as a commitment to the animating ideas and practices governing human rights today. Some of these included:

Requirement Against Worsening: A general commitment not to promote arrangements in which respect and protection for people's human rights is significantly worsened, ceteris paribus. So, in the absence of compelling countervailing reasons, states should not endorse situations in which protection for human rights deteriorates markedly.

Commitment To Action under Relevant Circumstances: A general commitment to show appropriate international concern as required by the practice, to undertake action when one is the agent capable and appropriately placed to have sufficient reason to act.

Accountability Requirement: A commitment to practices of accountability.

Ethos Requirement: A commitment to maintain an ethos conducive to respect for the practice of human rights, such as that everyone deserves to be treated with dignity and respect as a human being.

Let us discuss the relevance of these contribution requirements to the cases at hand, starting with the first two powerful constraints. In many cases, eviction contravenes these two constraints. Consider cases of sending those who have enjoyed TPS for decades back to countries of origin where their basic human rights would not be at all secure. Such actions cannot be part of what a legitimate state required to contribute to a legitimate state system can justifiably do. In many such situations, this would be a straightforward violation of the anti-worsening requirement. Sending TPS holders back to El Salvador where their basic human rights would become quite insecure is a clear example. Moreover, in such cases, the state in which the TPS holder has been residing is clearly an agent capable and appropriately placed to have sufficient reason to act. The requirement against worsening and the commitment to action under certain circumstances (when one is an agent capable and appropriately placed to have sufficient reason to act), are two important considerations. In addition, the ethos and accountability requirements could be invoked to add force to the argument.

Similar considerations would apply to many of the other cases as well. Consider, for instance those described as responses to the illegitimate state system – a system that makes inadequate provision for those finding themselves in states unwilling or unable to protect their basic human rights (case 2.5). By evicting those who, plausibly, are trying to defend themselves against an illegitimate state system, we would be violating the contribution requirement against worsening, ceteris paribus. As with the previous category, the evicting state is an agent capable and suitably placed to have sufficient reason to allow such migrants to remain, so there would be another important contribution requirement failure (other things being equal).

I have been arguing that states that carried out policies of ejecting long-settled members in instances such as 2.1–2.5 cannot be legitimate. They would not exercise power legitimately were they to follow through with such plans. This has important implications as I discuss below. For example, many agents would have no reason to respect such eviction policies and it would be permissible for those the state aims to deport to resist the state's attempts to carry out such illegitimate actions. We continue discussing these themes in Chapter 9.

4.5   Justified Occupation and Wrongdoing

Recall that the right of settlers to continued occupation may be justified so long as they do not engage in wrongdoing. But deporting long-settled community members would constitute wrongdoing under certain circumstances, such as the ones being considered in the five categories as we have been discussing in Sections 4.1–4.4. The wrongdoing can be described in various ways. One way is that such actions would unjustifiably inflict grave harms on people who are undeserving of such hardship. Reflecting on the situations of the Windrush generation, those with TPS status being deported to El Salvador, or DACA examples, we see how momentous these deportations are likely to be for those evicted. The hardship that mixed families experience adds to the severity of the suffering. But quite apart from family considerations, as I have also been arguing, uprooting long-settled people and significantly disrupting their located life plans, especially when this fundamentally affects their ability to meet their core needs, their prospects for human rights fulfillment, and causes no undue hardship for the communities in which they reside, does constitute wrongdoing, other things being equal. So, following this argument, those who take themselves to be the rightful occupants of the territory, able to make decisions about who should be permitted to join and stay on the territory, would no longer be justified in occupying the territory on which they reside.

In response to this reasoning, someone might remind me that straight after presenting this argument in Chapter 2 concerning the conditions on justified occupation, I also offered a defense of the state. Once that move was made, my objector might maintain, that shields states from these sorts of issues concerning whether they have a justified right to continue to occupy territory. However, a response to such an objector flows out directly from the argument that was made on behalf of states because that case depended crucially on states' abilities to facilitate justice. So, the defense of the state applies when and to the extent that it is able to facilitate justice, or at least to the extent that its actions are not unjust. States that insisted on ejecting long-settled members in the examples under discussion would not be facilitating justice, indeed would be facilitating injustice, so their grounding argument would not protect them from this conclusion.[29]

5 Are There Strong Countervailing Reasons to Block My Argument Concerning the Obligation to Regularize?

Here I consider some common objections to regularization and show how they can be addressed. One objection to allowing irregular migrants to stay is that we are being unfair to those foreigners who are respecting the rules and waiting patiently in line for their turn to be legally admitted. Unfortunately, in practice, there is effectively no line for those who do not have desired skills or relevant family members who are already citizens. This complaint invokes some imaginary construct that does not correlate well with any states' current admission policies.

Another objection to amnesty is that it sends a message that law-breaking can be advantageous and will be rewarded. However, in response we could note that the nature of lawbreaking varies tremendously. It is a

---

[29] In fact, the central case for the state was that it can provide good administration that facilitates good planning in bringing about justice in particular communities. The end goal is to have structures that can facilitate just communities. People resident on the territory can be factored into good plans, if we design good policy and generally encourage long-settled community members to make their intentions about remaining clear. Of course, currently most do not do this. On the contrary, unauthorised community members risk significant punishment in every interaction with agents of the state, especially if they have been there for a long time.

rare person who has not broken laws concerning speed limits. Widespread noncompliance with speed limits tells us nothing about the likelihood of the average adult's committing a more serious crime, such as murder. Some laws are more accurately described as administrative rather than criminal. Entering the country without permission should count as administrative law given its nonviolent nature.

Furthermore, even if settling without authorization violates immigration laws, it does not follow that we should punish people many years later, following the idea of a statute of limitations on being arrested and charged for crimes within a certain period, at least for certain kinds of crimes.

In addition, can we reasonably be expected to comply with a law that requires massive self-sacrifice? Can we reasonably be expected to comply with law that treats one unjustly? In attempting to answer such questions, we should consider whether law has the same status for everyone, especially when it treats segments of a population unjustly. According to an interesting argument by Bas Schotel, certain laws have no standing for excluded migrants in some cases. On Schotel's view, areas of the law that "aim to oppress and even destroy (groups of) individuals"[30] would not come close to the target of having authority for that group.[31] As he notes, "it may be the case that a legal system contains both areas that have legitimate authority and others that clearly do not even come close to target because they are 'oppressive and destructive'."[32] A good example of this can be found by considering law under the Nazi regime. While traffic laws may have some legitimate authority for everyone, it is not clear that laws requiring discrimination against Jews would have legitimate authority, especially for Jewish people being discriminated against. Schotel therefore introduces the idea of relative legal validity.[33]

I have argued that in unjustly evicting or excluding certain groups, immigration laws are unjust. Following Schotel's line of argument, those laws cannot have legitimate authority for those unjustly treated. As a result, and in those cases, the law cannot seriously claim authority over those migrants. The law does not have the same kind of authority for those the state unjustly excludes. In addition, for those the state classes as nonmembers and treats unjustly, they do not have obligations to obey the law

---

[30] Bas Schotel, *On the Right of Exclusion: Law, Ethics and Immigration Policy* (Abingdon: Routledge, 2012), 126.

[31] Ibid.   [32] Ibid., 127.

[33] We can make sense of this by looking at the functions of law, for instance separating its coordination functions from others.

insofar as it unjustly excludes them and treats them as persons who lack standing in that very community. So, there are no duties to obey immigration laws for those that the state treats unjustly in certain cases. As I have argued, in all the cases outlined in Section 2, the state would act unjustly should it proceed to evict such members. And the state would act unjustly should it refuse to offer a pathway to regularize the status of such members, so that they have a legal right to remain permanently on the state's territory. If the state makes and attempts to enforce unjust immigration laws then those so treated can act to resist such enforcement. They may act in ways designed to evade and deceive. And they may use proportionate force in what essentially becomes a matter of self-defense.[34]

In addition, many of the arguments that are used as to why there are duties to obey the law in general, may not apply in the particular case of migration law (let alone unjust migration law). Common arguments include ideas that citizens have consented to obey laws, that they have duties of fair play to contribute to the cooperative schemes from which they benefit, or that they have obligations to obey the law that derive from respect for participants in democratic procedures.

There is a general strategy that might go to the core of all these kinds of arguments concerning duties to obey the law, namely, that citizens are relieved of the duty to obey the law when it violates basic rights or has a strong tendency to encourage behavior that does. The authority of the law is called into question when it violates basic rights or is issued from a body that does not exercise power legitimately.[35]

6   Conclusions

In this chapter I have been considering whether legitimate states may permissibly eject long-settled migrants, such as those in my five core cases, who present as irregular migrants according to particular state legal systems. I have argued that states may not permissibly do so and that they

---

[34] For some excellent arguments for these kinds of positions see, for instance, Christopher Bertram, *Do States Have the Right to Exclude Immigrants?*; and Javier Hidalgo, "Resistance to Unjust Immigration Restrictions," *The Journal of Political Philosophy*, 23 (4) (2015): 450–470.

[35] Fair play accounts concerning duties to obey the law only have force when the benefits and burdens of the cooperative scheme are distributed fairly. In the cases of unjust migration laws (such as those discussed in Section 2), the benefits and burdens of cooperative schemes are not distributed fairly, hence releasing those who bear the brunt of this injustice from any such duties. In such cases the unfairness of the laws would undercut any obligations to obey them. At any rate, any obligations we have to obey such laws are likely to be fairly weak and easily defeated by stronger obligations to avoid contributing importantly to injustice.

have an obligation to offer such long-settled members pathways to adjusting the migration status of such residents who would like to remain. Several arguments were marshaled for this position. Common to some of them is the idea that when people have settled into ways of life, uprooting them would typically cause considerable hardship and disproportionate harm to them and those with whom they have formed significant relationships. Their claim to remain is frequently compelling. It is especially so when migration can be described as a response to an illegitimate state system.

Central arguments were made in Sections 4.4 and 4.5. Section 4.4 shows how evicting long-settled members would undermine legitimacy in several ways. Such actions threaten the state's rights to exercise power legitimately by undermining core internal, system, and contribution requirements. In Section 4.5, appealing to earlier arguments concerning the justification for residents of a state to continue rightfully residing on a territory, I drew attention to the ways in which this argument relies on occupants' respecting certain conditions. Those conditions place significant limits on what occupants may do now. Evicting long-settled members would trigger the constraining conditions, and undermine robust rights to continued occupation, thereby challenging the state's ability to exercise power legitimately now. Other sections offered important defense of premises key to these positions and supplementary considerations, such as why there is a right not to be kept in limbo and reviewing again why it is important to respect people's located life plans under certain conditions.

In Section 5, I considered frequently raised objections to why regularization is highly problematic, centering on the importance of obeying the law. A common theme in my responses involved questioning the standing that law should have in cases where people are being unjustly excluded. Importantly, I suggested that in such cases the unjustly excluded may well have insufficient reason to comply with such law, which would have no authority for them. When immigration laws are unjust, those unjustly treated may take steps to prevent officials of the state enforcing their unjust laws. For instance, they may attempt to evade detection, including using deception in order to do so.[36] We continue discussing the responsibilities everyone has in the face of unjust immigration laws in Chapter 9.

---

[36] A certain amount of proportionate use of force may also be justified. For a good argument along these lines see, for instance, Hidalgo, "Resistance to Unjust Immigration Restrictions."

CHAPTER 6

Refugees

1 Introduction

There is a clear connection between human rights and the status of being a refugee. Violations of human rights, or the high risk of such violations, are major causes of large-scale exoduses in attempts to seek safety. The need for refugee protection, and how the international community responds to that need, constitutes an important test case for the legitimacy of our state system.

On the strict 1951 convention definition of who counts as a refugee, a refugee is someone who "owing to a well-founded fear of being persecuted for reasons of race, religion, nationality, membership of a particular social group or political opinion, is outside the country of his nationality and is unable or, owing to such fear, is unwilling to avail himself of the protection of that country."[1] Other major regional human rights instruments take a much broader view of who counts as a refugee. For instance, the Organisation of African Unity (OAU) Convention states that the status of refugee applies "to every person who, owing to external aggression, occupation, foreign domination or events seriously disturbing public order in either part or the whole of his country of origin or nationality, is compelled to leave his place of habitual residence in order to seek refuge in another place outside his country of origin or nationality."[2] The Latin American Convention also has broader scope including persons "who have fled their country because their lives, safety or freedom have been threatened by generalized violence, foreign aggression, internal conflicts, massive

---

[1] It is worth bearing in mind some salient facts about the refugee situation in 1951 compared with that of today. Increasingly refugee movements take the form of mass exoduses rather than individual journeys and are often a result of state collapse, dysfunction or civil war.

[2] *The African Union Convention Governing Specific Aspects of Refugee Problems in Africa,* available at: www.achpr.org/instruments/refugee-convention/

violation of human rights or other circumstances which have seriously disturbed public order."[3]

Whether or not we adopt a narrow or a broad account of who counts as a refugee, by definition someone is a refugee because basic human rights are not being protected. Violations of human rights are among the main causes of mass exodus and so long as the situation persists, they make repatriation unlikely. Aiming to bring about environments in which human rights can be better safeguarded is thus critical to solutions to refugee related problems.

In addition to the intimate causal connection between prompting someone to flee and human rights violations, while someone is an asylum seeker or refugee, they are also more vulnerable to having their human rights violated. Asylum seekers and refugees experience many threats to their lives, liberty, and security. Indeed, refugees as a group must be among the most vulnerable people in the world, with their rights threatened before, during, and after fleeing their countries of residence.

The organization that has most influence on real world policy in this area is the High Commissioner for Refugees. It was established in efforts to ensure that persons have basic rights respected once they leave countries of origin. What arrangements has it put in place to protect human rights and provide safe haven? How effective are these at accomplishing their goals?

Refugees have a number of rights that apply to their status quite directly such as the right to seek and enjoy asylum in other countries (Article 14), and the right not to be forcibly returned (Article 33, 1951 Convention; also, Article 9, Universal Declaration of Human Rights) also known as protection against refoulement. Disturbingly, there is much evidence that states are increasingly denying asylum seekers the right to seek asylum, by making entry to their territory impossible. Boats of asylum seekers have been prevented from landing at certain ports. Refugees are interdicted and intercepted on the high seas and turned back. Penalties are regularly imposed against airlines and transportation companies for carrying those seeking asylum.

In addition, racism, xenophobia, national or ethnic tensions, and intolerance have made the rights of refugees insecure en route to seeking asylum. And even when they are granted admission, in many places, refugees are subjected to abuse and physical attacks by both state and

---

[3] Articles 1 and 2 confirm a prohibition against forcible return, especially when the person returned would be in danger of being subjected to torture. The Cartagena Declaration on Refugees, Part III, para. 3.

non-state actors, frequently violating their rights to life, liberty, and security. Refugees are often targets for racist aggression. Young men may be forced into fighting in civil wars, and women may be subjected to physical and sexual abuse.

As I argued in Chapter 3, for the state system to retain its legitimacy it must have some corrective mechanisms when there is a large gap between the grounds for endorsing the state system and the reality. The case of refugees is an excellent example of such a large gap. In many cases, especially of large populations of refugees such as, in recent years, the Rohingya Muslims or Syrian refugees, their basic human rights are seriously under threat. The state system has failed them. It therefore falls on the international community to act. But what should international agents do to assist? How should they go about trying to make arrangements for improved human rights protections under these circumstances? I believe this is an under-theorized question in current debates concerning refugees and, as it lies at the heart of the matter, I focus on it in this chapter, so the analysis of how to assist constructively has a robust grounding.

Three traditional approaches to addressing the plight of refugees in the longer term are voluntary repatriation to countries of origin, local settlement in host states, and resettlement elsewhere. Widespread persisting human rights violations in countries of origin make repatriation options in a reasonable timeframe unlikely and undesirable for many refugees. In addition, attempts to resolve the problems that give rise to large refugee flows through international political means frequently yield no meaningful changes to the underlying causes of displacement. Furthermore, the number of displaced people, and the tiny percentage being offered durable solutions, give us important reasons to consider expanding the option set that we are able to provide refugees, beyond these traditional options.[4] Consider, for instance, that currently there are around 70 million displaced people and that less than 1 percent are offered the resettlement option.[5] Fewer and fewer refugees are able to access so-called durable solutions through these traditional options. And tens of millions find themselves in a state of limbo, "with the average refugee situation now

---

[4] This is especially so as only a small fraction of those who wish to be resettled are standardly accommodated. For the latest figures see the UNHCR website at: www.unhcr.org/resettlement .html. In addition, we clearly need to have better systems of burden sharing for host states that bear much of the cost of hosting refugees. As I argue in this chapter, the form that assistance should take is crucial.

[5] For up to date current figures see the UNHCR website. See, for instance, www.unhcr.org/ 5b27be547.pdf

dragging on for over twenty-five years."[6] I begin the exploration of further options in the next section, Section 2, by analyzing some of the defects in our current refugee system and indicating some ways in which to improve. Section 3 discusses two different cases as illustrations of how we can improve. Although the cases are different, they have important common elements; they showcase the positive potential of a development oriented approach. Section 4 highlights how the focus on preparing for post-conflict recovery can also be beneficially linked to this development oriented approach. In Section 5 I cover several ways in which we should rethink refugee governance and responsibilities, emphasizing new partnerships and other institutional changes that are needed. Section 6 considers some of the many challenges that have been made to a development focused approach, showing how the main critiques can be addressed and bringing to bear further relevant research that supports the proposals. Section 7 takes stock of the challenges and the opportunities the empowerment model presents. We need to rethink what constitutes effective and feasible solutions to large-scale refugee problems. Such analysis has an important bearing on the shape and content of our responsibilities in relation to refugees.

Though I believe that, in the normative literature, far too much focus is on the issue of who counts as a refugee, perhaps I should briefly specify and situate my own view. According to the 1951 Refugee Convention, a refugee is someone outside her country of citizenship facing reasonable fears about persecution because of race, nationality, religion, political opinions, or memberships of particular social groups. Several theorists (such as David Owen, Alex Betts, and Matthew Gibney) have provided more inclusive accounts of who should count as a refugee.[7] These scholars tend to identify the core of being a refugee as the urgent need for protection, rather than focusing on the reasons why this is the case. On such accounts, a refugee is someone who needs protection from another state because the state in which they usually reside is either unable or unwilling to protect the fundamental human rights or interests of its citizens. I generally endorse this kind of more expansive account. However, within the category of refugees, I also believe that those fleeing violent conflict qualify as in especially urgent

[6] Megan Bradley, "Unresolved and Unresolvable? Tensions in the Refugee Regime," *Ethics and International Affairs*, 33 (1) (2019): 45–56.

[7] See, for instance, Alex Betts, *Survival Migration: Failed Governance and the Crisis of Displacement* (Ithaca: Cornell University Press, 2013); Mathew Gibney, *The Ethics and Politics of Asylum: Liberal Democracy and the Response to Refugees* (Cambridge: Cambridge University Press, 2004); Andrew Shacknove, "Who Is a Refugee?" *Ethics* 95 (1995): 274–284; and David Owen, "In Loco Civitatis," 269–289.

need of protection. Here I focus my attention on this large group, which would include cases such as has arisen from the protracted civil war in Syria, though some of the solutions discussed also apply to some so-called economic migrants and others who fit the broader definition. Because of the neglect in considering how to assist this large group in particular, they are my primary concern in this chapter.

2   Dysfunction in the Refugee System: Ways to Do Better

Much of the existing ethics and political theory literature that deals with responsibilities to refugees focuses on individual state's obligations to offer refugees asylum at their borders and, especially, obligations to admit refugees for settlement or resettlement.[8] But such approaches ignore the possibility that thoughtful joint action might present more effective and sustainable ways of discharging our obligations well.[9] Development oriented approaches are particularly promising in this regard and the international agencies charged with refugee responsibilities should help to secure the international coordination needed to promote them. Alexander Betts and Paul Collier offer the most prominent new proposals in this area, and I discuss them in detail here.[10]

Our current regime for dealing with refugees is defective. For instance, policy overseen by the United Nations Refugee Agency (the United Nations High Commissioner for Refugees (UNHCR)) focuses on offering refugees safety in camps. However, most refugees are not in camps, not least of all because life in the camps can be quite abysmal and the prospect

---

[8] There is a vast important literature on these key normative issues, along with how to define refugees. Some excellent accounts include Alex Betts, *Survival Migration*; Joseph Carens, *Ethics of Immigration*; Sarah Fine and Lea Ypi (eds.), *Migration in Political Theory* (Oxford: Oxford University Press, 2016); Mathew Gibney, *The Ethics and Politics of Asylum*; Matthew Gibney, "Refugees and Justice Between States," *European Journal of Political Theory*, 14, 2015, 448–463; David Miller, *Strangers in Our Midst*; David Miller, *National Responsibility and Global Justice* (Oxford: Oxford University Press, 2007); David Owen, "In Loco Civitatis," 269–289; David Owen, "Refugees, Fairness and Taking up the Slack," *Moral Philosophy and Politics*, 3 (2) (2016): 141–164; Andrew Shacknove, "Who is a refugee?," 274–284; and Christopher Heath Wellman and Phillip Cole, *Debating the Ethics of Immigration*.

[9] Alexander Betts and Paul Collier, *Refuge*, 102.

[10] I discuss other kinds of options in "Addressing the Refugee Crisis in Europe," a talk presented at the American Philosophical Association, Pacific Division Meetings (2017). There are a number of other innovative proposals now circulating. These include some interesting territorially based options, such as ideas about creating new spaces where refugees can form a new community. For a good summary see, for instance, Robin Cohen and Nicholas Van Hear, "Visions of Refugia: Territorial and Transnational Solutions to Mass Displacement," *Planning Theory and Practice*, 18(3) (2017): 494–504.

of having to live in them for years, even decades, has little appeal. Over half of current refugees live in cities. In fact, when we consider how refugees actually navigate our current refugee protection arrangements, at the moment what the refugee system offers refugees is "long-term encampment, urban destitution, or perilous journeys."[11]

The original Refugee Convention was set up to deal with threats that emerged from the Second World War and, in that context, persecution was an important factor prompting people to leave their home states. While targeted persecution is still a real and important threat for some refugees, the vast majority of refugees are fleeing insecurity, danger, and violence in fragile states.[12] Here we focus especially on such cases in which a society has collapsed into mass violence, not more isolated ones of bad things happening to a few people.[13]

The average period for refugee status is now over twenty years.[14] For that length of time, emergency food and shelter are just some of what people need. Other needs are salient as well, such as trying to enjoy some semblance of normal family life, education, autonomy, and community. Many will want the capacity to earn a living to support themselves and their families. Needs for autonomy drive many to seek employment. Most refugees not only want to work but will also find ways – whether legal or illegal – of doing this.[15] As we see in the case of Syria, many refugees avail themselves of the informal economies in adjacent states to seek work.

Facilitating opportunities for refugees to work legally is not only required to respond to refugees' expressed needs, but it is also essential if we consider how to make supporting refugees for two decades financially sustainable. Indeed, reviewing the Refugee Convention, we notice that much of it focuses on socio-economic rights, such as the right to work, so there has been a notable shift in thinking since 1951.[16] Some of the consequences of denying refugees the right to work have been disastrous. The refugees themselves have often felt despair and a sense of alienation. Unused skills begin to get lost with detrimental consequences, including the prospects for successfully rebuilding post-conflict societies. When we consider that many refugees stay in this state of limbo for decades, our failure to ensure they can work legally is a grave mistake. Denying refugees the right to work has an important effect on their sense of dignity, quality

---

[11] Betts and Collier, *Refuge*, 9.   [12] Ibid., 9.
[13] Ibid., 17. People seeking refuge are fleeing danger. In contrast to the aftermath of the Second World War, many refugees are not fleeing the political situation directly but rather the economic fallout from the political situation, such as in Zimbabwe.
[14] Bradley, "Unresolved and Unresolvable?"   [15] Ibid., 10   [16] Ibid., 156.

of life, and their ability to contribute to family and community well-being. In addition, we need to think about both current and future needs, not only of the refugees but also those in the societies that host them and those in societies they have fled. This wider perspective can get us to move away from seeing refugees exclusively as vulnerable victims rather than potential agents of positive change, as we emphasize development possibilities.

Most refugees remain in the region of the country they have fled and so, to be useful, that is where solutions should center. While there is often a great deal of panic when refugees reach the borders of Western states (as we see with refugees trying to enter Europe or the USA), the greatest needs lie elsewhere, "usually just across the border from conflict and crisis zones. And yet there is a mismatch in terms of attention and resources. We focus on the 10 percent who reach the developed world but neglect the nearly 90 percent who stay in developing regions of the world."[17]

As I discuss shortly, solutions need to take seriously refugees' right to work. And we need better regional solutions that will help refugees build their capacities. To see how this could be done in alternative ways, I consider briefly two very different cases.

3 Two Cases: Uganda and Jordan

3.1 Uganda

Uganda has a long history of hosting refugees and currently offers home to over 500,000 refugees. It is the third largest host country in Africa. The Ugandan approach rejects encampment and has allowed refugees opportunities to work. Refugees are allocated plots of land on which to grow crops for subsistence as well as exchange. It permits market activity and also allows refugees to start businesses. Uganda provides a successful case study into what can happen when refugees are allowed to work. Large numbers of refugees are engaged in entrepreneurial activities such as running small shops. In Kampala, approximately 21 percent of refugees run businesses, creating employment, with 40 percent of these jobs going to Ugandan citizens.[18] Refugees are therefore creating employment for both refugees and host nationals.

In addition, because refugees are allowed to work, within the camps there are valuable opportunities for skills transfer and informal apprenticeships in the many businesses being run by refugees in areas as diverse as

---

[17] Ibid., 127. [18] Ibid., 165.

construction, commerce, and garment production. These opportunities provide young refugees the chance to gain practical skills needed to make their aspirations for the future a reality.

3.2 Jordan

Most refugee-hosting countries do not allow refugees to work. Uganda may have some special circumstances that allow for a more generous stance, such as a surplus of arable land.[19] Many host populations have legitimate fears that must be taken into account when deciding how to accommodate refugees. For instance, citizens are concerned about competition for jobs, falling wages, increasing prices of goods (such as housing), security, rising tensions, and so on. Like many countries around the world, the challenge for Jordan is how to address their citizens' concerns, while offering fair and empowering opportunities to refugees. Approaches to job creation that assure mutual gains are worth consideration.

Jordan has long aspired to transition to a manufacturing economy. So, it needs geographically concentrated clusters to create the beneficial economies of scale such as in skilled labor or supply chains that firms seek. The displacement of large numbers of Syrians presents exactly such an opportunity. Many Syrian refugees are well educated and have relevant industrial skills. They also share a language with Jordanians.

On the zonal development model, displaced Syrians would be offered work in specially created economic zones, and they would also have access to education and training. Through financial incentives and trade concessions, the international community might encourage two types of operations in special economic zones (SEZs). International firms might be required to employ Syrian refugees and Jordanian nationals in particular proportions. Syrian firms unable to operate in war-torn Syria might be allowed to employ refugees only. Because the zonal development model generates jobs that would not otherwise exist for Jordanians, such strategies are beneficial for Jordanian nationals, so they have good reason to welcome these newly created opportunities that help them achieve their industrial development goals.[20]

---

[19] Also, it is a one-party state, so government officials do not need to worry about reelections.

[20] It is notable that prominent businesses, such as Ikea and Hewlett-Packard, are already contributing supplies and service to refugee agencies, and supporting the kinds of development oriented strategies discussed here. There is also some important precedent for such policies, for instance, Greece in the 1920s and Central America at the end of the cold war. For more see, for instance, Betts and Collier, "Help Refugees Help Themselves: Let Displaced Syrians Join the Labor Market," *Foreign Affairs*, September 11, 2015, 4.

A key part of this model is that the preferred policies can also assist in contributing to post-conflict rebuilding in the societies from which refugees are fleeing. Businesses could expand or relocate and follow refugees back to Syria when the situation is secure. Preparing to rebuild Syria is an important aspect and will work to the benefit of many, including internally displaced people, in fact a much larger population than those who have crossed a border fleeing the Syrian civil war.

Several state and non-state actors have been working together to find appropriate solutions along these lines, and promising new partnerships have been emerging in attempting to integrate refugees into labor markets. On the Jordan Compact Deal negotiated by David Cameron in February 2016, Jordan would receive around $2 billion in assistance and investment and would permit about 200,000 Syrians to work in Jordan. A central focus would be five new SEZs that would employ refugees who would work with Jordanians. The partners to this arrangement include the governments of Jordan and the United Kingdom, the World Bank (which offered loan-based finance), and the European Union, which agreed to allow trade concessions for some products (such as in the garment industry) exported from these SEZs. President Obama also supported the compact and he appealed to CEOs of major US corporations to bring jobs to refugees.

So, mutually beneficial relationships are possible and we can make important gains by working together.[21]

4 Lessons from Jordan and Uganda and the Importance of Preparing for Post-Conflict Recovery

As the cases of Uganda and Jordan show, different solutions might work well in different contexts. There is no one model that needs to be rolled out to apply to all cases. But what these two cases have in common is a shift from thinking of refugee issues in purely humanitarian terms to thinking about these issues in ways typically encompassed by a development approach, placing issues concerning employment and education at the center. They also both aim to create areas in which development can flourish in border locations.[22]

---

[21] Betts and Collier note that such approaches can yield the following win-win-win situations: Europeans get to address the migration crisis, Jordan transitions to manufacturing along with managing the security crisis unfolding in its neighborhood, business gets new markets, refugees get work opportunities, and the international community benefits if Syria enjoys peace.

[22] Other precedents for development oriented strategies being pursued in border locations can be found in Thailand (for Burmese refugees) and also in the Philippines (Betts and Collier, *Refuge*, 179).

The cases of Uganda and Jordan show us that quite different approaches can succeed. On the model exemplified by Uganda, the aim is integration. Refugees are put on a path to gaining full socio-economic and political rights, eventually on a par with citizens of host countries. By contrast, the Jordanian model creates separate geographical areas in which economic opportunities are made available on special terms. While different approaches may be best for different contexts, there are common threads as we aim to develop people's capacities, especially through economic empowerment.[23]

Another distinctive component of the development oriented approach (especially that of Betts and Collier) is the focus on taking into account the post-conflict situation and aiming to incubate recovery. We need to join together post-conflict recovery policy with better policy on how to assist refugees effectively here and now. Once conflict ends, societies are fragile and there can be high risks of return to violence, as we see in many places around the world. Good policies can reduce post-conflict recovery risks and potentially even bring about peace more quickly. And by integrating policies for recovery and refuge, policies can provide an important sense of hope for refugees that normal life will return one day.[24]

Much European coverage of the so-called refugee crisis has focused on Eurocentric concerns, such as how those who have made their way to Europe can be integrated and on how the European Commission should fairly apportion refugee related burdens among EU states. But these are not the core issues for the vast majority of those who have been displaced by the conflict: the six million Syrians who are internally displaced and the four million who remain in the region in neighboring states. For these people, especially those who have not left Syria, their future will depend on how quickly Syria can restore economic and community life within Syria.[25]

> The 4 million in the neighbouring havens may decide to forge new lives in their host societies, those in Turkey learning a new language. But most refugees in neighbouring havens aspire to return once peace permits. Even some of those who have reached Europe may find that they prefer to return home rather than reinvent themselves as Europeans, or remain as Syrians-in-Europe while their children absorb a culture not their own.[26]

An important reason to consider how to improve prospects for post-conflict recovery is that this is what the vast majority of the displaced both

---

[23] Ibid., 234.   [24] Ibid., 182.   [25] Ibid., 183.   [26] Ibid.

want and need, if their situation is to change in constructive ways.[27] Much needs to happen to reduce post-conflict risks. There is only so much international actors can achieve to affect change in some of these areas. But in economic matters, they can play an important role. Because reducing post-conflict risks is connected with how quickly the economy recovers, there is much the international community can do here. It is typically assumed that post-conflict reconstruction essentially involves physical reconstruction. In the case of civil wars, however, recovery is not so much about physical construction as organizational rebuilding. In particular, we need to restore government capacities in several areas. Creating organizational capacity primarily requires recruiting those with the right skills and motivation. Without key functions such as tax collection, law enforcement, and regulation being performed competently, the state cannot operate well. Those who are to perform these tasks require special training, especially tertiary education. And the international community can greatly assist here.

Encouraging participation by international firms can help facilitate the necessary changes that enable human, social, and organizational capital to flourish. International firms that set up in haven countries can also potentially expand to the country from which refugees hail. Once peace is restored, firms will have created a well-trained workforce many of whom will want to return.[28] This is not so wildly unrealistic, because successful firms aim to expand. So, operations can continue in the haven country while expansion is pursued in the post-conflict country.

There may need to be some public subsidy to attract sufficient firms to these haven countries. But the cost of such subsidy may well be worth it, given high costs that are often incurred with post-conflict stabilization.[29] Economic participation can also strengthen host societies, and this can be valuable in itself since they might themselves be fragile. The international community can encourage, support, incentivize, and subsidize such participation. For instance, many of the refugees from Syria, indeed the core group, are teenagers and young adults, and this presents a good

---

[27] Ibid., 184.   [28] Ibid., 189.

[29] Betts and Collier astutely observe that "the cost of temporarily subsidizing new jobs in firms coming to post-conflict economies is modest compared with the vast and often failed expenditures on stabilization that have been conventional. The attempt to stabilize Afghanistan is estimated to have cost American taxpayers $3tn to date. What, on standard policies, is going to be the bill for post-conflict Syria? And if stabilization policies fail, what would be the cost of a reversion to regional conflict? Linking refuge to incubation does not have to be free to be a bargain." *Refuge*, 190.

opportunity for international assistance in providing training needed for post-conflict recovery.[30] During conflict citizens lose skills and opportunities to add to their skill set.[31] This can be particularly worrisome in sectors likely to be needed in the recovery phase, such as health care, civil service, education, and construction. Training the future workforce during refuge can help meet projected skill shortages.[32]

Such policies deserve serious consideration, especially if we understand some of the Syrian context in particular. There has been a massive exodus of the more educated from Syria. This group has found leaving both more feasible and more rewarding than less-educated compatriots. The exodus from Syria has drained the country of roughly half its university educated population and about a quarter of those with secondary education. The scale of human capital loss as a result of conflict is probably unprecedented.[33] All of this is expected to significantly hamper post-conflict recovery.[34]

5   Rethinking Refugee Governance and Responsibilities

In Section 2 I canvassed just some of the ways in which the institutions that are charged with the responsibilities to protect refugees are failing. We need a new global governance architecture that better matches the times. Desirable features already discussed include how it offers scalable solutions that aim to protect refugees from a series of risks, both in their current phase and in the future. Protecting refugees' abilities to secure their autonomy through work is an important ingredient.

5.1   Reimagining the Relevant Partnerships

Our current arrangements assume that solving refugee issues is largely a state and humanitarian matter. But in many areas, state-centric approaches have been superseded by strategies that involve members of civil society, economic actors, and collaborations between these and other agents.[35]

---

[30] Ibid., 194.   [31] Ibid., 195.
[32] Ibid. In Betts and Collier's view, refugees who get internationally supported opportunities will have a matching obligation to countries of origin if peace returns within a certain period.
[33] Ibid., 199.
[34] Various policies might reverse this drain, for instance encouraging Syrian refugees in Europe to return to Syria once durable peace is restored. Policies that equip refugees with needed skills and encourage them to go back would help.
[35] Ibid., 214.

We need to rethink responsibilities at a number of levels, and here I have space to mention only a couple concerning rethinking state responsibilities and those of non-state actors.

Sometimes non-state actors are better equipped to solve problems, especially when actions from business or civil society are required. Businesses are increasingly important. At the local level, Ugandan social entrepreneurs have developed innovative products such as sustainable hygiene products made out of papyrus leaves.[36] The factory employs refugees exclusively and the products are sold to UNHCR to distribute to refugees in settlements, fostering jobs and further opportunities.[37]

A key message is that refugee governance needs to adopt a more localization agenda, in which it engages with local actors and forms partnerships with those that are efficiently assisting refugees in particular circumstances. The example of the sustainable enterprise that works in a particular context where papyrus leaves are abundant, is such a case. So business and civil society actors have roles to play, as a complement to, not a substitute for, state action.

5.2   A Pathway Out of Limbo

One important requirement that I have not yet discussed is that the refugee regime must provide a route out of limbo. We cannot reasonably expect anyone to live in a state of high uncertainty about where they will live for an indefinite period of time. The basic idea is that after having been a refugee for some years, refugees' situations must be assessed so they can have more certainty about their future. The assessment point would probably be between five and ten years. While any date may be arbitrary to some extent, having a clearly signaled rule also has benefits in clarifying expectations. At that point, an independent body would make a determination about prospects for repatriation. Those for whom it is judged there is no credible prospect of repatriation in the foreseeable future should be offered a pathway to formal resettlement, either in their haven country or another. So, while there should still be some scope for resettlement, for most displaced people it should come at the end of a process in which the focus is on restoring autonomy, building capacity, and finding local solutions for the vast majority who stay – *and want to stay* – in the region, that is, presenting refugees with more genuine opportunities that they themselves would like to see made available.

---

[36] Ibid., 214–215.   [37] Ibid., 216.

5.3   Other Institutional Changes Are Needed

We need to manage influxes of people better, so that they do not unnecessarily endanger lives. So, for instance, moving EU reception or processing areas to EU embassies already present in host countries or countries of origin would reduce the dangers to people who currently have to undertake risky journeys to access these. We also need to rethink the expertise UNHCR needs. Currently, it is focused on offering legal guidance and humanitarian operational matters, primarily distributing humanitarian aid in refugee camps. While not unimportant, today other expertise is essential as well, such as in development economics and politics. UNHCR should share responsibility for refugees with other official agencies, but also be permitted more scope to cooperate with NGOs, businesses, civil society organizations and, of course, refugees themselves.

6   Further Support for and Key Challenges to a Development-Focused Approach

While a development oriented approach – especially the version offered by Betts and Collier – has much to offer in providing fresh ideas concerning responsibilities in relation to refugees, this work has attracted considerable criticism. In this section, I have two main tasks. My first central objective is to show that there is much evidence in support of core aspects of the approach. For instance, looking at current trends and literature in refugee studies, we see a notable shift in favor of support for refugees' having labor market access. The second main task is to examine the most challenging criticisms in efforts to evaluate whether the central approach should be abandoned and replaced with alternatives. As I show, all the main concerns can be addressed.

6.1   Supporting Evidence and Current Trends

There is quite a rich body of literature that can be brought to bear in favor of development oriented accounts. There is growing awareness that we need to connect refugee studies with work on both development and conflict and peace studies.[38] In addition, much evidence suggests that

---

[38] Elena Fiddian-Qasmiyeh, Gil Loescher, Katy Long, and Nando Sigona "Introduction: Refugee and Forced Migration Studies in Transition" in Elena Fiddian-Qasmiyeh, Gil Loescher, Katy Long, and

allowing refugees to have formal labor market access can greatly assist in improved well-being, self-reliance and positive relations with local populations.[39] There is also a large amount of evidence that denying labor market access is a huge driver of refugee exploitation and deprivation.[40] Also noteworthy is growing appreciation among international policy makers and organizations that they should be facilitating the livelihoods of forced migrants by supporting rights to work.[41]

A dominant reason offered for why refugees are denied access to formal employment is the largely mistaken belief that refugees *must inevitably* reduce wages, compete with host citizens for jobs, and undermine the quality of services. However, none of these feared effects are inevitable and everything depends on the policy choices that surround how access to labor markets proceeds, along with other associated policies. Under the right complementary policy conditions, refugees can help raise incomes and employment rates for natives, contribute to net positive fiscal effects, and generally contribute to more efficient, innovative, and productive economies.[42] For all of this to work well, robust support systems should be in place so that potential costs do not accumulate, especially costs for local workers, which can be counter-productive if these trigger political backlash. So there needs to be well funded arrangements to assist any host citizens in adjusting to changes associated with granting refugees formal labor market access, by supporting job retraining programs, facilitating occupational upgrading, and the like.[43] Complementary policies aimed at mitigating costs, especially for local workers, are critical.[44] The right policies can also amplify benefits.

There is also recognition that an inclusive approach that supports the livelihoods of both refugees and host populations is worthwhile in many

---

Nando Sigona (ed.) *The Oxford Handbook of Refugee and Forced Migration Studies* (Oxford: Oxford University Press, 2014), e.g. 17–18.

[39] See, for instance, Michael Clemens, Cindy Huang, and Jimmy Graham, *The Economic and Fiscal Effects of Granting Refugees Formal Labor Market Access*; and Clemens, Huang, Graham, and Gough, *Migration Is What You Make It.*

[40] Karen Jacobsen, "Livelihoods and Forced Migration" in Elena Fiddian-Qasmiyeh, Gil Loescher, Katy Long, and Nando Sigona, *The Oxford Handbook of Refugee and Forced Migration Studies* (Oxford: Oxford University Press, 2014), 99–110.

[41] Ibid.   [42] Clemens, Huang, Graham, and Gough, *Migration Is What You Make it.*

[43] Clemens, Huang, and Graham, *The Economic and Fiscal Effects of Granting Refugees Formal Labor Market Access*, 8.

[44] Ibid.

circumstances.[45] Not only does this create goodwill among host populations (counteracting host population fears and hostilities), but host governments are more likely to view programs as desirable and support them in such cases. In addition, bringing refugees and host citizens together in an environment that fosters learning, such as vocational training or business services development, can create further benefits. These include the creation of valuable networks, potential partnerships, and generally building social capital with the host community, thereby reducing tensions as refugees are seen to be "bringing resources (in the form of programmes) and because working/learning together is good for social relations."[46]

Here I have space to discuss only some of the interesting research available in support of these claims. I start with a clear recent example of just how giving refugees formal labor market access to start or grow businesses has resulted in substantial benefits to host countries. Turkey allows refugees to own businesses. Between 2011 and 2017, Syrian refugees "started a total of 6033 formal companies ... employing 9.4 people on average – a total of 56 710 people, most of whom were hosts."[47] Being part of the formal economy, refugees were not only able to increase their incomes but they also paid more taxes.

Developing countries host 85 percent of the world's refugees and, more recently, in these countries, governments, donors, and private sector actors have been including refugees in labor markets in innovative ways.[48] Multinational corporations (MNCs) are one of the important partners in such endeavors, given their capacity to hire and help influence policy.[49] Economic activity and MNCs tend to cluster in urban areas, where 60 percent of working age refugees are also located. In most developing countries, refugees are not legally allowed to work, and yet many refugees do in fact work, rendering them more vulnerable to exploitation and deportation. Removing restrictions on working would

[45] Karen Jacobsen, "Can Refugees Benefit the State? Refugee Resources and African Statebuilding" *Journal of Modern African Studies*, 40 (4) (2002): 577–596.
[46] Karen Jacobsen, "Livelihoods and Forced Migration."
[47] Clemens, Huang, Graham, and Gough, *Migration Is What You Make It*, 19. See also S. Ucak, J. Holt, and K. Raman, *Another Side to the Story: A Market Assessment of Syrian SMEs in Turkey* (New York, New York: Building Markets, 2017).
[48] C. Huang, S. Charles, L. Post, K. Gough, *Tackling the Realities of Protracted Displacement: Case Studies on What's Working and Where We Can Do Better* (Washington, DC: The Center for Global Development and the International Rescue Committee, 2018); C. Huang *Global Business and Refugee Crises*.
[49] Cindy Huang and Jimmy Graham, "Are refugees located near urban job opportunities?" Center for Global Development, Policy Brief, June 18, 2018.

considerably increase their economic opportunities and, as examples such as Turkey illustrate, if well managed, can yield significant gains for host countries.[50]

Among other initiatives that are driven by the same grounding idea of creating mutually advantageous solutions for refugees and host populations, the work of *Talent Beyond Boundaries* is perhaps particularly notable.[51] The mission of this organization is to connect refugees with international job opportunities, in efforts to facilitate labor mobility as a complementary solution to other options currently open to refugees. As stated on the website: "War and conflict have forced millions of skilled people to find refuge in places where they are unable to work legally. *Talent Beyond Boundaries* is working to connect this often-excluded talent pool with employers around the world who are searching for skilled workers. The pathways that *Talent Beyond Boundaries* is establishing allow refugees to find stability and employers to gain new talent, while reducing the number of dependents on aid."[52]

There is growing momentum around granting refugees more formal labor market access and associated rights. In 2016, UN Member States unanimously adopted the New York Declaration for Migrants and Refugees, which encourages governments to open their labor markets to refugees in efforts to both foster the resilience and self-reliance of refugees and benefit host communities.[53] In this context there is increased interest in understanding what kinds of policies can harness the positive economic, fiscal, and other benefits of allowing labor market access while minimizing any negative effects that such access might create. And there is increasing research on these topics.[54] So, all in all, there is considerable movement in the direction of making more employment opportunities available to refugees as one important way to help address their plight. The next three sub-sections (6.2–6.4) address further dominant critiques of development oriented approaches.

---

[50] Huang and Graham "Are Refugees Located Near Urban Job Opportunities?"

[51] See https://talentbeyondboundaries.org/

[52] Ibid. Other initiatives that are worth further discussion include the skills partnership program advocated by Michael Clemens. See, for instance, Michael Clemens, "Global Skill Partnerships: A Proposal for Technical Training in a Mobile World," *IZA Journal of Labor Policy*, 4 (2) (2015) 1–18.

[53] New York Declaration. Retrieved from https://refugeesmigrants.un.org/declaration

[54] For a comprehensive survey of some of this research see, for instance, Clemens, Huang and Graham, *The Economic and Fiscal Effects of Granting Refugees Formal Labor Market Access*; and Jacobsen, "Livelihoods and Forced Migration."

*6.2   Can Global Capitalism, in the Form of Special Economic Zones,
Come to the Rescue? Would These Approaches Render Refugees More
Vulnerable to Exploitation?*

Heaven Crawley is one of the prominent critics who pursues these ideas.[55]
She is skeptical that "global capitalism can come to the rescue of the
refugee system through the creation of special economic zones."[56] And
she is doubtful that this solution will work well for all refugee populations,
such as in Pakistan, Iran, or Chad. Now, to be clear, the idea of creating
special economic zones (SEZs) is just one example of the kind of development oriented approach that it is worth exploring. Like Crawley, many
critics focus on SEZs as the main solution on offer, missing the more
general development centered approach, and taking the example to constitute the main solution to be advocated as a solution to all refugee problems
in all places. But this is not what is being proposed.

Consider how one of the central driving ideas of development centered
approaches is to facilitate economic empowerment, while another is to
encourage refugee driven innovation.[57] These core ideas will, of necessity,
have to be context specific. The idea is that local partners and particular
refugee populations come up with solutions that work given specific
circumstances, that will facilitate economic empowerment in particular
contexts. We need to make policy space for such refugee driven innovation. The international refugee system needs to allow for such local
solutions, but it also has a role to play in working with and on the policy
and political constraints.

Having said all of that, there is still a place for SEZs, and here lies one
core concern: Would these approaches render refugees more vulnerable to

---

[55] Heaven Crawley, "Migration: Refugee Economics," *Nature*, 544, 26–27, April 6, 2017, 2. She also
believes that the analysis largely omits "or misrepresents the role of international politics, foreign
policy, the arms trade or outside military intervention" (ibid., 2). But here she has been inattentive
to what is on offer, as mostly advocates of development oriented proposals assume that those
options are being tried or have been tried, and have so far yielded little success. The idea is to come up
with some other options in the face of a lack of relevant action. In general, there is plenty of
criticism in the literature that focuses on a target based on misreading of the work. Examples of this
kind include criticisms by Behzad Yaghmanian "How Not to Fix the Refugee Crisis – A Response
to 'Refuge'" *Refugees Deeply*, April 20, 2017, available at: www.newsdeeply.com/refugees/
community/2017/04/20/how-not-to-fix-the-refugee-crisis-a-response-to-refuge. See also Tom
Newby, "Refuge: Transforming a Broken Refugee System – but into What?" *Care Insights*,
Development Blog, May 30, 2017, available at: https://insights.careinternational.org.uk/
development-blog?start=98
[56] Crawley, "Migration," p. 3.
[57] For a very informative exchange between Heaven Crawley, Alexander Betts, and others, see "Are
Jobs the Answer?" available at: www.odi.org/events/4467-refugees-are-jobs-answer

exploitation? Special economic zones have a bad reputation as sites of considerable exploitation. And so, critics have been skeptical that they are a great option for refugees.[58] Would we be exploiting some of the world's most vulnerable people by developing such zones? I do not necessarily think so and there are plenty of measures that can be adopted to ensure that reasonable labor standards operate in them. With enough support from the international community and adequate monitoring, labor practices that include basic agreements on minimum wages and conditions could be in reach. As long as these zones extend the range of options open to refugees currently and do not involve forced labor (i.e. labor undertaken against laborers' will under threat of punishment), I think the approach of focusing on beneficial development and building resilient post-conflict societies, through work, training, and skill acquisition, can constitute an improvement over the status quo for at least some of the refugees currently facing an extremely constrained option set and who would welcome more opportunities to participate legally in labor markets.

We must ensure the option to work is voluntary and employment must be regulated to ensure it meets basic standards. International oversight at the organizational level coupled with media scrutiny can significantly reduce the risks of abuse. In fact, the status quo permits greater opportunities for exploitation as refugees work illegally or informally without legal protections.[59]

6.3   The Jordan Compact Was Not Perfect

Critics argue that the Jordan Compact (the deal discussed in Section 3.2, which received $2 billion in assistance to bring jobs to 200,000 people) was not the success it was predicted to be. In particular, it aimed to provide employment to more people than it was, in fact, able to deliver.[60] In response to these charges of implementation failures, we might note some key reasons involve remedial issues, such as a lack of public transport to and from the refugee camps. Ensuring adequate local transport is available

---

[58] For a few examples see Behzad Yaghmanian "How Not to Fix the Refugee Crisis." Also, Daniel Trilling "Should We Build a Wall Around North Wales?" *London Review of Books*, 39 (14): July 13, (2017) 15–18.

[59] The literature on current forms of exploitation for those denied legal rights to work is vast. For a good summary, see Karen Jacobsen, "Livelihoods and Forced Migration," 99–110.

[60] For some of these charges see Heaven Crawley at "Are jobs the answer?" available at: www.odi.org/events/4467-refugees-are-jobs-answer; also Tom Newby, "Refuge."

is an entirely fixable problem and may well be another source of job opportunities. Despite some failures, there were also noteworthy successes. For instance, the compact managed to secure the right to work for refugees in Jordan.[61] It also led to the allocation of about 100,000 refugee work permits, thereby extending labor right protections to those vulnerable to exploitation. It allowed Syrian businesses to operate and create jobs for Jordanians. And it created opportunities from which to learn, for instance, Ethiopia is currently trialing an improved version of the model.[62]

6.4 *The Proposals Aim to Keep Refugees Far, Far Away*

There has been much skepticism about the motivations of the authors in putting forward their proposals. On one common line, the charge is that the motivation for proposing ideas about local economic inclusion stems from a desire to reduce onward migration to high-income countries.[63] But this uncharitable interpretation of the project misses some key facts. About 85 percent of refugees stay in low- and middle-income countries, so it makes sense for us to focus our assistance in places where the refugees actually are.[64] In preceding discussion, I have also highlighted further facts not taken into account with this criticism, such as that refugees often prefer to stay in the region, if they can, in places where cultural affinity, religious practices, or social connections may be more familiar. Furthermore, the ones who migrate onwards are frequently not the most vulnerable and in greatest need of our assistance. In addition, post-conflict recovery for countries of origin is better assured if we focus particular attention on developing the capacities of those who choose to stay in the region, as many of these people are likely to be able to assist in the recovery process. In general, we might also note that we can help more people more effectively in countries more similar in terms of GDP per capita and culture.

7   Taking Stock: Important Qualifications and Opportunities

In this section, after noting a few important qualifications, I highlight some limitations. I summarize some significant advantages of a development

---

[61] Alexander Betts, personal communication.   [62] Ibid.
[63] Daniel Trilling, "Should We Build a Wall Around North Wales?" 15–18.
[64] For up to date current figures see the UNHCR website. See, for instance, www.unhcr.org/5b27be547.pdf

oriented approach. All things considered, and following some new trends in refugee studies, I believe there is a strong case that a development oriented approach deserves serious consideration when trying to understand the nature of our responsibilities to refugees and the option set we should make available to those suffering from forced migrations.

First of all, does the approach prevent people migrating? There are alternative avenues open to those who wish to migrate, for instance through pursuing labor migration and family reunification options that may be available to them. Such channels should be available through embassies in the haven countries. But the needs of refugees, such as refuge and autonomy, can be met in ways that do not involve migration as the default. We have failed to provide refugees some of the options they would most like to be available and the development oriented approach aims to remedy this.

Second, the work-based solutions will not work for everyone, such as young parents taking care of infants, the old, and some who are disabled. There is still an important role for complementary responses, traditionally described as humanitarian. To be sure, some will need to move far away from countries of origin rather urgently. For instance, some with complicated medical needs that cannot easily be accommodated in neighboring countries may need to relocate to situations providing appropriate care straight away. Similarly, some refugees may still be in significant danger while in nearby locations – for instance, they may continue to be genuine targets of persecution – and alternative arrangements far from countries of origin might well be appropriate for them.

Also, once peace is restored, some may not want to go back to countries they have fled, or not be able to do so, given continued threats to their safety. For those where threats to safety are ongoing, options to remain in the haven country or resettlement options should be available. And these can be offered also to those who simply do not wish to go back. But this would still be a much smaller number of refugees than those currently in limbo waiting for a more durable solution to their plight. I should emphasize again in this regard that currently formal resettlement is an option offered to only about 1 percent of the refugee population.[65] And it is also worth stressing that creating these other options would better match what refugees repeatedly express an interest in having secured.

While the prescriptions may not work for everyone, what they do offer is a huge improvement over current arrangements for the vast majority of

---

[65] Ibid.

currently displaced people, especially in providing more of the options displaced people value. There are further compelling features of the proposed strategies that are worth emphasizing. The proposals accommodate many salient needs, both the current and longer term needs of the refugees and also those of displaced populations. Needs for autonomy, as facilitated by work opportunities, are strong for many people. Needs to stay close to family, friends, and communities in the region are also widely shared. Those who are forced to flee often do not wish to go far away, when closer, attractive options present themselves. In addition, the proposals usefully take account of the challenges and opportunities for many home and host society citizens. Involving a more appropriate range of actors in working toward sustainable and effective solutions for refugees is also commendable. There are plenty of non-state actors that can and should play a role, and the focus on state-based solutions needs to change. The analysis also usefully shows the organizational changes required to reform refugee arrangements so they can better provide good support. And they aim to protect a wide range of agents who are affected by the situation for the duration of risk. In short, what is required is not solely a humanitarian response but rather we need to complement our efforts with a development response, especially one aimed at bringing about resilient post-conflict societies.

8   Corrective Mechanisms, Legitimacy, and Refugees

It is time to return to some important themes introduced in Chapter 3, concerning legitimacy. In Chapter 3 I argued that for the state system to retain its legitimacy, it must include some corrective mechanisms when a large gap opens up between the grounds for endorsing the state system and the reality. The case of refugees is an excellent example of such a large gap. In many cases of large refugee flows, states are not doing what they ought to secure core human rights. When particular states fail badly on securing basic human rights, it is quite understandable that citizens will seek refuge elsewhere. It therefore falls on the international community to ensure there are arrangements in place to cover such contingencies. The form our assistance should take must track the evidence concerning what would be effective in securing refugees' human rights. As I have been arguing, supporting measures that show good prospects for hastening the onset of robust peace and equipping citizens for post-conflict societies is an especially good way to discharge these responsibilities. We all have responsibilities to support such measures for a number of reasons, including that without such action the state system loses legitimacy and the legitimacy of our own state in exercising self-determination rights can be called into question. So, the international community has very good reasons to support the measures highlighted here. All relevant agents in the international community are therefore on the moral hook.

Particular capacities that various agents have will play an important role in how these responsibilities should be distributed among all the agents who can and should play a role. As is usual with our human rights practice, details matter. But one conclusion we cannot reach is that the situation of refugees is not of concern to states and those who reside in them. Indeed, their contributions, or failures to contribute, can be key determinants of their own claims to exercise power legitimately.

Recall some key points of the discussion concerning the contribution requirements, as introduced in Chapter 3. There I argued that the Commitment to Development Index (CDI), which measures state contributions to some of the grounding conditions that facilitate human rights protections, could be used to capture relevant state contributions. When we consider how states are contributing positively to sustainable development, we need to look at contributions in several domains, such as aid, trade, investment, migration, environment, security, and technology. The focus on empowerment, employment, post-conflict recovery, and so forth aligns very well with how we promote performance in these different domains and contribute more broadly to development.

In addition to the CDI, I also highlighted other aspects of contribution that can have an enormously powerful and pervasive effect on human rights practice, and so they should all act as important further constraints on state action. These included:

A commitment to maintain an ethos conducive to respect for the practice of human rights, such as that everyone deserves to be treated with dignity and respect as a human being (*Ethos Requirement*).

A commitment to practices of accountability (*Accountability Requirement*).

A general commitment not to promote arrangements in which respect and protection for people's human rights is significantly worsened, ceteris paribus. So, in the absence of compelling countervailing reasons, states should not reject arrangements in which protection for people's human rights deteriorates markedly, especially when such protections are reasonably secure (*Constraint Against Worsening*).

A general commitment to show appropriate international concern as required by the practice, to undertake action when one is the agent capable and appropriately placed to have sufficient reason to act (*Commitment To Action Under Relevant Circumstances*).

In the context of responsibilities in connection with refugees, all of these have a role to play. I have already highlighted how the constraint concerning commitment to action under certain circumstances means that capable and appropriately placed agents often do have responsibilities in connection with addressing refugee related problems, especially once a development and empowerment oriented set of effective solutions is brought into better view. Furthermore, the requirement to act in ways that promote accountability for human rights practice requires us to work with others and offer compelling reasons for how we are orienting ourselves to taking up a fair share of our responsibilities in relation to refugees.

There is much to say about what assuming a fair share of responsibilities to assist refugees might consist in. Here I have space to make only a few remarks. I focus on how to distribute residual resettlement obligations that might remain. As I noted, there is still some scope for resettlement to play a role and as this is an area in which much real world policy has focused, there is much literature on this issue.

According to current EU resettlement schemes, the number of refugee assignments per state is based on:[66]

(a)   the size of the population (using 2014 figures, 40 percent weighting).
(b)   the total GDP (using 2013 figures, 40 percent weighting).
(c)   the average number of spontaneous asylum applications and the number of resettled refugees per million inhabitants over the period 2010-2014 (10 percent weighting).
(d)   the unemployment rate (2014 figures, 10 percent weighting).

According to supporting documentation, (a) reflects the capacity of states to absorb refugees, (b) reflects the wealth of a country and is a further indicator of economic capacity to absorb and integrate refugees, (c) is an indicator of state efforts made in the recent past, and (d) is a further criterion used to indicate integration capacity.

These four factors strike me as a reasonable combination, to use in that they nicely balance capacity to assist with recent efforts made. While it may not be perfect, this resettlement formula has a good claim to be considered reasonably fair, and is certainly better than no attempt at collective action to solve the problem.[67] If this scheme were extended to

[66] See, for instance, Commission Recommendation EU 2015/914 of June 8, 2015 on a European resettlement scheme, available in the *Official Journal of the European Union* L 148/33 13.6.2015 available at: http://eur-lex.europa.eu/legal-content/EN/TXT/?uri=CELEX%3A32015H0914
[67] While the formula may not be perfect, I mention this example for several reasons. I think it is important to draw attention to the fact that there is an actual agreement concerning resettlement in

apply across all states of the world (not just those in Europe), this would strike me as a credible attempt to define fair shares. There is, of course, the issue of non-compliance; that is, we should plan for the distinct possibility that not all states will comply with their fair share requirements. And there is a debate about what obligations compliant states have in such situations. For my purposes it is sufficient to show how states in a state system could be regarded as legitimate if supported by a robust human rights practice. This requires both commitments to accountability and to action under certain circumstances. A robust human rights practice will have many ways to enforce fair treaties and fortify delivery on agreements. There is much we can do to ensure that states are accountable for their actions and failures to act, and multiple points at which we can hold them to account, as I discussed in Chapter 3 and will expand on in Chapter 9. I continue this discussion of holding the non-compliant to account in Chapter 9.

9 Conclusions

As we have seen in previous chapters, there are duties to contribute to arrangements capable of human rights protections. Clearly, refugees are in a vulnerable position with many human rights potentially at risk. Refugees are a clear case in which the state system has failed and where we need legitimacy correction mechanisms. For the state system to be credibly legitimate, it must have mechanisms in place that can assist in these circumstances.

I suggested that in order to know *how* to correct we must first analyze how our current arrangements are inadequate. As I have been highlighting, our current institutions are failing many refugees and internally displaced people. These institutions need to be dramatically reoriented. In this chapter we have analyzed some of the ways in which those arrangements are failing and ways to improve on our current broken systems. States and other actors are required to contribute to such projects. I have argued for a number of legitimacy corrective mechanisms. To recap some of these, I argued that we should redesign the global governance structures and institutions concerning refugees. We need to make more space for relevant

the EU, so there is some attempt to take collective obligations seriously in the EU. What many often believe to be impossible has been achieved in some regions. Also, we often have good reasons to support *an* agreement over none, even when the agreement has defects. One possible problem with the EU agreement is that the resettlement numbers are quite low relative to the vast numbers of refugees, which is why I favor thinking more seriously about the scale issue, as I do in the second half of this chapter.

partnerships, such as including making space for business and civil society actors to play important and necessary roles. We need to ensure that local partners who have innovative and effective ideas about how to assist in specific contexts can be included in relevant programs that the international community helps subsidize.

Institutional changes that are needed also include managing our refugee processing fairly, so that refugees may apply for asylum in processing centers that are more proximate to where the high need areas are. For instance, refugees should be able to apply for asylum in embassies within the country or nearby border locations, in efforts to minimize the amount of hardship asylum seekers currently suffer. There needs to be independent assessment for those who have been refugees for a long time (such as five to ten years). Independent bodies should be empowered to make determinations about repatriation prospects and, for those where these are not credible, viable pathways to more permanent solutions to their situation should be made available. Some resettlement options should be made available for those at the end of this process and fair ways to distribute any associated burdens should be internationally determined, perhaps along the lines of the current EU model, which I discussed.

As this analysis shows, the shape and content of our duties to large-scale refugee populations needs to be rethought. Assuming that we have located at least one kind of under-discussed set of options that promote empowerment, we should be supporting more beneficial policies including (where appropriate in particular circumstances) supporting and subsidizing enterprises that promote labor market access, generate jobs, ensuring favorable trading arrangements are available (such as tariff-free access to high-income country markets), supporting policy conducive to stabilizing post-conflict societies, such as assisting with education and training, ensuring regulatory bodies such as labor inspectorates are adequately resourced to strengthen labor market protections, and, of course, playing our part in any resettlement programs that are still needed to supplement the programs focusing on development and post-conflict recovery.

We can also appreciate why many of the solutions that have been the focus of attention are not necessarily wonderful solutions for all those who are affected, at least not unless they are supplemented with policies that offset the disadvantages they also create, including for refugees and those left behind. So, for instance, resettlement in Germany may work well for the refugees and Germans who benefit from new citizens, but there can be an enormous net loss for those left behind in Syria that makes Syrians in Syria much worse off and considerably hampers their future well-being.

This kind of analysis shows that unless we adopt something like a developmental approach, our current policies may just be setting us up for more human tragedy in the future.

One final noteworthy positive feature of this approach I raise here is that it puts front and center what constitute effective and feasible solutions to the deep problems surrounding refugee crises. Once we have that more firmly in view, it also gives us a much better model for what can be achieved if many key agents work together. This gives us a clearer vision that can inform discussion of our refugee related responsibilities, so that we can indeed help them, and those close to them, in ways that are likely to be more effective than our current, limited option set. Considering effective and feasible solutions highlights some of the key agents and focal points for action that should be part of any normative account of what we ought to do for the millions of displaced people around the world, providing a better grounding for discussing the shape of our responsibilities to refugees.

So, the three traditional approaches to addressing the plight of refugees in the longer term (voluntary repatriation, local settlement, and resettlement) must be expanded. Given the scale of the refugee problems, we need to supplement these with new approaches, especially as persisting human rights violations in countries of origin make repatriation options less likely and give us important reasons to consider increasing the option set that we are able to provide refugees. Providing environments in which human rights can be better safeguarded is thus critical to solutions to refugee related problems. Preventing new refugee flows is also a major issue. The causes of new refugee flows are often complex and each case needs to be studied in context. However, some common solutions to managing diverse cases often combine elements of tackling poverty and addressing underlying tensions that spill over into violence. Continuing contributions to development aid (including capacity building), monitoring by UN human rights bodies, appointment of special commissions to study particular situations, and so on, can assist.

In these and other ways, mechanisms aimed at establishing a legitimate state system are urgently needed. In the absence of good faith and credible efforts at making such changes, our current arrangements for assisting refugees simply cannot be regarded as adequate. A state system that offered these up as the ways for dealing with refugees could not be regarded as legitimate.

CHAPTER 7

Temporary Labor Migration

1 Introduction

Nations have long made use of migration schemes to fill labor shortages. On such schemes, Chinese labored in Malaya, Indians worked in Fiji, Mexicans were seasonal migrants in the USA, and Turks filled many postwar labor shortages in Germany, to name just a few examples. Today, the scale of labor migration is vast. According to the International Labor Organization (ILO), in 2017 migrant workers made up 164 million of the 258 million international migrants.[1] In some countries foreign nationals make up over 50 percent of the labor force. For instance, migrant workers constitute more than 80 percent of the labor force in the United Arab Emirates, Qatar, and Kuwait.[2] There are also hardly any nations not affected by labor migration, either as countries of origin, transit, or destination countries for migrants.

It is reasonably easy to understand why people are willing to engage in labor migration schemes. Faced with more limited prospects for earning similarly good wages in their home countries, many are attracted to the idea of working abroad, at least for a while. And the demand for such workers is huge as well. Prospective employers often perceive considerable advantage in recruiting migrants. Employers often assume that migrants will work for lower wages and be more compliant, and in many cases these assumptions have proven to be correct. Given the plentiful demand and supply, there is a market opportunity that many recruitment organizations have been keen to seize. Indeed, migration has become increasingly commercialized, with many private recruitment companies seeing considerable opportunities to profit in this sector, so much so that temporary

[1] See the ILO website here: www.ilo.org/global/topics/labour-migration/lang-en/index.htm
[2] Helene Harroff-Tavel and Alix Nasri, "Trapped and Tricked" (Geneva: International Labor Organization, 2013); and International Labor Organization, "Labor Migration (Arab States)" www.ilo.org

labor migration is now dominated by these operations. Most migrant workers enlist the services of such agencies and in some countries, migrants are required to operate through them as well. And, as we see, therein lies many of the new challenges migrants face.

Economists frequently argue that migration assists both countries of origin and destination in achieving various goals, such as in increasing economic growth or development. Migrants have, it is claimed, facilitated strong economic growth in both developed and developing countries. To take some examples where the gains to developed countries are clear, the agricultural sectors of Europe and America are heavily dependent on migrant workers. Massive infrastructural projects in Gulf countries have been heavily reliant on migrant workers. And domestic workers imported largely from the Philippines have enabled Hong Kong citizens, especially women, to make productive economic contributions.[3]

Migrant worker schemes are often thought to be of benefit to developing countries as well, through the transfer of skills and ideas, the creation of valuable interpersonal networks that can facilitate trade, and remittances, which often vastly exceed official development assistance in many countries.[4] Working abroad can assist with unemployment, under-employment and vulnerable employment in home countries, problems that can be quite significant in many developing countries. Global unemployment for 2019 is projected to be 193.3 million.[5] In 2017, 1.4 billion people were estimated to be in vulnerable employment, with the figure expected to rise by 17 million per year in 2018 and 2019.[6] In developing countries about 76 percent of people are in vulnerable employment.[7] The figures for youth unemployment are even more troubling, with a global unemployment rate of 13 percent. The challenges are particularly acute in Northern Africa where there is a youth unemployment rate of 30 percent.[8]

However, notwithstanding the benefits of such arrangements to both home and host countries, along with the migrants themselves, there have also been immense costs. Migrant workers are often prominent in jobs that are rejected by locals and concentrated in sectors where exploitation is prevalent. The programs have sometimes involved appalling work

---

[3] See, for instance, Michael Clemens, Cindy Huang, Jimmy Graham, and Kate Hough, "Migration Is What You Make It."
[4] For instance, in 2016 remittances were worth about US$479 billion.
[5] ILO, *World Employment and Social Outlook – Trends 2018*, ILO website, 1.   [6] Ibid., 1.
[7] Ibid.
[8] Ibid., 2. It is possibly worth noting that the migrant worker schemes also create some job opportunities in sending countries.

conditions, underpayment or non-payment of wages, and highly abusive treatment. They can also present home countries with significant challenges, such as human capital depletion with concomitant social, economic, and cultural costs.

So, what are we to make of temporary labor migration schemes? Can they ever have a place in an account that aspires to offer guidance on migration justice? Or rather, sullied by more than a whiff of exploitation, along with other heavy burdens, should countries aiming to treat people fairly stay well clear of them?

In this chapter I argue that temporary labor migration schemes that meet certain conditions can have a place in a just migration framework. In a world with large-scale global unemployment and under-employment that often lacks sufficient opportunities for pro-poor development, migrant worker programs that follow certain guidelines can constitute *one* important strategy in dealing with these issues. As I discuss in this chapter, here we are in the messy world of second-best options, but it is important to dwell in this space if we hope to offer useful guidance in navigating the actual migration challenges that we currently face.

In Section 2 I discuss some of the new features of temporary labor migration programs that warrant our attention. As signaled, temporary labor arrangements have been in place for centuries; however, as I discuss, some new features not only raise further cause for concern, but also present unprecedented opportunities for global collective action in addressing them. Section 3 canvases some long-standing problems associated with temporary labor migration schemes and why many have thought them to be morally problematic. As I argue in Section 6, there are new policy tools that allow us to address many of these problems in ways that are sensitive to a number of features including the "rights versus numbers" issue, which I cover in detail in Section 4. The main issue here is that there is a general tendency for states to trade off rights and access: the more rights temporary migrants are accorded, the less access they are granted to migration opportunities in high-income countries. I outline the many interests at stake as we try to resolve whether arrangements that secure fewer rights in exchange for greater labor market access can be defensible. Section 5 offers a close look at some of the successful international initiatives that aim to address all the issues canvassed in Sections 2–4. Preeminent among these prominent initiatives is The Global Compact for Safe, Orderly and Regular Migration, along with its related policies on recruitment developed by the International Organization on Migration and the ILO. I identify several key principles that are embedded in our human rights practice, as

articulated in these documents. Importantly, we see how there are requirements to respect the basic features required for fair contracting, especially
in labor matters. A key aspect is ensuring migrants' agency is protected in
all aspects of fair contracting processes. Armed with the core principles, we
can evaluate which rights should always be ring-fenced for protection and
which, under suitable conditions, minimally fair contracts may justifiably
restrict. That case is marshaled in Section 6. I show how there can be a
place for mutual (sufficient) advantage approaches to have a role in reducing migration related injustice in our contemporary world. Section 7
concludes and emphasizes some key connections to our responsibilities
derived from earlier chapters.

Before I move on to develop the arguments, I pause to cover some
definitional matters. Who is a temporary labor migrant? And, how do
temporary labor migration programs typically work?

By temporary labor migrant, I have in mind those who migrate for a
temporary period for the purpose of work. There are, of course, vast
numbers of people who have migrated on a temporary basis for other
purposes but now seek to participate in the labor market. Such migrants
are not counted in official figures concerning temporary labor migration
and, for the purposes of this chapter, these people are not my primary
concern. So, for instance, international students who hold part-time jobs,
may also be subject to many of the same problems I discuss, but I do not
focus on them here. My primary concern is with migrants who are in
much more vulnerable positions.

Temporary labor migrants can have a range of skills, though often those
most subject to exploitation are those on the low skill level side of the
spectrum. Temporary migrant workers are often heavily featured in the
sectors and jobs that local workers do not find desirable, where levels of
pay and unionization are low, conditions are poor, and more generally, the
overall position of the worker is more vulnerable to abusive treatment. The
position of high skill level migrants is not as precarious as this.

On these temporary labor programs, foreign nationals are invited to a
country for the express purpose of working in a particular industry that has
a labor shortage. The industry may require high or low skill levels.
Typically, employers must demonstrate that they have attempted to fill
positions with citizens, but were unsuccessful. It is then permissible to
offer foreign nationals temporary labor contracts, though employers must
comply with many onerous terms, and all of this does not legally proceed
without extensive involvement of various state-level authorizing labor and
immigration bodies. Such contracts often include a range of restrictive

terms, including that employees must return to their states of origin on completion of the contract, they may not be permitted to seek alternative employment while on the contract, they may be prohibited from seeking citizenship while on the contract, and they may be restricted in bringing family members with them. It is notable that the conditions can vary greatly and many high skill workers are typically not subject to nearly as many restrictions as low skill workers. For instance, high skill workers may not be tied to a particular employer,[9] they may not be restricted in bringing family members, and they may be offered the opportunity to transfer their status from temporary to permanent.[10]

2   What's New?

Since this book is about new challenges, someone might wonder whether there are any new problems concerning temporary labor migration, since many of the ethical problems briefly noted in the introduction are long-standing. As I see it, there are at least these three features that warrant our attention:

(i)   The increased scale of temporary labor migration flows is note-worthy, as is the widespread use of such temporary schemes by many countries to solve labor and development problems.

(ii)   There are some new problems created by the recruitment industry's extensive role in commercializing and facilitating migration.

(iii)   Most importantly, there are several credible proposals for remedying some of the most problematic aspects of temporary migration programs, along with much support for collective action in efforts to solve these.

   The features are related. The sheer number of labor migrants is unprecedented. Given the increase, a vast private recruitment industry has emerged, especially through Asia and Africa, to capitalize on migration opportunities. Many of the new forms of mistreatment are traceable to systemic misconduct on the part of these private recruitment agents or agencies. Fortunately, there are several reform avenues that have been suggested and, if properly implemented, would constitute good solutions to many contemporary forms of mistreatment. These new guidelines deserve extended discussion as they raise normative questions concerning

[9] This is the case in the UK, for instance.
[10] Canada and New Zealand offer this to low skill workers as well.

the nature and content of some of our important responsibilities toward migrants.

Over the last couple of decades, there has been a huge increase in individuals seeking temporary work abroad. In recent years, the flows of low-wage laborers between South and Southeast Asia and the Middle East have been particularly notable. The mistreatment that this group of migrants has faced has been widely reported.[11] Because of the 2022 FIFA World Cup preparations in Qatar, there has been criticism of the conditions for construction workers in particular.[12] But the problems are quite widespread. In many male-dominated sectors in the region, such as construction, seafaring, and manufacturing, workers have been routinely deceived on such basic issues as the living and working conditions, the type of work to be performed, salary, and even whether there is any actual job for them in the destination country. And in the female dominated domestic work sector, women are extremely vulnerable to exploitation and abuse, because of their relative isolation in private homes. Common issues for all migrant workers include deception concerning living or working conditions or the type of employment, non-payment of agreed wages, inhumane housing and work conditions, excessive working hours, confiscation of passports, identity, and travel documents in attempts to control workers, interference with privacy, physical, verbal, or sexual abuse, and employment of children below working age.[13]

The situation in the Gulf States has been especially acute because of the "kafala" system and its legacy. In the United Arab Emirates, for instance, foreign workers make up 99 percent of the low-skilled job sector and they have traditionally been bound to particular employers directly through a system of foreign worker sponsorship, known as the kafala system. Governments delegate responsibilities for migrant workers to citizens and companies, an arrangement that has, in practice, facilitated a form of modern-day slavery. Employers have rights over workers until either their contract expires or they

[11] See, for instance, Maleeha Riaz, "A Culture of Slavery: Domestic Workers in the United Arab Emirates," November 30, 2016, *Human Rights Brief,* available at: http://hrbrief.org/2016/11/culture-slavery-domestic-workers-united-arab-emirates/; and Laura Smith-Spark, "Report: 600 000 forced labor victims in Middle East," *CNN,* April 9, 2013; Pete Pattisson, "Death toll among Qatar's 2022 World Cup workers revealed," *The Guardian,* December 23, 2014; Pete Pattisson, "Revealed: Qatar's World Cup 'slaves'," *The Guardian,* September 25, 2013.

[12] Pattisson, "Death toll among Qatar's 2022 World Cup workers revealed"; Pete Pattisson, "Revealed."

[13] United Nations Committee on Migrant Workers, *General Comment No. 1 on Migrant Domestic Workers,* UN Doc CMW/C/GC/1 (2011). Also, Bassina Farbenblum, "Governance of Migrant Worker Recruitment: A Rights-based Framework for Countries of Origin," *Asian Journal of International Law,* 7 (2017): 152–184.

grant permission for employees to leave. Workers have been abysmally treated under this system, with frequent reported issues being inadequate compensation, given their contractual terms, and no time off at all. Domestic workers have been particularly badly affected and they frequently report horrendous emotional, sexual, verbal, and physical abuse.[14]

Abusive treatment in host countries is nothing new. But the role of private recruitment companies in facilitating exploitation of the most vulnerable, is a phenomenon that has not received as much attention. As Bassina Farbenblum notes, scholars have

> ... only recently begun to consider the rampant, systemic abuses that migrant workers encounter during recruitment in their countries of origin. These abuses invariably form the first chapter – or, in some cases, the entire book – of the migrant worker exploitation story, particularly in South and Southeast Asia. In these regions, private recruitment agencies and sub-agents have become particularly integral to international migration, and have increased exponentially in number over the past three decades. It is also in these regions that abusive recruitment practices have become endemic – the norm.[15]

Migrant worker recruitment can involve many private actors, acting both nationally and internationally. The private recruitment agencies are dominant players, and are usually located in major cities in countries of origin. Much less visible are the individual subagents who operate at the village level and who aim to recruit suitable workers. Recruitment agencies and subagents can perform valuable functions in facilitating access to employment for millions of aspiring low-wage workers who would otherwise lack such opportunities. They can provide important information about foreign employment and can assist prospective migrants in the complex processes involved in securing such employment. However, these relationships are often at the heart of much of the abuse migrant workers suffer. For instance, these agents often charge high and unauthorized fees, which can become part of the migrant worker's debt, and they frequently justify these charges by misrepresenting the remuneration and conditions that migrants can reasonably anticipate. Based on false information about the salaries and conditions, migrant workers may sell assets or take out

---

[14] Even though one of the states that operates the kafala system, the UAE, has recently passed reforms in efforts to dismantle it, it remains in place in other Gulf states. In addition, so far progress in the UAE on implementation is not yet clear. For instance, domestic workers (15 percent of the foreign worker population) are not covered by the reforms. It is also not clear what oversight there is to ensure reforms are being made. See, for instance, Maleeha Riaz, "A Culture of Slavery."

[15] Farbenblum, "Governance of Migrant Worker Recruitment," 153.

loans from dubious local moneylenders who charge exorbitant interest rates. This debt burden forms a significant factor in why migrant workers often feel compelled to continue in abusive arrangements. And this debt burden is often the central feature why these arrangements might be characterized as modern forms of slavery. Here are two tales that illustrate further ways in which deception, trickery, extortion, and lack of oversight have led to forms of enslavement.

> When a recruitment agency in his own country offered him a job overseas, with a salary of 270 pounds a month, it sounded too good to be true. It was, but Rafiq did not find out until it was too late. Like many migrants from his south Asian nation, Rafiq handed over 3160 pounds as a recruitment fee to the agent – three times the average annual income in his country. But at the airport, just hours before departure, he was given a contract to sign, which offered a salary amounting to half of what he was originally promised. "I had no option but to sign it," says Rafiq. "I had already paid so much. We were forced to get on the flight. His co-worker was a victim of the same scam, "I was shocked to see the contract. I literally became red. Then slowly I realized there was nothing I can do about it," he says.[16]

> Violet C., a 34-year-old Filipina worker, went to her agent after a year of working 18 hours per day for 2 households with no rest and no day off. She told the agent that she wanted to return home but first he refused this and sent her to another family and then, when she persisted, a manager asked her, "Do you have Dh8500 ($2314)?" indicating that she would be required to pay the recruitment costs. She said the agency confiscated her clothes, money, passport, and other documents and locked her and 9 other domestic workers in an office for 18 days before she was able to escape.[17]

3 Reasons to Be Concerned about Temporary Worker Programs: Not So New Concerns

In this section I assemble six dominant kinds of reasons to find temporary worker programs unjust.

First, the programs can be very bad for migrant workers. I have already alluded to a range of troubling practices. To add to the list, there are many migrants who engage in work without contracts. When there are contracts,

---

[16] Pete Pattisson, "Migrants claim recruiters lured them into forced labour at top Qatar hotel," *The Guardian*, October 29, 2018.

[17] Rothna Begum, Human Rights Watch, "I Already Bought You: Abuse and Exploitation of Female Migrant Domestic Workers in the United Arab Emirates" October 22, 2014, available from the *Human Rights Watch* website at www.hrw.org

they may include unjust terms and conditions. And even when there are contracts that purport to follow fair guidelines, employers regularly fail to comply with these. There is often little proper oversight, regulation, or enforcement and, generally, there are massive failures to protect migrants in such cases. Migrants have little recourse. Even if there are grievance procedures available, migrants are often unwilling to use them for fear of reprisals, dismissal, and even deportation. In addition, rights that are commonly denied to these workers include rights to change employers, the right to bring family members, the right to join unions, or the right to strike. In authoritarian states, migrants are often denied even basic civil rights, such as the right to marry citizens or co-habit with them.

Second, temporary migrant programs can exploit highly vulnerable populations. Temporary migration programs may seem attractive for desperate people. But seeking to contract with such vulnerable people simply takes advantage of their bargaining weakness.[18]

A third reason to find the programs objectionable is that they seem to serve the interests of capital more than that of labor. Temporary migrant programs often assist capitalists in maximizing profits as they reduce the cost of labor, someone might object.

Fourth, and related to the previous point, importing laborers from abroad might well worsen the situation of local laborers, as it might undercut their bargaining power and suppress their wages.

Fifth, we might query whether temporary migration programs are always effective tools of development, as they frequently involve a variety of costs. Some of the social costs of these programs include long-term separation of family members, which can mean that children go for long periods without seeing their parents. These programs can also change work incentives in countries of origin. Young adults may wait for a chance to migrate rather than take up local employment options at lower wages.[19] This can lead to large populations of unemployed youth. These programs can allow sending countries to ignore their responsibilities to create desirable employment opportunities.[20]

In addition, brain drain can undermine the human rights fulfillment of those in countries of origin. When highly skilled citizens depart countries

---

[18] I explore this argument in Gillian Brock, "Global Poverty, Decent Work, and Remedial Responsibilities: What the Developed World Owes to the Developing World and Why" in Diana Meyers (ed.), *Poverty, Coercion and Human Rights* (New York: Oxford University Press, 2014), pp. 119–145.

[19] For more see Gillian Brock, *Global Justice*, chapter 8.

[20] For more see Gillian Brock, *Global Justice*, chapter 8.

of origin, this can have a detrimental impact on the basic needs and rights of fellow citizens.[21] In some domains, such as health care, this has been particularly pronounced. The out-migration of large numbers of nurses and doctors, for instance, can lead to a lack of human resources necessary to ensure basic health care delivery.[22] Similar effects have been documented in a range of other sectors involving skilled professionals. In many cases the costs of migration are born by those who are left behind.[23] And even factoring in the progressive power of remittances, the combined effects might still leave those who remain considerably worse off.[24]

Sixth, some believe these programs are in principle unjust because they do not typically allow temporary migrants to become permanent residents of communities. On this view, migrant worker schemes have an inbuilt injustice and that involves the inability to adjust status to being a permanent resident.[25] This feature sets up a dynamic that ensures the migrant is always at an unacceptable disadvantage in any employment arrangements.

As I have signaled, I believe we can address many of these concerns, and that there are new resources available that can help us do so, as we discuss in Section 5. On balance, there is a place for such programs in an account of migration justice, so long as several conditions are met.[26]

Before we can get to these resources, we must discuss a basic challenge that must also be confronted in working out what justice demands for temporary labor migrants and that is the numbers versus human rights issue.[27] This constitutes an important challenge for just temporary labor migration arrangements. I explain the challenge in the next section.

---

[21] These are issues I cover in detail in Gillian Brock and Michael Blake, *Debating Brain Drain*.

[22] See, for instance, Brock and Blake, *Debating Brain Drain*, chapters 3 and 10.   [23] Ibid.

[24] For more arguments on how and why this the case see Brock and Blake, *Debating Brain Drain*, chapters 3 and 10, and Brock, *Global Justice*, chapter 8.

[25] See, for instance, Patti Tamara Lenard and Christine Straehle, "Temporary Labor Migration: Exploitation, Tool of Development, or Both?" *Policy and Society*, 29 (2010): 283–294; and Patti Tamara Lenard, "Why Temporary Labor Migration Is Not a Satisfactory Alternative to Permanent Migration" *Journal of International Political Theory*, 8 (1–2) (2012): 172–183.

[26] For two other kinds of noteworthy defenses of Temporary Migrant Programs in the face of these kinds of problems, see Matthew Lister, "Justice and Temporary Labor Migration," *Georgetown Immigration Law Journal*, 29 (2014): 95–123; and Christian Barry and Luara Ferracioli, "On the Rights of Temporary Migrants," *Journal of Legal Studies*, 47 (2018): 149–168.

[27] This is nicely articulated by Martin Ruhs. See, for instance, Martin Ruhs and Philip Martin, "Numbers vs. Rights: Trade-Offs and Guest Worker Programs" *International Migration Review*, 42 (1) (2008): 249–265. See also Ruhs, *The Price of Rights: Regulating International Labor Migration* (Princeton: Princeton University Press, 2015).

4   The Numbers versus Human Rights Issue

There is a relationship between the rights that migrants are accorded and the numbers of migrants that states typically admit. Looking at countries around the world, there is a noteworthy general trend: the more rights migrants on temporary labor programs are accorded, the lower the number of low-skilled migrants that are permitted to work in destination countries. Countries tend either to admit large numbers of low-skilled migrant workers but offer them relatively few rights or, if numbers of migrants are smaller, this is typically associated with more migrant rights.[28] The main reason for this relationship is that the more rights migrants are accorded, the higher the potential cost of labor. From the destination country's economic perspective then, migrants with fewer costly rights may well be preferred, and so admitting higher numbers of migrants is typically associated with fewer costly rights. If we are forced to choose, is it better to have programs that allow larger numbers of migrants with fewer rights, or fewer migrants with stronger rights? This is the dilemma we must confront.

Singapore and the Gulf States are good examples of countries operating a "high numbers, low rights" policy toward low-skilled migrants. Both allow large numbers of migrants to fill low-wage jobs but accord them few rights. For example, Singapore prohibits those in low-wage jobs from cohabiting or marrying Singaporean residents, apparently in efforts to limit settlement possibilities and therefore migration costs. By contrast, Canada's live-in caregiver program allows small numbers of migrants to work as in-home helpers but they can become permanent residents after being employed for two years. Sweden, along with other Scandinavian countries, requires migrants to enjoy full employment rights with citizens, and so there are much lower numbers of migrant workers in these countries.

The international market for low-skilled migrants is enormous and many low-skilled migrants are willing to accept jobs in high-income countries at wages and employment conditions much below those mandated by local laws. Migrants' frame of reference, after all, is their home country, where many of those conditions do not prevail. They may not care much about being denied certain rights or equal treatment in high-income countries, especially if they plan to be in those countries for only a

---

[28] For good empirical evidence of this pattern see Martin Ruhs and Philip Martin, "Numbers vs. Rights," 249.

short time.[29] But they often care very much about access to employment opportunities that deliver good wages. So, from the migrants' perspective, employment on restrictive conditions might still be highly desirable. Many workers are willing to accept fewer rights if the wage is attractive to them. In addition, migrant-sending countries are often faced with similar conflicts that reflect their citizens' preferences: promote the rights of their nationals who participate in these migration schemes or maximize economic benefits of emigration by facilitating the movement of more citizens to labor in foreign countries?

One needs to be careful in navigating these issues, as there are many stakeholders whose interests are affected by decisions to adopt one policy or another. For instance, focusing exclusively on improving human rights protections of current migrants might negatively affect the prospects for even larger cohorts of future migrants who might benefit greatly from accessing labor markets in higher-income countries. If granting more generous rights to current migrants limits the access current and future migrants have, this can overall be bad for beneficial development.

So, we seem to have a justice dilemma. While more migration and more rights for migrants might both be valuable, when it is not possible to secure both, how should we choose between them?

5   Some Policy Solutions

Fortunately, various international initiatives aim to address these issues, mindful of the problems, tensions, and trade-offs discussed in Sections 2, 3, and 4. If states complied with their requirements, this would constitute a credible and effective set of solutions to many of the most egregious problems. As we come to see, these agreements draw on several aspects of our human rights practice, and show good synergies in promoting core human rights goals, especially concerning protecting vulnerable people in significant danger of rights violations. These policies give us considerable insights about how our human rights practice aims to navigate problematic features inherent in temporary migration programs, and with the challenges discussed in the previous section. Drawing on some of the principles embedded in the practice, we can discuss the key guiding principles that help us navigate other problems such as the numbers versus human rights issue. I consider this issue in Section 6.

---

[29] Of course, not all rights create significant costs for employers. But since several might, we explore the normative implications of this view.

As we come to see in this section, our human rights practice incorporates measures that can offer important solutions to many of the problems identified. With 85 percent of states agreeing to comply with – and promote – the terms and conditions of the main documents I discuss, some significant solutions with considerable authority are in sight.[30] I discuss only some aspects of The Global Compact here with more discussion to follow in Chapter 9. Importantly for the purposes of this chapter, the Global Compact requires adopting nations to comply with two sets of recruitment guidelines that offer considerable remedies for the problems we have noted. We discuss the guidelines offered by the International Organization for Migration (IOM) in Section 5.2 and those of the ILO in 5.3. In Section 5.4 I extract three key guiding principles that we can use to navigate the rights versus numbers issue, and I discuss how to resolve that issue in Section 6.

5.1   The Global Compact for Safe, Orderly, and Regular Migration

This inter-governmentally negotiated policy is significant as it sets out the terms for a new understanding about global best practice in the area of migration. While 193 member states of the UN originally agreed to the terms of the document in July 2018, at the adoption ceremony in December 2018, only 164 countries formally adopted the compact. I believe this is still a highly significant achievement because 85 percent of the world's states formally adopted the framework, and as noted, it currently has considerable authority with the adopting nations.

The compact is embedded within a platform of conventions already adopted by the United Nations and ILO, and builds on these previous foundations. The compact is a non-legally binding, cooperative framework aimed at solving migration challenges, while upholding the sovereignty of states.[31] It sets out shared understandings and responsibilities.[32]

Importantly, the preamble also notes that "[w]e commit to continue the multilateral dialogue at the United Nations through a periodic and

---

[30] I discuss the question of authority in more detail in Chapter 9. As the Global Compact notes, the "authority rests on its consensual nature, credibility, collective ownership, joint implementation" along with agreements to follow-up and review. The commitments states have already made to implement these solutions, give them considerable importance.

[31] International Organisation for Migration, *Global Compact for Migration* (GENEVA, IOM, 2018), 2, available at: www.iom.int/global-compact-migration

[32] Ibid., 2.

effective follow-up and review mechanism, ensuring that the words in this document translate into concrete actions for the benefit of millions of people in every region of the world."[33] And this follow-up and review part is especially noteworthy as this involves significant opportunities for states to be called to account for their performance on these standards. It also provides opportunities to share experiences of best practice as nations work toward implementation in sometimes challenging conditions.[34]

The compact is based on several key principles, notably recognition that no state can address migration issues properly on its own, and the need for "international, regional and bilateral cooperation and dialogue. Its authority rests on its consensual nature, credibility, collective ownership, joint implementation, follow-up and review."[35] The cooperative framework has twenty-three objectives for safe, orderly, and regular migration. Here I highlight only a few that are particularly relevant for dealing fairly with temporary labor migrants.

The framework enjoins state parties to collect and use accurate data as a basis for evidence-based policies (Principle 1). It calls on parties to "minimize the adverse drivers and structural factors that compel people to leave their country of origin" (Principle 2). It encourages parties to "provide accurate and timely information at all stages of migration" (Principle 3), and to "ensure that all migrants have proof of legal identity and adequate documentation" (Principle 4). Principle 6 requires signatories to "facilitate fair and ethical recruitment and safeguard conditions that ensure decent work," and to "address and reduce vulnerabilities in migration" (Principle 7). Principles 8–10 enjoin parties to strengthen their responses to addressing human trafficking across borders, while Principle 14 recommends enhanced "consular protection, assistance and cooperation throughout the migration cycle."[36]

Other principles encourage more investment in skills development (Principle 18), the promotion of "faster, safer and cheaper transfer of remittances" (Principle 20), more cooperation in "facilitating safe and dignified return and readmission, as well as sustainable reintegration" (Principle 21). Principle 23 recommends strengthened "international cooperation and global partnerships for safe, orderly and regular migration."

---

[33] Ibid., 3–4.   [34] Ibid.   [35] *Global Compact for Migration,* 4.
[36] Two other highly notable principles to be discussed in the next chapter include: Principle 16, which enjoins parties to "empower migrants and societies to realize full inclusion and social cohesion" and Principle 17, which recommends that we "eliminate all forms of discrimination and promote evidence-based public discourse to shape perceptions of migration."

For our purposes Objective 6 is particularly relevant, and merits further discussion. Objective 6 encourages states to:

- "(g) develop and strengthen labour migration and fair and ethical recruitment processes that allow migrants to change employers and modify the conditions or length of their stay with minimal administrative burden, while promoting greater opportunities for decent work and respect for international human rights and labour law."[37]
- "(l) Develop and improve national policies and programmes relating to international labour mobility, including by taking into consideration relevant recommendations of the ILO General Principles and Operational Guidelines for Fair Recruitment, the United Nations Guiding Principles on Business and Human Rights, and the IOM International Recruitment Integrity System (IRIS)."[38]

So, as we see then, the Global Compact makes reference to further international documents that provide guidance on fair recruitment. These merit further discussion, as they incorporate good remedies for many of the noted problems. I discuss these additional documents in Sections 5.2 and 5.3.

5.2   IRIS

The IRIS is a set of fair standards for recruitment, based on elements of our contemporary international human rights instruments and labor conventions. It was developed by the IOM via extensive consultation with all stakeholder groups. It is primarily designed as a practical tool to give guidance to recruiters and employers to fulfill their human rights and other international obligations. There are five central principles along with useful benchmarks for operationalizing these principles. I discuss some of the central aspects next.

The first general principle covers respect for laws and rights at work. It enjoins labor recruiters to comply with all relevant agreements, regulations, policies, and laws governing recruitment of migrant workers that apply to the countries of origin, transit, and destination. Human trafficking, forced labor, and child labor (migrants under the age of eighteen), along with the recruitment of migrant workers to replace workers on strike are all prohibited. Explicitly mentioned as requiring respect are rights of freedom of association and collective bargaining, along with respect for equality of

---

[37] *Global Compact for Migration*, 13.   [38] Ibid., 14.

treatment and non-discrimination on the basis of race, ethnicity, gender identity, caste, political affiliation, religion, and so forth, in accordance with applicable law.

The second general principle discusses respect for ethical and professional conduct. Labor recruiters are required to have in place policies and processes, including due diligence, to ensure that their activities are consistent with the IRIS principles and that treat "migrant workers with dignity and respect, free from harassment, or any form of coercion or degrading or inhuman treatment."[39] So, for instance, the labor recruiter must check that employers, subcontractors, and other partners are complying with applicable standards.

More particular principles discuss core troubling aspects of the recruitment process that make migrants vulnerable to human rights violations. The first particular operational principle prohibits charging migrants recruitment fees or imposing costs related to job placement or employment.[40] The second protects freedom of movement and prohibits practices of withholding documents (such as passports, identity documents, or work permits) or wages. It also prohibits practices requiring monetary deposits as employment conditions. The third principle requires respect for contracts and transparency. It includes the following requirements. Labor recruiters must ensure that migrants have written contracts in languages they understand prior to departure. These contracts should outline the terms and conditions of employment, including expectations about the nature of the work, working hours, name and address of the employer, the deductions that will be made from pay, conditions of termination, and benefits of employment, inter alia. Written consent should be obtained before departure. Recruiters must ensure that the terms and conditions of work offered in the contract are accurate and comply with applicable laws. The recruiter must also ensure that migrant workers receive appropriate orientation and necessary training. The fourth principle ensures that data are protected and that there is respect for confidentiality of personal data supplied. Any data they collect must not be communicated to others without the migrant's consent. The fifth principle enjoins recruiters to ensure that migrant workers have access to grievance mechanisms or other ways to seek remedy

---

[39] "International Organization for Migration, International Recruitment Integrity System" (Geneva: IOM, 2018), 2, available here: https://iris.iom.int/

[40] It might still be permissible to charge prospective migrants for any standard payments associated with visa applications, in my view.

should there be breaches with the standards described. They must be assured effective access without fear of dismissal or reprisals.

The ILO also offers general principles and operational guidelines for fair recruitment. They are similar to the IRIS ones just covered, but provide more detail in some areas. I pick out only a few further areas for discussion that add more content in the next section.

5.3   The ILO Guidelines for Fair Recruitment

The ILO "fair migration agenda" highlights the need for decent work in countries of origin. It also highlights the need for fair migration schemes that are well regulated. The general principles include the following highlighted next.

> Principle 1: "Recruitment should take place in a way that respects, protects and fulfills internationally recognized human rights, including those expressed in international labour standards, and in particular the right to freedom of association and collective bargaining, and prevention and elimination of forced labour, child labour and discrimination in respect of employment and occupation."[41]

> Principle 2. "Recruitment should respond to established labour market needs, and not serve as a means to displace or diminish an existing workforce, to lower labour standards, wages, or working conditions, or to otherwise undermine decent work."[42]

> Principle 5. "Regulation of employment and recruitment activities should be clear and transparent and effectively enforced. The role of the labour inspectorate and the use of standardized registration, licensing or certification systems should be highlighted. The competent authorities should take specific measures against abusive and fraudulent recruitment methods, including those that could result in forced labor or trafficking in persons."[43]

Principle 7 emphasizes again that "no recruitment fees should be charged, or otherwise borne by, workers or jobseekers."[44] Principles 8, 9, and 10 all deal with fair contracting, and are similar to those covered under IRIS, highlighting the needs for accurate information, timely presentation of contracts, voluntary consent, and to be free from deception and coercion. Principle 11 underscores that workers should be free "to move within

---

[41] ILO, "General Principles and Operational Guidelines for Fair Recruitment" (Geneva: ILO, 2016), 1, available at: www.ilo.org/global/about-the-ilo/multimedia/maps-and-charts/enhanced/WCMS_626548/lang--en/index.htm
[42] Ibid.   [43] Ibid.   [44] Ibid.

a country or to leave a country"[45] and that none of their identity documents should be withheld or destroyed. Principle 12 emphasizes that workers should be free to terminate employment and return to countries of origin, and should not need the employer's or recruiter's permission to do so nor to change employer.[46] Principle 13 stresses the need for workers, to "have access to free or affordable grievance and other dispute resolution mechanisms in cases of alleged abuse of their rights in the recruitment process, and effective and appropriate remedies should be provided where abuse has occurred."[47]

Operational guidelines cover much the same territory as those of IRIS. Some noteworthy features that deserve emphasis include that governments have responsibilities to "ensure that there is an effective and sufficiently resourced labor inspectorate and that it is empowered and trained to investigate and intervene at all stages of the recruitment process for all workers and all enterprises, and to monitor and evaluate the operations of all labor recruiters."[48] In addition, governments should ensure that employers and recruiters are held accountable, individually or jointly, for respecting workers' rights in the recruitment process. Governments should ensure workers have access to grievance and other dispute resolution mechanisms without fear of retaliation especially deportation.

5.4   *Summary of Some Key Relevant Principles*

Inherent in these three international documents are a few key basic principles. The main one is this:

> (1) There are requirements to respect the basic features of fair contracting, especially fair labor contracts.

Fair contracting will have a number of elements, but for the purposes of discussion, two are particularly relevant and I add them as further specific orienting principles, as they are both deeply embedded in the commitments embodied in our human rights practice:

> (2) There are requirements to respect freedom to exit employment.

In addition, the policies are mindful of the need to take account of the interests of all relevantly affected workers and other stakeholders. I add this as a third core principle that the guidelines draw from our human rights practice.

---

[45] Ibid.   [46] Ibid.   [47] Ibid.   [48] Ibid.

(3) Fair labor contracts take account of significant negative externalities for third parties.

As I discuss in the next section, using these key principles inherent in our human rights practice concerning employment, we can address the central worrisome features about contemporary labor migration schemes.[49]

Before we close this section, it is perhaps important to note that there can be permissible qualifications and conditions governing freedom of exit. For instance, there may be reasonable obligations to abide by some contract terms, such as giving appropriate notice to employers so they can ensure their obligations to others are met. Another condition might be that in the case of a dispute as to whether an employer has met relevant employment contract terms and conditions, the employee should usually seek resolution before exiting. The right to exit freely may well have *some* conditions attached to it, mindful of fairness issues to all who are significantly affected by an employee's decision to leave.

6   Toward Fair Temporary Migration Programs

As I argue in this section, there is a place for mutual sufficient advantage to have a role in designing fair labor migration programs. There are a number of key sets of agents affected by temporary migration programs, including employers, other members of host societies, migrants, and members of destination countries. For all these agents, we need to consider the interests of both current and future generations. There should be sufficient advantage to the key stakeholders and there are a number of other criteria that must be met.

There is scope for each country to set the terms of temporary labor migration contracts (above some minimum threshold) and there is scope for each migrant to judge whether those employment contracts offer sufficient advantage to the migrant that she is willing to accept labor contracts offered on those terms. But like all fair contracting, there are some minimum requirements that must be met if the contracts are to constitute fair agreements. There are, for instance, some very basic human rights, such as civil and political ones, that should not be on the table for compromise discussion, or so I will argue.

---

[49] Using these basic principles, we can also easily derive the core ILO tenets, such as a prohibition on child labor. Children, especially young children, cannot easily satisfy the conditions for validly giving free consent, for instance.

The guiding principles that assist in deciding on that minimum are those that I have indicated are widely supported by the animating principles of our current human rights practice. They are the need to respect rights necessary for guaranteeing fair contracting, those necessary for freedom of exit, and those necessary to deal with significant human rights related negative externalities for third parties.

States have responsibilities to ensure that offers of contracts for employment are minimally fair. Fair contracts have many requirements. First of all, contracts need to be embedded in fair processes that determine whether there are genuine labor shortages in the first place. And these processes must allow scope for comprehensive discussion on how to fill any shortages identified, given that there are always several options available and these will have implications for local workers, especially their wages. One option for dealing with labor shortages is, of course, simply to raise the wages of local workers rather than searching further afield. More generally, many effects on stakeholders in both countries are relevant to whether a contract is fair. If compelling data are available about harmful effects, steps should be taken to address these, or at least to cooperate with countries in addressing these.[50]

In considering which rights migrants have consistent with fair contracting, while there can be a place for compromise on some rights, in the case of others, compromises would jeopardize principles of fair contracting. In beginning to marshal my defense for this position, note that in our contemporary world, migrant workers often make decisions to work in other countries that restrict their rights, and they often do so because they judge that some aspects of their well-being, or that of their families, will be enhanced by such decisions. Typically, in the case of low-skilled migrants, these decisions revolve around access to employment opportunities that will raise income for themselves or their households. While guest worker programs that limit rights might make many of us uncomfortable, exclusion that forces people to live in abject poverty should make us even more so.[51] And the fact that millions of migrant workers make these choices

---

[50] Dealing appropriately with the harmful fallout from migration requires a great deal of care, as I argue at length in *Debating Brain Drain*. Typically, this involves extensive cooperation between home and host countries to ensure recruitment follows any guidelines between the two countries, especially guidelines concerning mitigating harmful effects for countries of origin. Host countries must also assist with the enforcement of any contractual agreements migrants have with their home country.

[51] Several authors make similar points including Howard Chang, "Liberal Ideals and Political Feasibility: Guest-worker Programs as Second-best Policies," *North Carolina Journal of*

every day is quite important as we reflect on charting a justified course in these murky real-world waters.

Here we are in the realm of second-best options since there are no clean hands alternatives available. In this messier space, we should pay attention to relevant evidence. There is a huge amount of evidence that, under the right conditions, temporary migration programs can promote beneficial development. And we have no compelling evidence that shutting doors to temporary migration generally leads to better outcomes for migrants and sending countries.[52] This should be relevant in deciding what policy to adopt here and now that helps us reduce global injustices. As Bell and Piper helpfully suggest, "unequal rights under a guest worker program could be morally justified if three conditions are met (a) if they benefit migrant workers, as decided by migrant workers themselves; (b) they create opportunities for people to improve their lives; and (c) if there are no feasible alternatives to (a) or (b)."[53] Much will hang on the options we consider to be feasible. And much of this book is concerned with just such reflection. However, what we must consider is that migrants and prospective employees are presented with an option that many migrants currently entertain: whether they should pursue a job that will bring them a wage they consider attractive, given their perception of the options available, even though some rights would be temporarily restricted.

There is good evidence that a decent job is the single most transformative factor in assisting people out of poverty.[54] The scale of unemployment and vulnerable employment in the world is enormous. At least 600 million productive jobs need to be created to produce enough jobs to match demographics.[55] Even were this target to be reached, 900 million workers are still expected to live below the poverty line. Youth unemployment is yet more troubling. In some countries 40–50 percent of the youth population is unemployed.[56] In 2017 about 42 percent of workers (1.4 billion) were in vulnerable forms of employment worldwide and the figure is worse

---

International Law and Commercial Regulation, 27 (2002): 465–481; Daniel Bell and N. Piper "Justice for Migrant Workers? The Case of Foreign Domestic Workers in Hong Kong and Singapore" in Will Kymlicka and H. Baogang (eds.), *Multiculturalism in Asia* (Oxford: Oxford University Press, 2005); and Robert Mayer, "Guestworkers and Exploitation," *Review of Politics*, 67 (2005).

[52] Ruhs, *The Price of Rights*, chapter 7. Consider also again those figures I cited concerning massive global unemployment and vulnerable employment. If closing doors is so good for would-be migrants, the figures would not be of this scale.

[53] Daniel Bell and N. Piper, "Justice for Migrant Workers?," 214.

[54] Brock, "Global Poverty, Decent Work, and Remedial Responsibilities."

[55] ILO, *Global Employment Trends* (Geneva: ILO, 2012).

[56] World Bank, *World Development Report: Jobs* (Washington, DC: World Bank, 2019).

in developing countries, at 76 percent.[57] These figures are expected to worsen in the next few years. In the face of such data, we should consider the possibility that some kinds of job contracts that restrict some rights might present one desirable option, given our highly imperfect world.

So, what kinds of employment contracts may justifiably be offered? Are employment contracts that restrict some rights (those thought to carry costs to destination countries) normatively permissible? As foreshadowed, I think we can get to the issue of which rights are "tradable" by focusing on fair contracting requirements, freedom of exit, and blocking significant negative externalities for third parties. So, as I see it, some human rights will need to be ring-fenced for guaranteed protection, while there is scope for further reflection on others.

6.1   *Protecting Some Core Rights*

In efforts to attempt a more systematic analysis, I go through the central articles of the Universal Declaration of Human Rights, since they cover the main candidate areas. Considering these articles, I believe at least the following list should all be part of the minimum protected core in virtue of their close connection to the agency of those engaged in fair contracting. So, if migrants are to have the ability to make fair contracts and to protect their ability to exit when there are breaches of contractual terms, some rights deserve special protection. I abbreviate and summarize them next.

Article 3: Everyone has the right to life, liberty and security of person.

Article 4: No one shall be held in slavery or servitude; slavery and the slave trade shall be prohibited in all their forms.

Article 5: Prohibitions on torture, cruel, inhuman or degrading treatment.

Article 6: The right to recognition as a person before the law

Article 7: Relevant protection from the law

Article 8: The right to "an effective remedy by all the competent national tribunals for acts violating the fundamental rights granted him by the constitution or by law."

Article 9: Prohibitions on arbitrary arrest, detention or exile.

Article 10: "Everyone is entitled in full equality to a fair and public hearing by an independent and impartial tribunal, in the determination of his rights and obligations and of any criminal charge against him."

Article 11: Presumption of innocence, inter alia.

---

[57] ILO, World Employment and Social Outlook – Trends 2018.

Article 12: No arbitrary interference with privacy.

Article 13: The right to freedom of movement within the state.

Article 14: The right to seek asylum.

Article 15: The right to a nationality.

Article 18: The right to freedom of thought, conscience and religion.

Article 19: Freedom of expression.

Article 20: The right to freedom of peaceful assembly and association, which also means that 23 (4), the right to join trade unions, must be protected.

The list just assembled constitutes the main non-tradable rights. They are the ones that are required as the core minimum needing to be upheld in fair contracting. Protecting these is essential if migrants are to retain the ability to enter into fair contracts and to preserve their exit options. I assume their close connection to these activities is clear enough, without the need for much further argument. Rather, I expect the argumentative burden to lie largely elsewhere, namely in the area of which, *if any*, rights may permissibly be restricted. I proceed to that important task next.

6.2   Justifying Possible Restrictions

Recall that in the background of this discussion, there is an important challenge that must be confronted, namely that offering more rights generally leads to fewer migration opportunities being made available. The demand for completely equal rights may well lead to worse outcomes for migrants, as judged by those migrants and prospective migrants. So, mindful of this constraint, we are trying to evaluate how and when compromise should be permitted. Here I discuss some of the controversial rights often raised as candidates for compromise in practice, and discuss whether they are tradable under the fair contracting framework I have adopted.

So, our attention turns to the question of which rights may one justifiably restrict and for how long? Some rights do seem to create costs, especially fiscal costs, for destination countries, such as rights to health care, education, housing, and other social benefits that come with permanent residence.[58] Which, if any of these, may a destination country permissibly restrict?

---

[58] In practice, the main rights restrictions in contention in liberal democracies are: selected social rights, the right to free choice of employment, the right to family reunion, and the right to access permanent residence. We might well wonder what genuine costs are associated with these rights? And who actually bears the costs of protecting the rights? There are important issues about what a

6.2.1   The Rights to Health Care, Education, and Public Welfare

Consider what is involved in fair contracting and fair exit options. Some access to basic or emergency health care should be available, either through the employer or the state, to preserve robust rights to work according to the terms and conditions of the contract or to exit from these. Migrant workers may permissibly be restricted from more generous access to other forms of health care that are perhaps not integral to these capacities (elective surgery, for instance). One consideration in favor of guaranteed access to some basic health care is that for many illnesses, such as in the case of infectious diseases, there can be relevant effects on others, both within the state and in home countries, so we must include appropriate care for infectious diseases by the third principle, which tries to ensure that we do not inflict significant harms on third parties.

The case for rights to other public benefits, such as education or public welfare, is much weaker. Insofar as these are indeed costly benefits to sustain, and workers are on the territory to *work*, the need for them is less clear and it seems permissible for these to be restricted.

6.2.2   The Right to Free Choice of Employment

There can be some restrictions on this right, but as I argue in this section, the justified restrictions in this area are not as limited as many often suppose. In the case under consideration, we should understand the right to free choice of employment as a permission to change employment *within certain sectors or occupations*. Employment should not be tied to particular employers, or that would significantly damage freedom of exit. The freedom to exit and remain on the territory would not be available. But if there is a genuine labor shortage, this option should be available, as it would benefit both destination and home countries, along with migrants.

So, the right to free choice of employment needs to be protected in the ways I have emphasized, or the possibility of exit would not be meaningful. There should be a process by which one can apply, to the destination

---

fair distribution of costs might be and, in some cases, it might not be unreasonable for employers to bear some of the costs of hiring workers from whom they derive much benefit.

Also worth a note is why I have selected these particular rights for discussion here. Because these are the main rights that are in contention in practice, I do not discuss other options of rights that might be tradable. Someone might wonder, though, why not discuss restricting all sorts of rights governing occupational health and safety or hours of work, and more generally the conditions that often characterize sweatshops. In my view, such trades would be ruled out by my approach, as the platform in which the practice is embedded precludes such trades via its many commitments to decent work, ILO core commitments, the fair work agenda, and so forth.

country government authorizing body that issues labor visas, to change employer, if employers are found to be in breach of their contract requirements.

So, while I think there can be a restriction on the right to free choice of employment outside of a particular sector or occupation, there should be more latitude in allowing migrants to change employer within those categories.

6.2.3   *The Right to Family Union or Reunion*

There can plausibly be some restrictions on the right to have family members join the migrant in the destination country. Relevant to this assessment is that many citizens choose occupations that take them away from their children or spouses for considerable periods of time. Consider how this is the case with service in the military, work on ships, or employment on the international space station. If choosing such jobs that require separation from families for long periods of time can be reasonable, then of course so can it be similarly reasonable to choose a migrant work scheme that carries similar restrictions. So, in principle, I do not think there is a major problem with these sorts of requirements, and individual migrants should be free to decide how much this issue matters to them. For instance, for some migrants who have no children or partners, this restriction might have no bearing on their decision to work for one year in a foreign country at a job that is attractive to them.

Having said that, we might note that there are different ways to specify restrictions. As Martin Ruhs points out, we can distinguish two kinds of restrictions: one prohibits family reunion completely and another kind makes it unlikely as the right to family reunion is tied to providing evidence that the worker can support family members in ways that do not create net fiscal burdens for the state.[59] A fiscal constraint might be the less obnoxious way to phrase the restriction.

However, it is also plausible that even were the absolute restriction in force rather than the income-based one, this would be permissible. States may defensibly prohibit migrants from bringing family members to a destination country for the term of the labor contract. Consider again how this regularly applies to employment in various occupations, such as the military or work on ships. So, here we might note that even if this is

---

[59]   Ruhs, *The Price of Rights.*

not a very generous approach for a destination country to take, it seems permissible, under the conditions we are entertaining.[60]

6.2.4   *Right to Permanent Residency*

A temporary work contract may prohibit a migrant from seeking to adjust status to becoming a permanent resident while on that contract. There can be a place for such contracts, on the general rationale that I have been considering. While I think such contracts can be permissible, I also note that there should also be a general tendency for states to recognize eligibility for full membership over time. The longer a migrant has been resident on the territory, the stronger the case. This discussion folds into a more general discussion of whether countries should be more generous in admitting migrants, one that I pursue in Chapter 9. As I argue, everyone has a right to a fair process concerning the determination of rights pertaining to migration and, as I argue, this involves due consideration of several potentially relevant factors that apply in the case of labor migration.[61]

---

[60] Someone might wonder how I reconcile the view that we can restrict the right to family (re)union with positions argued for in previous chapters, such as Chapter 5, on the justifiability of deporting the long-settled. As Delphine Nakache argues, "International law allows for restrictions on the enjoyment of family rights, where these restrictions are lawful, pursue a legitimate aim and are proportionate to the aim pursued ... decisions to expel must be proportionate to the aim pursued, which means there must be *'relevant and sufficient reasons for the measure, that no less restrictive measure is feasible, that adequate safeguards against abuse should be in place, and that the measure should be imposed by way of a fair procedure'.*" (Delphine Nakache, "Migrant Workers and the Right to Family Accompaniment: A Case for Family Rights in International Law and in Canada," *International Migration*, March 2018. In the quote she refers to an International Commission of Jurists guide [ILO, *Migration and International Human Rights Law: A Practitioners' Guide*. Geneva: ICJ, 2014]. My view is that there are vast differences between the cases of deporting family members and migrants electing to undergo limited separations under certain conditions. For instance, there is a difference between choosing to take up a sufficiently attractive opportunity that requires some separation from family members, and having a forced separation thrust upon one. There are also differences in proportionality. (Not being able to see one's children ever again is different from seeing them on an annual basis, for instance.) Importantly, note that in the case of current deportations, none of the conditions mentioned in the italicized portion apply to the cases I discussed in Chapter 5. Having said that, migrant worker schemes should be mindful of these conditions, and there is more to say about how fair processes should operate. I return to these issues in Chapter 9.

[61] May a state keep renewing temporary labor contracts without offering the migrant a pathway to citizenship? There are important normative arguments here that have considerable force. For instance, consider the basic notion of fair play. A principle of fair play requires that there be some fair distribution of the benefits of cooperation to all those who contribute to those benefits and bear the burdens of cooperation. Denying permanent residency might be construed as the state taking the contributions of temporary migrants without offering them all the benefits of that cooperation. Now, justice certainly does require fair terms of cooperation. But what can be disputed is which are the salient benefits, whether they are sufficient for the contribution made, and what counts as a fair distribution of benefits. I believe temporary migrants have a right to make their case

At any rate, a legitimate state may permissibly offer a contract that includes restrictions on the right to convert status from temporary to permanent while on a particular labor contract and within certain time-frames. But I also believe a legitimate state will have some obligations in connection with those temporary migrants who have resided on the territory for many years. As I argue in Chapter 9, those who have resided on a territory for many years and who have made substantial contributions to community well-being (as labor migrants generally do) have a strong case to remain.[62]

7   Conclusions

As I have argued in this chapter, there is a place for mutual advantage type approaches in our quest to reduce migration injustice, so long as migrants are offered fair contracts that they are free to accept or reject, and so long as they have exit options should contractual breaches arise. I discussed why minimally fair contracts must take account of relevant harms to third parties and must protect the ability of migrants to contract fairly. Those offering employment contracts have important responsibilities. And the state has a key role to play in regulating fair terms of employment. Effects on stakeholders in both countries are relevant. I also noted that some basic core human rights must be ring-fenced, because they are necessary for migrants' rights to contract fairly. These rights protect migrants' abilities to

---

and to have that case fairly adjudicated. (These are issues I discuss in Chapter 9.) And it is plausible that a compelling argument can be marshaled that migrants' contributions and participation in the destination country deserve strong weight and should give them a right to remain. After all they are doing jobs that citizens do not wish to do and they are jobs that are necessary to keep the society going. These workers clean houses, they take care of the elderly, sick, and young, they tend gardens, wash dishes, construct homes, pay taxes, and the like. This is a case in which I think the normative arguments pull in one direction and the empirical ones suggest another. In this book, I am constantly navigating this tension between normative and empirical considerations. The human rights practice approach I pursue here aims to straddle this divide showing how we can be faithful to our human rights normative commitments while also appreciating some current important real-world constraints. We cannot easily dismiss the empirical constraints when taking such an approach, even though I believe migrants' claim to remain strengthens over time. For an outstanding argument invoking the notion of fair play, see Sarah Song, *Immigration and Democracy*.

[62] For excellent treatment of the issues I am also concerned with, see Martin Ruh's account in *The Price of Rights*. His view is that some rights restrictions are justifiable but only if there is clear demonstrable evidence that the rights result in net fiscal losses for the receiving country and that empirical fact influences there being a more restrictive policy. While there are some similarities in the recommendations we support, our argument structures are different. I seek a principled way to navigate the normative issues by extracting core principles embedded in commitments to our human rights practice. His approach seems somewhat *ad hoc* to me.

make informed choices about employment and provide rights of exit should arrangements violate contract terms and conditions. Importantly, so long as the core rights are protected, migrants should be the ones judging whether to accept or reject these contracts. The approach centrally aims to respect migrants' agency as authors of their own lives, while trying to provide the best decision environment or option set available at a given time.

Recall the argument I developed in Chapter 3, according to which states must support the conditions for adequate human rights fulfillment in all communities. States must contribute to the legitimacy of the state system, such as by participating in international arrangements that can deliver on human rights protection, and their own legitimacy depends on such participation. So, legitimate states must comply with migration treaties that can credibly protect migrants' human rights, such as the core documents we have been discussing here (The Global Compact for Safe, Orderly, and Regular Migration, IRIS, and the ILO guidelines on fair recruiting). States will have significant responsibilities in relation to these policies, for instance regulating and overseeing the activities of employers and recruitment agents. They also need to ensure relevant grievance mechanisms and opportunities for redress are available to those migrants who suffer from compliance failures. I continue to discuss these themes at the end of Chapter 9. To foreshadow the view I argue for there, when other states are the ones guilty of compliance failures, compliant states should raise such issues with noncompliant states in attempts to get noncompliant states to discharge their duties. Many elements of the human rights practice provide excellent channels for ensuring that such concerns can be raised in appropriate accountability settings. For instance, the periodic review system provides the architecture and good channels for critical engagement along with guidance on how to improve performance and offers to assist in constructive ways. And the explicit implementation and follow-up procedures that are outlined by the Compact for Migration, provide further excellent venues for exactly such constructive dialogue in migration settings.[63] I return to these themes again at the end of Chapter 9.

---

[63] So, for those states that are signatories to the compact or related policies, we have important channels for holding states to account for performance. What about those states that are not signatories? In those cases, the same principle applies but alternative channels for communicating the need for improved performance must be sought. But since 98 percent of states have adopted, endorsed, and/or ratified one or more human rights conventions, and these all have follow-up and review processes, these and other channels will provide relevant further opportunities for such constructive criticism and dialogue.

CHAPTER 8

Terrorism and Migration

Seeking to control terrorists and terrorism can certainly be part of the policy, but if we already are rather safe, efforts to make us even safer are likely to be, at a minimum, inefficient. In the end, if we really want to deflate terrorism's impact we will need particularly to control ourselves.[1]

1 Introduction

Fears concerning terrorism and security seem to have significantly set back the prospects for migration justice recently. These alleged terrorism-related security threats were behind several draconian measures introduced in 2017, such as the executive order to ban citizens from seven predominantly Muslim countries entering the USA, the suspension of refugee admissions, and new extreme vetting procedures for all who aim to arrive or transit through the USA. Trump's anti-immigrant plans also include the notorious wall on the USA–Mexico border, more border agents and immigration judges, limits on family-based migration,[2] and the elimination of the green card lottery system.[3] The combined effects of these changes would be a cut to legal immigration by about 500,000 annually.[4]

---

[1] John Mueller, *Overblown: How Politicians and the Terrorism Industry Inflate National Security Threats, and Why We Believe Them* (New York: Free Press, 2006), 143.

[2] Spouses and minor children of US citizens might still be able to migrate to the USA, but parents and siblings would not be eligible candidates.

[3] This is an immigrant visa program aimed at increasing the diversity of immigrants and those from countries with historically low rates of immigration to the USA are eligible to apply to participate in the lottery.

[4] See David Nakamura, "Study: White House plan slashes legal immigration rates by 44 percent – 22 million fewer immigrants over a half-century," *Washington Post*, January 29, 2018, available at: www.washingtonpost.com/news/post-politics/wp/2018/01/29/study-white-house-plan-slashes-legal-immigration-rates-by-44-percent-22-million-fewer-immigrants-over-a-half-century/?noredirect=on&utm_term=.7f737410dc06. They cite a study from David Bier and Stuart Anderson, which estimates that, if enacted, these plans would cut legal immigrants by about a half million annually.

What are we to make of these alleged new security and terrorism threats and how, if at all, should they bear on migration policy?

In this chapter, I discuss some of the problems associated with assessing the weight that should reasonably be placed on terrorism and security in contemporary admissions policies. As I argue, while there is some threat level, key issues include deciding what measures would be effective in combating risks commensurate with that threat level, while not ignoring the opportunity costs pursuing such policies might entail, especially ones that might better promote the goals of a strong and inclusive society capable of resilience to such threats, among many other valuable goals. I also consider whether some risks can be further reduced without compromising our values, principles, and other important justice goals. A further set of concerns arises concerning the measures that may be taken to protect against the perceived threat and whether they violate additional demands of justice.

This discussion provides much salient data about risk analysis that is helpful to a more focused analysis of how security threats get to be so readily coupled with migration issues. Here we find some familiar dynamics along with some new developments. Politicians have often been successful in adopting strategies such as scapegoating and exclusionary constructions of national identity. New developments include changing demographics and structural changes that have resulted in limitations on upward mobility, which can promote conflict and resentment. These sentiments can be amplified and harnessed to promote an anti-immigrant ethos in which unwise policies can flourish.

As I argue in this chapter, each legitimate state has the right to have its own conversation about how best to combat terrorism and to make policy decisions accordingly, so long as it fulfills all its legitimacy requirements. There are also justice constraints on how that dialogue may permissibly unfold. Making good decisions about public funding should start with an accurate assessment of risks, for instance. Wasteful and excessive spending in one area (relative to risk) when other core dimensions of justice are widely neglected is a justice-relevant consideration. In general, excessive spending on shoring up some human rights where further important gains are unlikely to materialize, especially when other human rights are neglected or not yet sufficiently secure, is relevant to how we evaluate society's behavior against a justice standard. So, excessive spending on the right to

The original study is available at: www.cato.org/blog/white-house-plan-bans-22-million-legal-immigrants-over-5-decades

security, when rights to basic education, food, housing, and health care remain unfulfilled is relevant to assessing how well justice is achieved in particular societies.[5] While each nation should be able to decide on its own spending priorities, according to the framework developed in this book, there are constraints on that spending. When there is large-scale under-fulfillment of some human rights, further ineffective expenditure on securing other human rights is unjust.

2   How Safe Are We?

There has been considerable analysis of whether terrorist threats have increased, decreased, or remained the same since 9/11. And plenty of it focuses on the US context, perhaps because of the spectacular events of 9/11. As so much of the anti-immigrant policy is exported from the USA these days, I take it to be a core case in this chapter and worthy of considerable analysis.[6] One commonly shared view is that the USA might be safer from orchestrated attacks on the scale of those perpetrated on 9/11, but that plenty of threats remain.[7] In fact, some of the greatest threats do not seem to receive the kind of attention they ought to, commensurate with their threat level. For instance, access to various harm-causing agents, such as military-grade weapons or nuclear materials, remains too easy. Three kinds of threats are often noted as particularly worrisome – domestic lone wolves, dirty bombs, and cyberattacks – and I discuss them next.

2.1   Domestic Lone Wolves

Plenty of security experts agree that individuals currently residing within the United States who are inspired to commit violence through the

---

[5] Given that we have been considering the USA as a key case study in this chapter, it is relevant to point out that there are currently massive deficiencies in these areas and the trend in the USA is towards deterioration. For a concise synopsis of key issues affecting basic human rights, especially including how health rights are being eroded, see the Human Rights Watch, *World Reports*, especially "United States: Events of 2017" available from the Human Rights Watch website at: www.hrw.org/world-report/2018/country-chapters/united-states

[6] While there are much rich data from the USA, shades of the same phenomena exist in many places.

[7] For assessment from apparently quite diverse parts of the political spectrum see, for instance, Steven Brill, "Is America any safer?," *The Atlantic*, September 2016, Alex Nowrasteh, "Post 9/11 America is Remarkably Safe," *Cato at Liberty* website, September 12, 2017, and Janet Napolitano, *How Safe Are We? Homeland Security since 9/11* (New York: Hachette Book Group, 2019). Interestingly, on the latter's analysis, the risks of dying in a terrorist attack are lower in the post 9/11 world than they were in the fourteen years prior to those attacks.

internet or posts on social media pose the country's greatest danger.[8] Such people operate independently of organized terrorist groups and can and do perpetrate mass attacks.[9] Many security experts also agree that the USA is ignoring important threats from domestic attackers. The terrorist landscape has changed dramatically over the last two decades to make the threat of lone wolves much more likely. Bin Laden imagined that he was an important historical figure who wished to be known for bringing about the spectacular. If he aimed to blow up ordinary targets such as malls and marketplaces, that would not be very impressive and would not set him apart from other terrorist organizations. Al-Qaeda positioned itself as an elite organization. By contrast, ISIL has a rather different conception of who can join, and it also encourages everyone to just do what they can. "It tells people, 'It's okay to lash out at people you hate – in our name. It's okay that you're a loser. You can still have an impact. You can be a hero.' It's elixir for someone sitting in the glow of their laptop in their parents' basement."[10]

One of the main ways in which the FBI attempts to guard against the threat of lone wolves, is searching through social media. However, there is much traffic to sift through and it is difficult to do a good job here. Furthermore, it is not clear all would-be killers use social media to communicate their attitudes or plans.[11] More recent homeland security programs include ones attempting to combat extremism – for instance, the Countering Violent Extremism program. This program aims to reach those so alienated or unstable that they are vulnerable to ISIL recruitment. This aligns with other initiatives, such as the Department of Homeland Security's campaign: "If you see something, say something." The office for community partnerships works with local leaders, particularly Muslim leaders, to encourage them to identify anyone, especially young adults or teenagers, in their communities who appear disaffected. In many cases, at least some people around perpetrators of terrorist attacks knew something was going on, but were either unsure of how to report this or felt reluctant to do so. Building sufficient willingness from community-members and

---

[8] Heather Timmons, "Trump's obsession with immigration is making the US more vulnerable to terrorism," *Quartz*, December 18, 2017; also, Peter Bergen, *United States of Jihad: Investigating America's Homegrown Terrorists* (New York: Crown Publishing Group, 2016).

[9] Timmons, "Trump's obsession with immigration is making the US more vulnerable to terrorism," 2.

[10] Brill, "Is America any safer?," 40.

[11] As one example, Omar Mateen, who killed forty-nine people in Orlando, did not seem to be in contact with anyone about his plans. Brill, "Is America any safer?," 44.

providing the right opportunities for such reports takes significant organization and care. One final important strategy worth mentioning is targeting ways to counter ISIL's online recruiting. Recruiting peer-to-peer messengers and creating "peer-to-peer anti-jihad social media campaigns" have been successful.[12]

2.2   Nuclear Threats and Dirty Bombs

The so-called dirty bomb is one of the most talked-up ominous terrorist threats. A dirty bomb consists of a conventional explosive combined with some radiological material. The latter is readily available as it is widely used for radiation treatments in hospitals and also commonly used in industrial facilities to irradiate food (a process which kills bacteria). It would be relatively easy to execute such an attack and its repercussions would be huge, given the likelihood of inducing widespread fear leading to overreaction. Even though only a few people would be killed in the initial explosion, the contaminated area would require massive resource expenditure. So, for example, an explosion at the National Gallery of Art in Washington would yield a contaminated area of around 40 blocks, including the Supreme Court, the Library of Congress, and the Capitol.[13] Those buildings might have to be abandoned for decades. But putting this in perspective, it might mean "an extra one in 10 000 people would die of cancer if people were not evacuated and if the area were not completely scrubbed. The decontamination process could take years and cost billions, because radioactive material adheres stubbornly to cement, which means that many roads, sidewalks, and buildings would have to be replaced."[14] Again, to put that in perspective, in a city of 500,000 there would probably be an extra 50 cancer deaths over several years.

As noted, the necessary radiological material is available in the USA in multiple places. Large amounts of radioactive material are improperly secured and even unguarded in the USA. In addition, there are no standard requirements on background checks for drivers and warehouse employees who handle this material regularly. It is also easy to import such material in cars or containers, as monitors cannot detect radiological material when it is wrapped in lead. Only about 3 percent of containers entering the USA are X-rayed.

---

[12] Brill, "Is America any safer?," 49.   [13] Ibid., 56.   [14] Ibid.

2.3   Cyberattacks

Successful cyberattacks have the potential to wreak great havoc.[15] A skillfully targeted attack on a chemical plant, electric grid, nuclear facility, or blood bank could create widespread panic and fear. As one prominent example, Ted Koppel argues that the USA is not prepared for a cyberattack on key infrastructure such as the electric grid.[16] As he notes "tens of millions of Americans could be left without power for weeks or even months – and, therefore, also without access to water, ATMs, the towers that transmit their cellphone messages, and other lifelines."[17] A skillfully focused cyberattack could cause large parts of a country to lose power. It would take months to get the necessary replacement parts and skilled repair teams in place for a full recovery, and neither power companies nor government have enough measures in place to deal with such events.

One of the notable features of cyberattacks is that they can be conducted from anywhere in the world. Perpetrators do not physically have to be anywhere near the scene of their target. The possibilities for creating mayhem through cyberattacks are massive.[18] Given that people do not actually have to travel to a territory to cause large-scale harm, in the case of cyberattacks the focus on demonizing migrants is quite out of kilter with the actual risks of harm.

3   Is Overreacting to the Threat of Terrorism a Further Danger?

Since 9/11, a perception of an inflated threat level has produced widespread anxiety and led to wasteful spending on ineffective policies.[19] Moreover, the overreaction has assisted terrorists in achieving their goals. In fact, as John Mueller shows, the overreaction to terrorism has caused substantial damage as measured in human lives, civil liberties, and economic harm. As Mueller observes, "international terrorism generally kills a

---

[15] Mike Allen, "Ten Biggest National Security threats facing U.S," *Axios AM*, available on the Fortuna's Corner website.

[16] Ted Koppel, *Lights Out: A Cyberattack, a Nation Unprepared, Surviving the Aftermath* (New York: Penguin Random House, 2015).

[17] Ibid., 53.

[18] Notably, cyberattacks have been implicated in undermining democracies in fundamental ways, as we have seen in recent years in the USA and UK, with the potential for more devastation quite real. See, for instance, Carole Cadwalladr, "Cambridge Analytica has gone. But what has it left in its wake?" *The Guardian*, May 6, 2018.

[19] John Mueller, *Overblown*.

few hundred people a year worldwide – not much more, usually, than the number who drown yearly in bathtubs in the United States."[20] But the overreaction to this relatively small risk kills many more. The fear of flying in the aftermath of 9/11 caused more deaths as people chose to drive rather than fly. While the events of 9/11 killed nearly 3,000 people, "more than 3000 Americans have died since 9/11 because, out of fear, they drove in cars rather than flew in airplanes, or because they were swept into wars made politically possible by terrorist events."[21] Osama bin Laden boasted that the 9/11 terrorist attacks "cost al-Qaeda $500 000, while the attack and its aftermath inflicted, he claims, a cost of more than $500 billion on the United States. Shortly after 9/11, he crowed, 'America is full of fear from its north to its south, from its west to its east. Thank God for that'."[22] Overplaying the dangers of terrorism plays nicely into the terrorists' hands, assisting their aims. A judicious response should focus rather on reducing damaging fears and overreactions, along with open-minded and careful consideration of effective policy options. A reasonable discussion would keep in view key points, such as the following.

First, as a general rule, terrorism does not actually do much damage. Second, not only are overreactions to terrorist threats costly, they confirm that terrorist ambitions have been realized. Third, focusing excessively on worst-case scenarios can be unwise and wasteful but also, and more importantly, because of the ways in which this distorts judgment, making the highly improbable seem more likely.[23] Fourth, given the more limited nature of the terrorism threat, sound policy might focus on the ability to respond well to terrorist attacks when they do occur, focusing on how to minimize their harmful effects. Fifth, we might be wise to treat terrorism as more of a criminal problem that requires a policing response rather than a military one. In particular, we should support international policing efforts aimed at prevention. Indeed, we would have obligations to do so in virtue of requirements to contribute to our human rights practice in appropriate ways.

We should not underestimate the powerful interests that have incentives to obstruct greater appreciation of these points (as we see in later sections). On John Mueller's account, members of the terrorism industry, which

---

[20] Ibid., 2.   [21] Ibid., 3.   [22] Ibid., 3.
[23] See Richard Heuer, *Psychology of Intelligence Analysis* (Washington DC: Center for the Study of Intelligence Analysis, 1999). See also John Mueller and Mark Stewart, *Chasing Ghosts: The Policing of Terrorism* (Oxford: Oxford University Press, 2015).

includes politicians, experts, and the media, "profit in one way or another by inflating the threat international terrorism is likely to present."[24] But despite these powerful opposing forces, we should seek to put terrorism in perspective, by emphasizing that the USA can handle almost any damage terrorism can inflict. (For instance, as a point of comparison, the USA absorbs about 40,000 traffic deaths per year.)[25]

We should seek to reduce fear and anxiety while also supporting international policing. Terrorism should be treated as more of a criminal activity. We should seek to reduce anxieties and fears around terrorism. But this is more difficult than one might think, "because fears, once embedded, are not all that susceptible to rational analysis and because the terrorism industry will likely continue assiduously to cultivate those fears."[26] As John Mueller astutely notes:

> Terrorism generally becomes a high-consequence phenomenon not because of its direct effects, but because it manages to scare people and, partly as a result, to inspire unwise policies. Most to be feared is not terrorism itself, but fear itself, and the central focus should be on dealing with the costly and often unnecessary fear and with the costly and often unwise overreaction terrorism so regularly inspires. As Benjamin Friedman aptly notes, 'One way to disarm terrorists is to convince regular Americans to stop worrying about them. That, of course, is much easier said than done.[27]

As Mueller also goes on to note, many perceived problems just disappear by themselves. So, there

> ... should be at least two cheers for complacency ... Complacency can, of course, charm one into a false sense of security. But on average, this may well be better than the alternative: a false sense of insecurity that can lead people to become too cautious to live, and can cause them to spend unwisely and to lash out foolishly and self-destructively at threats they have exaggerated – or even at ones that may not, in fact actually exist, like the one supposedly posed by domestic Japanese during World War II.[28]

---

[24] Mueller, *Overblown*, 6.
[25] The frequent rhetoric that suggests terrorism would do away with our way of life should be challenged as the nonsense that it is. The only way this could happen is if we allowed it to do so. As Edward R. Murrow said "No one can terrorize a whole nation, unless we are all his accomplices." CBS television broadcast, March 7, 1954.
[26] Mueller, *Overblown*, 8.　　[27] Ibid., 142.　　[28] Ibid., 143.

4   Making Good Decisions about Public Funding: Is a Sensible Conversation on Combating Terrorism Possible?

Steven Brill argues that, as a nation, the USA has not been able to adjust, politically and emotionally, so that it is able to make rational decisions concerning terrorism.[29] He notes that this is hardly a surprise in a highly divided democracy "where attention spans are short and civic engagement is low."[30] In such cases, there will be a tendency toward oversimplification in public discussion. Making sound decisions concerning how to spend public money best, requires paying attention to relevant evidence, even when this is hard and involves complex issues such as security matters. Relevant to deliberations are what measures are effective, what is a good investment compared with the frequency of other grave risks that kill more people, and so on. Drawing comparisons with other dangers from which we should be protected is entirely justified in such deliberations.

So far, a great deal of public money has not been well spent. According to Brill, between 2001 and 2016 the USA wasted about $100–$150 billion on homeland security programs or equipment that has not worked.[31] However, much more than that has been well spent on items such as equipment for port inspections, on protecting New York's subway tunnels, and holding emergency drills in Boston. Other security measures that are cost-effective include secondary cockpit barriers and armed pilot training. Insofar as establishing the TSA provided important reassurance to those too afraid to fly, this was also money well spent. As is now widely reported, according to a University of Michigan Transportation Research Institute study, in the three months following 9/11, there were approximately 1,018 more traffic fatalities than would have taken place, as people were too scared to fly and preferred to drive. Establishing the TSA, therefore, provided the necessary reassurance to change this more lethal pattern, which, if it had continued, would have resulted in about 300 deaths per month.[32]

Massive efforts to screen all communications are also likely to be wasteful, which some have characterized "as trying to find a needle in a haystack by adding more hay."[33] In addition, collecting huge surveillance banks of data is likely to create highly attractive targets for criminal activity.[34] There are also issues about whether such surveillance programs

---

[29] Steven Brill, "Is America any safer?", 3.   [30] Ibid., 3.   [31] Ibid., 25.   [32] Ibid., 35–36.
[33] Mueller, *Overblown*, 146.   [34] Ibid., 146.

make us marginally safer, and whether that small gain is worth sacrificing our personal liberties, privacy, and trust in public institutions. Responsible policy making should take all of this into account.[35]

As John Mueller argues, it is unlikely there will be another terrorist event on the scale of 9/11.[36] The attackers had the element of surprise on that day, and 9/11 is likely to be an outlier. If you consider that the costs of overreacting can be great, especially if they involve being dragged into costly overseas wars, the most cost-effective counterterrorism measure is avoiding overreaction.[37] There are smarter investments democracies can make than funneling resources into programs and technologies that do not work in some desperate attempt to solve a problem that cannot be entirely eliminated. One such example would be the $800 million a year spent on an air marshals program that stopped zero incidents and which would have been better invested in early-childhood education or replacing the lead pipes that exist in a significant portion of water systems in the USA. Either of these projects would have contributed more to citizen well-being.[38] In such conversations about evaluating the success of expenditure, relative to risk of harm, it is also entirely within scope to ask about whether allowing such easy access for everyone (including terrorists and those with severe mental health issues) to buy assault weapons should continue.

The reality is that terrorism is just something we have to live with, much like crime. There is no way to end all crime. You cannot protect a city against acts carried out by single individuals who have bombs in backpacks or who decide to use vehicles as weapons. However, you can do much to contain damage when it does occur. Investing in effective response programs when attacks happen, for instance through preparing well for when these occur, could also see significant gains, as was the case with the well planned and executed response to the Boston bombing in 2013. This is similar to our strategy of providing ambulances for dealing with inevitable car crashes or violent crimes, even though we aim to prevent these from happening. So, spending resources on recovery and mitigation (that is, reducing damage from attacks when they do occur) can be useful.[39]

In assessing value for money, it is worth bearing in mind that the USA can absorb just about any terrorist attack. That is not to say that

---

[35] The screening has also led to the pursuit of questionable methods to secure convictions. Over the last fifteen years or so, the FBI has been accused of regularly overstepping constitutional boundaries in efforts to discover plans that may be hatching, and even entrapping suspected terrorists into carrying out attacks. See, for instance, Peter Bergen, *United States of Jihad*.

[36] Mueller, *Overblown*.   [37] Ibid., 252.   [38] Brill, "Is America any safer?," 69.   [39] Ibid., 71.

expenditures on preventive and protective measures are not worthwhile. On the contrary, it is worth spending some funds on containing the development of nuclear weapons, and this will require a certain amount of international cooperation. Second, to minimize the damage terrorism can do, there should be efforts to reduce or limit the erratic and foolish fears it characteristically inspires, insofar as this is possible. Third, there is a significant role for leaders to play in responding effectively to terrorism. Risks need to be put in context rather than used to exacerbate fear and, more generally, "there should be an effort by politicians, bureaucrats, officials, and the media to inform the public reasonably and realistically about the terrorist context instead of playing into the hands of terrorists by effectively seeking to terrify the public."[40] The world is not actually a terribly dangerous place when you consider the incidence of violent deaths.[41] Most people – indeed, almost all – wish to live in peace and security.[42] We need leaders who can help us make sense of the problems, the real risks we face, and help citizens put risk and danger in a proper context. Terrorism in one form or another may be inevitable, but it is not necessarily a dire threat unless we treat it as such. Rather than ramping up fears and spreading alarmist, hate-filled views, we need leaders who can help put the threat of terrorism in perspective, and who can help us adjust psychologically to this reality. That politicians do not do this enough, but rather often play up the fears and seek to intensify them, invites questions about why they choose such strategies. This is worth exploring, as I do in the next section.

As noted already, the reality is that, just like crime, the threat of terror cannot be eliminated. As Stephen Brill remarks:

> In fact, despite our best efforts, terror is destined to become, yes, routine – a three- or four-times-a-year headline event, perhaps almost as routine in this country as people with mental-health problems buying a semiautomatic and going hunting at a school or movie theatre. But if, as seems to be the case, Americans have come to accept mass killings carried out by those who are mentally unstable as horrifying but not apocalyptic, why do they perceive an attack linked – even if just rhetorically by the perpetrator – to Islamist terrorism differently?"[43]

This is an important question worthy of analysis. White male perpetrators of mass shootings (e.g. in Las Vegas, Charleston, Aurora, and Newtown) are dismissed as instances of angry and disturbed people lashing out.

---

[40] Mueller, *Overblown*, 151.   [41] Ibid., 153.   [42] Ibid., 153.
[43] Brill, "Is America any safer?," 64.

But when the perpetrator is Muslim and seems to be influenced by terrorist ideologies (e.g., Fort Hood, Boston, San Bernardino, or Orlando), the fear is increased. Of course, Americans are far more likely to be victims of gun violence than terrorism, so this level of fear around Muslim perpetrators requires explanation. Consider also that violent attacks by Muslims have killed fewer people than white nationalists.

> Far right extremists have been attacking Americans for a long time – in total, from 1990 to 2016, rightwing extremists killed more than twice as many people in the US as Islamic extremists did (this excludes both the Oklahoma Bombing and the September 11 2001 attacks, which the DHS considers 'outliers events'). They also killed many more law enforcement officials in that time period, a DHS and University of Maryland report says. And these counts don't include mass shootings that don't seem to have any political motive.[44]

I explore some explanations for the enhanced anxiety around Muslim perpetrators of violent attacks in the next section. As I note, there are great difficulties in communicating risk accurately, but more importantly, I discuss how fear can be socially constructed to serve political ends. In Chapter 9, I cover some further issues that some argue relate to base-level ethnocentrism.

5   The Difficulties of Risk Communication, Irrational Fear, and the Social Construction of Danger

5.1   Communicating Risk Is Not Easy

Sadly, sometimes accurately informing people about risks can make them more frightened.[45] When people's emotions are intensely engaged, people attend to the bad outcome itself and are inattentive to the fact that its occurrence is unlikely. Even communication that aims to assure people that risks of danger are tiny, can cause anxiety.[46] So, it is difficult to deal with people's often irrational fears about remote dangers. And it is difficult to alter strongly held beliefs. Sometimes the best way to ease anxiety in emotionally charged situations is to change people's focus. In fact,

---

[44] Heather Timmons, "Trump's obsession with immigration is making the US more vulnerable to terrorism," *Quartz*, December 18, 2017, 3.
[45] Mueller, *Overblown*, 155. For excellent work on these topics, see Cass Sunstein, "Terrorism and Probability Neglect," *Journal of Risk and Uncertainty*, 26 (2/3) (2003): 121–136.
[46] Sunstein, "Terrorism and Probability Neglect."

sometimes the best available way of reducing fear of very low-probability risks is to change the subject.[47]

It is also worth noting that the end-goal of the war on terror is often said to be something like a return to ordinary life, as conveyed in Donald Rumsfeld remarks: "Our victory will come with Americans living their lives day by day, going to work, raising their children and building their dreams as they always have – a free and great people."[48] This mission can easily be accomplished by just getting on with our lives, here and now. So that seems to be an entirely achievable goal, which leaders can help make a reality by encouraging people to just live their lives. It is also a cost-effective way of lowering the anxiety level. The fact that leaders do not often pursue this option deserves attention and brings us to the issue of why fear is useful.

5.2   The Usefulness of Fear

Danger is very often manufactured. H. L. Mencken once remarked, "The whole aim of practical politics is to keep the populace alarmed (and hence clamorous to be led to safety) by menacing it with an endless series of hobgoblins, all of them imaginary."[49] While all of them may not be imaginary, quite a few are exaggerated. Hyping events to alarming levels can often get people's attention. People are also more alarmed by dramatic fatalities. But there is considerable advantage in exacerbating a fearful environment, since "a fearful atmosphere inspires politicians to outbid each other to show their purity (and to gain votes), a process that becomes self-reinforcing as, to justify their wasteful and ill-considered policies and expenditures, they find it expedient to stoke the fears that set the policies in motion in the first place."[50] So politicians and opinion elites have been quite willing to exacerbate fear and have seen considerable advantage in doing so. Fear seems to sell well.

Where does people's fear of terrorism come from? On some accounts, the fears around terrorism are bottom up.[51] On this account, although opinion elites are quite willing to cultivate fears for their own advantage, they did not create the fears initially.[52] But I am skeptical of such analyses. People are selective about what to be afraid of, suggesting that fear and

---

[47] Ibid. and Mueller, *Overblown*, 156.
[48] Donald Rumsfeld, "A new kind of war," *New York Times*, September 27, 2001.
[49] Mencken, H. L., *In Defense of Women* (London: J. Cape, 1929).   [50] Mueller, *Overblown*, 150.
[51] John Mueller and Mark Stewart, *Chasing Ghosts*, 250.   [52] Ibid., 250.

perceptions of risk are more socially constructed than we might like to think. And various societies seem to construct fear differently. Americans are apparently concerned about nuclear power but are not afraid of genetically modified food, whereas the reverse is true of French. Germans worry about both.[53] As what we are afraid of varies considerably by country, even if there is a base-level of fear that is widespread, the variation suggests it can be altered by social factors.

6   Why Are People So Afraid?

Why are people so afraid of migrants spreading terrorism and posing massive enhanced security risks in the USA? This is a relevant case study because, as I noted earlier, it is the USA that currently advocates for highly anti-immigrant policies, and other states have followed their lead. Before we focus particularly on explaining these issues, it is worth drawing attention to some general trends that are operating in the background. As Khalid Koser observes:

> Large and rising numbers of immigrants have been entering advanced industrial societies at the same time that many of these societies are faced with immense structural changes. These include economic, demographic and technological changes that are transforming society, the labor market, and community. Among their outcomes have been painful changes in social safety nets, despite growing needs, burgeoning physical infrastructure demands, and brewing social and cultural crises. The wider context is of global economic uncertainties and a heightened sense of insecurity.
>
> Immigration and immigrants provide a tangible, visible, and convenient explanation for the malaises of modern society.[54]

So, there is a general trend toward connecting immigrants with a decline in life prospects that many face. Fear and resentment toward migrants can seem like a rational response to perceived competition and scarcity brought by foreigners. No doubt each country has its own particular set of factors in play concerning why fear levels are high; however, we can discern important patterns, drawing again on the immense amount of data we get from the USA. So, why are people so afraid in the USA? In particular, how does immigration get connected to being the massive security threat it is taken to be in the popular imagination? And what is the link to terrorism?

---

[53] John Mueller argues such points very nicely in multiple places, such as John Mueller and Mark Stewart, *Chasing Ghosts.*
[54] Khalid Koser, *International Migration*, 90.

6.1   One Story

Part of the complex explanation involves an examination of changing demographics, which funnels into a cultural story. Another part of the story involves reduced economic opportunity, brought about by globalization, outsourcing, automation, and changing market demands. Arguably, the economic explanation has been dominant. But less attention has been paid to explanations concerning status anxiety, so we start with these.[55] As Amy Chua observes:

> ... the United States today is starting to display destructive political dynamics much more typically associated with developing countries: ethno-nationalist movements, the erosion of trust in our institutions and electoral outcomes, and above all, the transformation of democracy into an engine of zero-sum political tribalism. Why? In part, it is because of the massive demographic transformation that we have been seeing, with whites on the verge of losing their majority status for the first time in US history. For basically 200 years, whites were just comfortably dominant in every way – economically, politically, culturally. So, it felt like we had no tribalism and that democracy always worked because there was a very dominant tribe.[56]

However, today every group feels threatened. Indeed, 67 percent of working class whites believe that whites are more discriminated against than minorities.[57] Groups become more tribal – more insular and defensive – when they feel threatened. An environment in which groups feel threatened triggers a rise in identity politics.

Another relevant part of the story is the division between working class, rural, Southern whites, and those who are largely concentrated in cities, who are typically more educated, tolerant, have more cosmopolitan values, and are used to frequent contact with immigrants. There is a perception

---

[55] For excellent accounts and evidence for these claims see, for instance, Niraj Choksi, "Trump voters driven by fear of losing status, not economic anxiety, study finds," *New York Times*, April 24, 2018; Arlie Hochschild, *Strangers in Their Own Land*; Robert Jones, Daniel Cox, and Rachel Lienesch, "Beyond Economic: Fears of Cultural Displacement Pushed the White Working Class to Trump," *Public Religion Research Institute/The Atlantic Report*. PRRI. 2017; Diana Mutz, "Status Threat, Not Economic Hardship, Explains the 2016 Presidential Vote." *PNAS*, 115 (18) (May 8, 2018): E4330–E4339.

[56] Amy Chua, invited talk at the Carnegie Centre on "Political Tribes: Group Instinct and the Fate of Nations," available from the Carnegie Centre website, transcript, 9. For fuller treatment of the views, see Amy Chua, *Political Tribes: Group Instinct and the Fate of Nations* (London: Bloomsbury, 2018).

[57] Chua, "Political Tribes," 9.

among Southern whites that elites, who embrace cosmopolitan values, are minority and immigrant friendly and are more concerned with the fate of the poor in distant lands than their compatriots.[58] And so, it is now as if the urban and coastal whites are practically like a different ethnic group from the working class, rural, Southern whites.

In the United States, wealth is highly concentrated on the east and west coasts – in places like Silicon Valley, Hollywood, Wall Street, and Washington. Those in the middle of the country view coastal elites as having a pro-minority stance and caring more about poor people in foreign countries than about other Americans. This sort of common dynamic in developing countries can easily give rise to populist movements and demagogues. It is common in developing countries for leaders to play up similar dynamics and the threat posed by arrogant, minority elites who hold power. So, this is why we see the prevalence of populist movements in which demagogues call on their people to "take back their country."

However, in seeking explanations for this fear, we have to take account of both cultural and economic factors. The economic component should not be underestimated. Many of those from working class and rural environments have this sense of regressing economically. Contributing to this feeling is that in the past someone from a working-class family could go on to achieve great success with a public education; the American Dream was a realistic aspiration. But this is no longer easily achievable. One reason concerns the enormous expense involved in gaining an education at top universities. And without such advantages, many avenues for upward mobility are no longer available. There has been a reduction in genuine opportunities for advancement.

How might concern about immigration fit into all of this? Immigration is an easy target, because it taps into the fear that the country is being overtaken by others who are holding one back. These others include immigrants, but also fellow citizens who would adopt pro-immigrant policies. And it invokes the fantasy of a time when things were perceived as different, and different because arrangements were more favorable to those identified as part of the group now perceived as suffering disadvantage.

And how does this all link to terrorism and security? Fears for your physical security are rational ones to have, especially when they present as grave harm. The more immigration can be linked with grave threats, the more rational the fear may seem to become. The constant cultural,

---

[58] Ibid.

political, media, and social chatter about how grave the risk of terrorism and security from migration is, the more people tend to assume it is common knowledge. But all that chatter comes from people choosing to talk about these issues, and opinion elites and members of the terrorism industry (including politicians) have a specific agenda they wish to promote. We have already seen that there is considerable advantage in doing so. We explore these and related issues further in the next section.

6.2   Another Story: The Social Construction of Fear Continued

Another dynamic worthy of comment is how the idea of a nation is frequently constructed. State identity is often secured through a "representation of danger."[59] As I discuss in this section, ideas about "otherness," difference, and danger play an important role.[60]

The imagined community plays a key role in our vision of what the nation is and should be.[61] The imagined community combines our hopes and fears. It is our hope to create resilient communities that can protect us from what we perceive as fearful. The idea of danger plays an important role in constructing our imagined communities. Danger is not some objective condition but, rather, it is relative to what we perceive as a threat. And that perception is subject to social manipulation.[62] In such a context, immigrants can easily be cast as a danger to be resisted. A concise version of one such argument might go like this.

(1)   Nations are imagined communities.
(2)   Ideas about danger, fear and otherness all play a role in creating national and state identity.
(3)   If elections are about voting for candidates that can understand and reflect one's hopes and fears, then reflecting a sense of danger around widely shared fears is a good strategy. If some groups (such as white Southerners) fear otherness, presenting a vision in which otherness will be blocked makes good sense.

---

[59] David Campbell, *Writing Security: United States Foreign Policy and the Politics of Identity* (Minneapolis, MN: University of Minnesota Press, 1998).
[60] Campbell, *Writing Security*.
[61] Benedict Anderson first came up with this expression in *Imagined Communities: Reflections on the Origin and Spread of Nationalism* (London: Verso, 1991).
[62] Campbell, *Writing Security*.

(4) Citizens will vote for candidates that can make policy around their hopes and fears (promoting their hoped-for states of affairs and reducing those which they fear).

(5) Domestic and foreign policy help to consolidate identity as a nation and define the parameters of otherness.

(6) Advertising that one will introduce policy that will reflect hopes and fears will attract voters, so focusing on how one will block otherness will win votes.

(7) Citizens will be especially drawn to those candidates who not only seem to understand voters and what they care about well, but also those candidates who can make their hopes and fears seem sensible and important.

(8) Playing up the threats – especially security threats – that others present will make hopes and fears seem quite sensible, and will serve to validate voters' views. Voters who feel validated will be motivated to support candidates who confirm and reinforce their worldviews.

It is important to note that robust data to substantiate the claims about increased security threats from increased migration, as some general rule or as a generalization that applies within the USA, cannot be found.[63] This is probably one reason why those who press this mode of thinking appeal so often to anecdotes about terrible crimes in which victims are citizens and perpetrators are illegal migrants. However, looking at large sets of data, these patterns do not exist.[64] In fact, a 2017 US study found that "immigrants are less likely to commit crimes or be incarcerated than the US born population" and that "the 2014 incarceration rate for immigrants – both authorized and unauthorized – ages 18 to 54 was considerably lower than that of the US born population."[65]

While immigrants have often been cast as a danger to be feared and resisted, it is possible to tell an alternative story in which immigrants do not constitute a danger but rather are a key part of the conditions for many to enjoy good opportunities, creating the strong nation as it exists today. For instance, immigrants can bring valuable cultural and economic revitalization to neighborhoods badly in need of new members and renewal.

---

[63] Anna Flagg, "The myth of the criminal immigrant," *New York Times*, March 30, 2018.

[64] Ibid.; also Graham Ousey and Charis Kubrin, "Immigration and Crime: Assessing a Contentious Issue," *Annual Review of Criminology* 1 (2018): 63–84.

[65] Centre for American Progress and Michael Nicholson, "Some Facts on Immigration Today: 2017 Edition from the Center for American Progress." Available at: www.americanprogress.org/issues/immigration/reports/2017/04/20/430736/facts-immigration-today-2017-edition, 5

Much evidence supports the economic thesis that immigrants can, under the right conditions, assist in solving economic problems rather than presenting a drain on the economy.[66] Indeed, the USA would not be the country it is today without immigration. This is obviously true, historically, but underappreciated are the great positive contributions immigrants make that continue to affect its present character. Immigrants have made, and continue to make, many valuable contributions to the USA, including helping to make it the largest economy in the world, and supporting the economy's growth and dynamism.[67] Immigrants, migrants, and refugees participate in the economy in various roles, such as job creators, entrepreneurs, taxpayers, and consumers, adding trillions of dollars to the US GDP. They have a vital role in contributing to US society, especially in the face of changing demographics such as an aging population that will challenge the existing social safety nets. Immigrants added an estimated $2 trillion (of the $18.62 total) to the US GDP in 2016.[68] As at 2010, "more than 40 percent of Fortune 500 companies were founded by immigrants and their children. ... These companies employ more than 10 million people worldwide."[69] The net fiscal impact of immigration over the long run is very positive.[70] Immigrants rely less on public benefits and social services than comparable US born households.[71]

Indeed, there are many myths about migrants that should be corrected. One such is that migrants pose threats in competition for jobs. But this is not necessarily true. In fact, in many cases migrants tend to create more job opportunities than if they were not permitted to migrate.[72] It all depends on who is migrating, where they are migrating to, and the policies that operate in particular environments. For instance, in many cases, immigrants tend to complement, rather than compete with, US born American workers, thereby enhancing productivity. Research indicates that US and foreign-born workers often have different skill sets and work in different kinds of industries, "even when they have similar educational backgrounds."[73] The right policies can ensure mutually beneficial results. So, much of the hype around competition for jobs is overplayed. In addition, the effects on wages are small, but immigrants tend to have a

---

[66] See, for instance, Michael Clemens, Cindy Huang, Jimmy Graham, Kate Hough, "Migration Is What You Make It," May 28, CGD note.

[67] Centre for American Progress and Michael Nicholson, "Some Facts on Immigration Today."

[68] Ibid., 10.   [69] Ibid.   [70] Ibid.   [71] Ibid.

[72] See, for instance, Michael Clemens, Cindy Huang, Jimmy Graham, Kate Hough, "Migration Is What You Make It."

[73] Ibid., 10.

positive effect on the wages of US born individuals over the long run.[74] Furthermore, over the next 20 years as so-called Baby Boomers retire, immigrants will play a central role in refreshing the aging workforce. In addition, it is notable that refugees start businesses at the same rate as US born citizens. And refugee entrepreneurship has enhanced the economic growth and development of many communities nationwide – notably, rust belt cities such as Dayton and Columbus, Ohio.[75]

The right kind of leader might emphasize such facts and contributions. She might also draw attention to the considerable role immigration has played in revitalizing communities, sustaining prosperity, and helping to constitute important parts of people's current identities. And we have seen many local leaders, especially mayors, successfully deploying such strategies and winning elections as champions of an inclusive immigrant ethos, even in the face of hostility and divisiveness.[76]

7   Synthesizing Discussion: Core Questions for Sensible Policy on Terrorism and Its Relation to Migration

For sensible policy concerning terrorism, a number of questions should be discussed, such as the following:

(1)   What are the risks of terrorism? What should our tolerance for risk, including terrorism risk, be?[77]

(2)   What strategies are effective at combating terrorism? Which strategies are counter-productive?

---

[74] Ibid.   [75] Ibid., 25.

[76] For some important cases see the *Cities of Migration* website. For one good resource see, for instance, *Practice to Policy: Lessons from Local Leadership on Immigrant Integration* (Toronto: The Maytree Foundation, 2012), available at: http://citiesofmigration.ca/

[77] What should our tolerance for risk of terrorism be? One answer comes from analyzing the statements from the DHS, as John Mueller does. In the wake of concerns that body scanners using X-ray technology cause cancer, the "DHS official in charge, John Pistole, essentially said that, although the cancer risk was not zero, it was acceptable. A set of studies, he pointed out, 'have all come back to say that the exposure is very, very minimal' and 'well, well within all the safety standards that have been set' . . . on the basis of a 2012 review of scanner safety, that cancer risk per scan is about 1 in 60 million. As it happens, the chance that an individual airline passenger will be killed by terrorists on an individual flight is much lower – 1 in 90 million. Therefore, ... the risk of being killed by a terrorist on an airliner is already fully acceptable by the standards applied to the cancer risk from body scanners using X-ray technology. But no official has drawn that comparison." John Mueller, *Are We Safe Enough? Measuring and Assessing Aviation Security* (Amsterdam, Netherlands: Elsevier, 2018), 254.

(3)   If the probabilities of terrorist attack are already very low, is further resource expenditure warranted?

(4)   Should we spend resources on policies that are reassuring but do not actually change risks?

(5)   How should we weigh up terrorism risks against other expenditures we could make that protect us against greater risks or which help us achieve other goals a just community seeks to achieve?

(6)   How can leaders help put risks including risks concerning terrorism and migration in context for citizens and help reduce unnecessary fear?

(7)   If elevated risks of terrorism concerning migration emerge, what kinds of measures are warranted? Should changes be made to current application processes? Or are the current processes sufficiently robust given the risk level that has emerged?

In beginning to answer some of these questions, we might emphasize a few facts, such as that terrorism today overwhelmingly happens in civil war situations as an instrument of warfare. Furthermore, those arrested on terrorism charges, especially in the USA, are mostly described as "incompetent, ineffective, unintelligent, idiotic, ignorant, inadequate, disorganized, misguided, muddled, amateurish, dopey, unrealistic, moronic, irrational, foolish and gullible."[78] Screening processes for migrants are already very robust and the terrorism danger presented by migrants is tiny.[79] In addition, the opportunity costs of focusing excessively on terrorism are routinely overlooked. Spending resources in one way often precludes spending them in another, where we could save more lives more effectively and at lower cost. For instance, diverting only *some* of the billions of dollars spent on airport security could save many more lives at very low cost if spent on expanded immunization programs, bicycle helmets, smoke alarms, tornado shelters, and flood protection systems, or a public health system (for that matter), to name just a few.[80] Leaders might help with explaining all of this better than they currently do.

We need to bear in mind that anyone who works in the terrorism security industry has a disincentive to promote such discussion, as that would inevitably entail budget cuts. And politicians have an incentive to maintain a fearful environment. We have seen that even if citizens have irrational fears, politicians can succeed if they reflect the rationality of

---

[78] John Mueller, *Are We Safe Enough?* , 200.
[79] Centre for American Progress and Michael Nicholson, "Some Facts on Immigration Today," 10.
[80] See, for instance, Brill, "Is America any safer?"

being afraid rather than challenging irrational fears. But this is a fool's strategy if the politician really does care about improving security. Obsessing about the terrorism dangers immigrants bring can increase security threats rather than make a country safer, as US security experts warn.[81] Anti-Islamic policies and Muslim travel bans are also viewed as provocations that leads to increased anti-US sentiment, reduced willingness to cooperate from the very groups essential to preventing violence, thereby generally making the fight against terrorism more challenging.[82] In fact, obsessing about terrorism perpetrated by Muslims makes us less safe. Many of the policies pursued during the Trump Presidency have been counter-productive. Importantly, policies that restrict Muslim immigration strengthen anti-Western sentiment, which feeds into propaganda that extremists can use to recruit new members. Hardline policies toward Muslims make it easier to argue that the West is involved in a war against Islam. In such contexts, moderate Muslims can lean toward sympathizing with more extreme groups. In addition, the Trump administration's policies, statements, and continuous attacks on many ethnic groups including Mexicans, Muslims, Asians, and African Americans have been emboldening US white nationalists fueling increased hate crimes, as I discussed in Chapter 5.

It is also worth noting that immigrant screening is already quite robust. And refugees in particular undergo extensive vetting. Applicants undergo comprehensive security checks. First, they are screened by the UNHCR, then resettlement support operated by the US Department of State, which does extensive biometric, biographical, and security checks. Another round of screening and security checks occurs before resettlement can proceed. The layers of screening around refugees in recent years have been highly robust.

8 Conclusions

Screening migrants who wish to enter a particular state is quite permissible; however, when the process is already very comprehensive, and much greater threats are routinely tolerated, further large amounts of resources

---

[81] Timmons, "Trump's obsession with immigration is making the US more vulnerable to terrorism," *Quartz*, December 18, 2017.
[82] M. A. Hersh, "Terrorism, Human Rights and Ethics: A Modelling Approach," *Journal of Socialomics*, 5 (2) (2016): 148; Paul Hoffman, "Human Rights and Terrorism," *Human Rights Quarterly*, 26 (4) (2004): 932–955; and James Walsh and James Piazza, "Why Respecting Physical Integrity Rights Reduces Terrorism," *Comparative Political Studies*, 43 (5) (2010): 551–577.

should not be devoted to this task. We should be more clear-eyed in our approach to risk and policies aimed at reducing risks. We should aspire to make well-informed decisions about which risks are acceptable and how effectively to address those we find unacceptable. While we might expect that many will have different views about how to weigh these risks, how to prioritize them, and which policies to adopt in light of them, we also need to be aware of opportunity costs: what we are foregoing by attending to one risk and ignoring another. How to have a genuine conversation about all of this is difficult in new and mature democracies. But in aiming at such a conversation, we should be mindful of well-known dangers. For instance, we must avoid the obvious trap that has been used since the beginning of politics, of scapegoating one group as a way to deflect attention from core issues. We have seen that there are many obstacles to having a more informed conversation, such as politicians' interests in perpetuating a fearful environment and people's irrational fears. Politicians know that fear can make voters pay attention more, so ramping these up helps people pay attention to the politicians who talk about them, and can be helpful to their election prospects.

In trying to understand why people are so afraid, we see that there are cultural and economic components.[83] Changing demographics, the sense of being left behind and no longer having genuine opportunities for upward mobility or a secure middle class life, are some of the drivers of fear and a sense of resentment directed at immigrants. However, a more accurate assessment of immigrants' contributions reveals that they have helped create, and can continue to create, the large, dynamic, strong economy that has made the US economy the largest in the world, and which can be the very engine of prosperity for many, if properly managed and coupled with policies that seek to distribute gains widely. Cultural affiliation and identity can easily obscure such views. We should not underestimate how resilient are the connections between identity and group affiliations. And we need to be aware that identity is often created and strengthened in contrast to a sense of "the dangerous other." Immigrants can fill this placeholder very easily, so it is not difficult to understand how an anti-immigrant ethos can gain a foothold. And we should be wary of politicians' attempts to link migration with enhanced security and terrorism threats, understanding the useful role they play in sanitizing fears to make them seem like good common sense.

---

[83] There is allegedly also a base level of ethnocentrism. We discuss this issue further in Chapter 9.

In addition, while some of the ethnocentric dynamics concerning migrants triggering perceived threat levels may exist, these tendencies can be, and have been, managed in better and worse ways. We can learn more about better ways to manage these. We also know that these dynamics have been successfully managed through innovative programs and positive messaging. For instance, all nations contain citizens who migrated from some other place but whose credentials as a citizen are now beyond reproach. Who we consider to be part of our community is a socially constructed and changeable aspect of our lives. We should challenge those who suggest migrants are necessarily a threat to justice within communities. Indeed, several kinds of organizations aim to create inclusive communities and their work deserves more prominence. I discuss such issues in Chapter 9.

As I have been discussing, political leaders have important responsibilities here, such as to assist in dissipating fears about migrants reducing security, to help put risks in context, to help facilitate sensible conversations about judicious public expenditure, and generally to help maintain, or bring about, just communities. As I have been stressing, wasteful spending in one area relative to effectiveness at addressing the particular problem is a justice-relevant consideration. Excessive expenditure on immigration policies – through costly border walls, the employment of a very large number of immigration enforcement officials, or unnecessary and invasive screening, especially when such actions do not reduce the risks they target – constitutes important injustice. When those resources could be more effectively deployed on other projects, such as in assisting those who currently have inadequate protection for core human rights, such expenditure is unjust.

CHAPTER 9

Migration in a Legitimate State System
Problems, Progress, and Prospects

1   Introduction

How open should states be to migrants? A core issue in normative debates about migration concerns the right of self-determining states to be able to control their borders. It is widely held that self-determining states have legitimate authority to control admissions and to exclude people from their territory.[1] By contrast, an increasingly commonly held contrary view is that borders should generally be open.[2] And there is a vigorous debate between these two sides.[3]

Enormous numbers of people seem to want to move across borders, especially to middle- and high-income countries. Are such states obliged to take in all or most of these applicants? Would failure to do so constitute important violations of their human rights? These are important questions. My answers to them will shed light on the debate between proponents of open borders and their critics, by offering a human rights oriented middle ground.

Another important central set of issues in migration justice debates concerns responsibilities to reduce migration injustices. So, for instance, what obligations do states have to cooperate in global endeavors aimed at migration justice? What obligations do citizens have to support fair

---

[1] David Miller, Michael Walzer, and Christopher Wellman have offered articulate defenses of this view. See, for instance, David Miller, *Strangers in Our Midst*; Michael Walzer, *Spheres of Justice* (New York: Basic Books, 1983); and Christopher Wellman and Phillip Cole, *Debating the Ethics of Immigration* .

[2] Joseph Carens, *Ethics of Immigration* (New York: Oxford University Press, 2013); Phillip Cole, *Philosophies of Exclusion: Liberal Political Theory and Immigration* (Edinburgh: Edinburgh University Press, 2000); Christopher Wellman and Phillip Cole, *Debating the Ethics of Immigration*; Kieran Oberman, "Immigration as a Human Right" in Sara Fine and Lea Ypi (eds.), *Migration in Political Theory: The Ethics of Movement and Membership* (Oxford: Oxford University Press, 2016), 32–56.

[3] For an excellent example, see Christopher Wellman and Phillip Cole, *Debating the Ethics of Immigration*.

treatment for migrants? Do citizens have obligations to resist unjust immigration laws perpetrated by the state in which those citizens reside?

In this chapter, I explore these important sets of questions. As we see, there are important international initiatives that can greatly assist in reducing migration injustice, so these questions about obligations to cooperate with global endeavors are far from academic. In Section 2 I argue that states have obligations to support institutions that can exercise effective oversight and regulate migration matters in ways that align with a robust human rights practice. And so, states have obligations to support credible arrangements capable of supporting justice for migrants. In Section 3 I cover some anticipated common objections to my project. These would include concerns that states cannot be expected to support such arrangements, especially given widely held perceptions that increased migration has been problematic for justice at the state level, and that if authority to enforce migration policy is not held at the state level, this would undermine state self-determination. Others might also worry that given apparent recent setbacks to respect for human rights, a regime based on a robust human rights practice is doomed to become an anachronistic throwback to a former rules-based order that no longer exists (if, indeed, it ever did). In order to rebut such objections, in Section 4 I introduce key elements from the Global Compact for Safe, Orderly and Regular Migration, which 85 percent of states adopted in December 2018. This extraordinary global cooperative framework deserves attention because of its sensitivity to many of the issues noted as objections, and its ability to forge a path forward that can make real progress in the right direction.

While the Compact makes for an impressive start at realizing migration justice, in one important area I believe it fails to offer sufficient progressive guidance, and that is on the issue of opening borders, how open states should be to increased migration. As I argue in Section 5, a legitimate state system must include rights to a fair process for determining migrants' rights, especially concerning rights to admission and to remain in particular states. This will generally entail a more open and transparent process for admission, and is expected to lead to an opening of borders, but with important constraints. In Section 5 I argue that our human rights practice is committed to the fair process rights for which I argue; a legitimate state system must include them as core features of its legitimacy. I show why citizens' many migration-related biased beliefs are problematic for migration justice and why we have obligations to correct them. I then discuss further aspects of the fair process contours, why justifications for decisions on the determinations of those rights must be human rights compliant, and what that entails. I offer an example of an alleged justification that fails the test of being human rights compliant and of one that passes.

Section 6 shows how my account can allow appropriate scope for self-determination, while also allowing proper authority for migration matters to rest in multiple places. As we see, some of the authority of the Global Compact derives from our state-level commitment to action: states have committed to act in certain ways and agreed to follow up, review, and hold each other to account. It is these state-level commitments that are an important source of the authority. We see how authority for delivering on the agreement lies in the Compact's consensual nature, along with commitments to joint implementation, follow-up, review, and accounting processes.

As we try to understand the proper place for self-determination, it is important also to recall some of the key arguments made in earlier chapters. We are reminded about the necessary conditions for states to have robust rights to self-determination. As we see, far from joining the Compact constituting an interference with self-determination, it is a necessary condition for states to have such rights at all.

Section 7 covers citizens' obligations to support institutions that will assist with sustaining migration justice. There are some important obligations for citizens at the local level. Newcomers settle in particular communities, and it is here that we have special obligations to make them feel welcome, and where tensions between the long-settled and newly settled should be well managed. Citizens have important obligations to assist in this adjustment process and to help build connections between newer immigrants and older residents, helping to reshape the boundaries of "us" and "them" in partnering to create inclusive communities.

In Section 8 I address the objections noted in Section 3, drawing on arguments made throughout the book, especially those from this chapter. We see how compelling rebuttals are available to each, why institutions that can support migration justice are available and why encouraging trends toward implementing these are emerging. Section 9 concludes, emphasizing the direction we must take to make our state system legitimate and capable of supporting justice for people on the move.

2   State Responsibilities to Support Fair Arrangements for Migrants

What are states' responsibilities to bring into being a legitimate state system in which migrants can be justly treated? As I argued in Chapter 3, states have obligations to contribute to a legitimate state system. So, they have a range of obligations in connection with that general requirement. A brief reminder of those arguments may be welcome and this follows.

Recall that Chapter 3 sought a justification for states' claims to have rights to self-determination that entail the right to control admission to their territory. In seeking such a justification, we discovered that rights to self-determination within the context of a state system generate many responsibilities. As I argued, in order for states to exercise power defensibly, they must adequately fulfill their human rights commitments, both within the state and beyond. Importantly then, states have obligations to cooperate in a host of transborder activities, programs, agreements, institution, (and so on) that aim to secure arrangements capable of effective human rights protection. These are some of the important contribution requirements that legitimate states must meet. Performance on these contributions affects both the issue of whether we have a legitimate state system and a particular state's rightful claim to self-determination. Because contribution to the legitimacy of the state system is an especially underappreciated area that is relevant to state legitimacy, I believe it deserves particular emphasis. The right of a state to self-determination is conditional on a state's contributing to conditions necessary for supporting self-determining, just communities. And the content of these responsibilities derives from activities (and so forth) that would align with a robust human rights practice.

So, because of these important arguments to meet legitimacy requirements, states have a number of important general responsibilities to promote arrangements capable of respecting, protecting, and fulfilling human rights. And they will have particular responsibilities to support institutions, initiatives, and so forth that can secure everyone's rights including migrants'. So, states have responsibilities to support or improve arrangements that can exercise oversight in migration matters in ways that align with a robust human rights practice, capable of supporting justice for people on the move. There is no need to create new institutions for these purposes. The important functions I identify can be performed through existing institutions, such as the United Nations (UN) and the International Organization for Migration (IOM). And there are some constructive moves in the right direction. I highlight some of these when we discuss the global initiatives that could form part of an important constellation of arrangements capable of supporting migration justice. The human rights aligned robust migration institutions that I believe are necessary will have a number of key important functions. They would coordinate, promote, oversee, and help enforce robust human rights practice in relation to migration. In Section 4 I show what this involves.

One very important framework that has been adopted by 85 percent of states deserves extended treatment in considering our prospects for implementing the architecture necessary for migration justice, and that is the Compact on Migration, introduced briefly in Chapter 7. I cover this in Section 4 as one important example of the arrangements that can perform the necessary tasks. First, we must consider some key objections to the very idea of institutions with global reach that can play a legitimate role in migration matters.

3   Some Key Objections

In this section I focus on five often-raised objections that are supposed to provide important challenges to any project that argues for institutional arrangements aimed at reducing migration injustice that have global scope and authority. These are summarized next.

Objection 1: Ordinary citizens will not support the kinds of pro-migrant regimes that I claim are necessary for legitimate states existing within a legitimate state system. Real people will not elect (and cannot be expected to elect) office holders who will support a legitimate state system, if that entails a commitment to the robust human rights practice envisioned.

Objection 2: Over the last few decades, immigration has been bad for justice at the state level. For instance, it is claimed that the influx of migrants has resulted in increased civic tensions, resentments, and polarization, along with decreased willingness to cooperate and sustain the welfare state, all with devastating consequences for democracy.[4] According to this line of thinking, there is some tension between promoting justice at the state and global levels. And since states are the primary units for implementing justice in our world today, policies that are damaging to state-level justice must be rejected.

Objection 3: There would be no scope for self-determination under the so-called legitimate state system proposed. Global actors far away from particular states would be telling states what to do. This would completely undermine states' rights to determine the kinds of communities in which

---

[4] For some of these sorts of concerns see Will Kymlicka, "Solidarity in Diverse Societies: Beyond Neoliberal Multiculturalism and Welfare Chauvinism," *Comparative Migration Studies*, 3 (17) (2015): 1–19.

they wish to live and the kinds of values their communities wish to give expression to in their societies.

Objection 4: No organization would have proper authority to enforce any measures allegedly required by the account of a legitimate state system I present. Given this lack of enforcement authority, states will generally not comply with the requirements purportedly necessary for a legitimate state system.

Objection 5: An account that gives a prominent place to human rights practice cannot be relied on to deliver migration justice. Respect for human rights has recently deteriorated considerably. Human rights discourse will not continue to motivate people well into the future, whatever successes it has had in the past.

These objections are related. For instance, the perception that increased migration has been bad for state-level justice might be the reason why some are skeptical that ordinary people will elect politicians who are inclined to support institutional regimes that would reduce migration-related injustice. Has migration been bad for justice in communities? The thought is that increased migration or immigrant-friendly policies have been responsible for phenomena such as decreased cohesion and solidarity among citizens, a decrease in support for the welfare state, a general swing toward right wing populism, Brexit, and Trumpism. We examine this line of argument in Section 8.

Objections 3 and 4 raise issues about preserving space for self-determination, and who should have the proper authority in matters that affect national sovereignty. We can also see how the concern that immigration has been bad for local justice might feed into a desire for stronger self-determination and a rejection of arrangements that seem to remove authority away from national communities. This chain of reasoning was prevalent among those supporting the campaign for Britain to leave the European Union in 2016, for instance.

As we see in Section 8, I use several strategies to disarm these objections. The so-called evidence for the claim that migration has been bad for state-level justice deserves scrutiny. I also look at some contrary evidence. In addition, I show how there is scope for self-determination even when we participate in international initiatives aimed at migration justice. And I show how this self-determination sits comfortably with the proper authority that these international mechanisms have, and why there are reasons to be optimistic that a robust human rights practice can endure, despite any alleged setbacks that our contemporary moment brings.

However, in order to rebut all these objections convincingly, we need some detail about influential migration cooperation frameworks that have recently been adopted. Given the enormous achievement represented by the Global Compact for Safe, Orderly and Regular Migration, and the important progressive role it can play, I discuss it next. If properly implemented, the Compact would go a long way toward bringing into being the kinds of human rights aligned institutions for which I am advocating. Detailed knowledge of this Compact can also assist greatly in showing why the objections do not derail my project. I resume tackling the objections in Section 8.

4   The Global Compact for Safe, Orderly and Regular Migration

The Global Compact for Safe, Orderly and Regular Migration (henceforth, in this chapter, "the Compact") is a global cooperative framework for managing migration issues. This inter-governmentally negotiated and agreed comprehensive policy is significant in that it sets out the terms for a new understanding about global best practice in the area of migration and commits many people to taking important actions. In July 2018, all 193 members of the UN agreed to the terms of the document. However, at the adoption ceremony in December 2018, only 164 countries formally adopted the Compact.[5] However, this is still a highly significant achievement, as 85 percent of the world's states have committed to undertaking many actions that would reduce migration injustices.

The Compact is embedded within many layers of conventions already adopted by the UN and International Labor Organization, and builds on these previous foundations. This framework acknowledges that no state can single-handedly address migration and "expresses our collective commitment to improving cooperation on international migration," setting out common understandings and shared responsibilities.[6] The Compact resulted from "an unprecedented review of evidence and data gathered during an open, transparent and inclusive process."[7] States recognize the need for continuous international efforts to improve understanding of migration by collecting and disseminating quality data. And they recognize the need to provide "citizens with access to objective, evidence-based, clear

---

[5] In a subsequent vote at the UN General Assembly, five countries voted against the compact (USA, Israel, Hungary, Czech Republic, and Poland), several more abstained and twenty-four were not present. However, there was still clear support from 152 member states, which makes the level of support still around 80 percent.

[6] "The Global Compact for Safe, Orderly and Regular Migration," p. 2., available at: www.iom.int/global-compact-migration

[7] Ibid., 2

information about the benefits and challenges of migration, with a view to dispelling misleading narratives that generate negative perceptions of migrants."[8] The Compact includes statements of commitments such as to "unite, in a spirit of win-win cooperation, to address the challenges and opportunities of migration in all its dimensions through shared responsibility and innovative solutions."[9] And they committed "to continue the multilateral dialogue at the UN through a periodic and effective follow-up and review mechanism, ensuring that the words in this document translate into concrete actions for the benefit of millions of people in every region of the world."[10] There is a recognition that success in these tasks relies on determination, trust, and cooperation.

The Compact is based on several key principles, and here I highlight four:

> "*International cooperation.* The Global Compact is a non-legally binding cooperative framework that recognizes that no state can address migration on its own due to the inherently transnational nature of the phenomenon. It requires international, regional and bilateral cooperation and dialogue. *Its authority rests on its consensual nature, credibility, collective ownership, joint implementation, follow-up and review*" (emphasis mine).[11]

> "*National sovereignty.* The Global Compact reaffirms the sovereign right of States to determine their national migration policy and their prerogative to govern migration within their jurisdiction *in conformity with international law*" (emphasis mine).[12]

> *Sustainable development.* "The Global Compact is rooted in the 2030 Agenda for Sustainable Development, and builds upon its recognition that migration is a multidimensional reality of major relevance for the sustainable development of countries of origin, transit and destination, which requires coherent and comprehensive responses. Migration contributes to positive development outcomes and to realizing the goals of the 2030 Agenda for Sustainable Development, especially when it is properly managed."[13]

> *Human rights.* The Compact is based on international human rights law and "upholds the principles of non-regression and non-discrimination."[14] Implementing the Global Compact, aims to "ensure effective respect, protection and fulfillment of the human rights of all migrants."[15]

---

[8] Ibid., 3.   [9] Ibid., 3–4.   [10] Ibid.   [11] Ibid., 4, emphasis mine.

[12] Ibid., emphasis mine. It continues: "Within their sovereign jurisdiction, States may distinguish between regular and irregular migration status, including as they determine their legislative and policy measures for the implementation of the Global Compact, taking into account different national realities, policies, priorities and requirements for entry, residence and work, in accordance with international law."

[13] Ibid.   [14] Ibid.   [15] Ibid.

The Compact is based on further principles, such as respect for the rule of law and due process and others described as "Gender-responsive" and "Child-sensitive." The cooperative framework has twenty-three objectives for safe, orderly, and regular migration, which are worth citing in full:

1   Collect and utilize accurate and disaggregated data as a basis for evidence-based policies.
2   Minimize the adverse drivers and structural factors that compel people to leave their country of origin.
3   Provide accurate and timely information at all stages of migration.
4   Ensure that all migrants have proof of legal identity and adequate documentation.
5   Enhance availability and flexibility of pathways for regular migration.
6   Facilitate fair and ethical recruitment and safeguard conditions that ensure decent work.
7   Address and reduce vulnerabilities in migration.
8   Save lives and establish coordinated international efforts on missing migrants.
9   Strengthen the international response to smuggling of migrants.
10   Prevent, combat and eradicate trafficking in persons in the context of international migration.
11   Manage borders in an integrated, secure and coordinated manner.
12   Strengthen certainty and predictability in migration procedures for appropriate screening, assessment and referral.
13   Use migration detention only as a measure of last resort and work towards alternatives.
14   Enhance consular protection, assistance and cooperation throughout the migration cycle.
15   Provide access to basic services for migrants.
16   Empower migrants and societies to realize full inclusion and social cohesion.
17   Eliminate all forms of discrimination and promote evidence-based public discourse to shape perceptions of migration.
18   Invest in skills development and facilitate mutual recognition of skills, qualifications and competences.
19   Create conditions for migrants and diasporas to fully contribute to sustainable development in all countries.
20   Promote faster, safer, and cheaper transfer of remittances and foster financial inclusion of migrants.
21   Cooperate in facilitating safe and dignified return and readmission, as well as sustainable reintegration.

22 Establish mechanisms for the portability of social security entitlements and earned benefits.

23 Strengthen international cooperation and global partnerships for safe, orderly and regular migration.[16]

Here I discuss only a couple of the objectives in slightly more detail as they are either good illustrations of some theoretical points already made or they play a key role in arguments I marshal in later sections. In this first category is objective 2, which is a good illustration of how to add important responsibility-related content to the contribution requirement. Recall that the Compact aims to minimize factors in countries of origin that drive people to leave. In describing objective 2 in more detail, the Compact says: "We commit to create conducive political, economic, social and environmental conditions for people to lead peaceful, productive and sustainable lives in their own country and to fulfill their personal aspirations, while ensuring that desperation and deteriorating environments do not compel them to seek a livelihood elsewhere through irregular migration."[17] To achieve these objectives, states that adopted the Compact endeavor to invest in programs that help people achieve the Sustainable Development Goals, such as by assisting with "food security, health and sanitation, education, inclusive economic growth, infrastructure, urban and rural development, employment creation, decent work, gender equality and empowerment of women and girls, resilience and disaster risk reduction, . . . as well as creating and maintaining peaceful and inclusive societies with effective, accountable and transparent institutions."[18] They also agreed to take actions to create conditions that facilitate sustainable development in their own countries through fostering foreign direct investment, trade, investment in human capital, education, training, skills development partnerships, and creating productive employment in efforts to reduce unemployment, and avoid brain drain.[19]

Objective 16 plays an important role in giving shape to some of our specific migration-related responsibilities. It concerns aiming for good migrant inclusion and social cohesion. A number of salient commitments are articulated, such as those that empower migrants to become engaged members of society and those that increase public confidence in migration-related policies.[20] To realize these commitments, states commit to drawing from actions such as promoting "mutual respect for the cultures, traditions and customs of communities of destination and of migrants by exchanging

---

[16] Ibid., 5–6   [17] Ibid., 8.   [18] Ibid.   [19] Ibid., 9.   [20] Ibid., 23.

and implementing best practices on integration policies, programs and activities, including on ways to promote acceptance of diversity and facilitate social cohesion and inclusion."[21] They also undertook to develop national policy goals and plans on how to promote inclusion of migrants in societies – including through good labor market integration – by fostering partnerships with relevant stakeholders. In addition, they also committed to eliminating gender-based discriminatory work-related restrictions and to supporting the establishment of local programs that are capable of facilitating migrant participation in the receiving society by involving community members, migrants, and local authorities in intercultural dialogue, mentorship programs, and the development of other ties that can improve integration outcomes such as fostering mutual respect.

Other commitments include supporting multicultural activities (such as sports, music, arts, culinary festivals, volunteering, and social events) that would promote mutual understanding and appreciation of migrant and destination country cultures. And they committed to promoting "school environments that are welcoming and safe,"[22] and supportive of migrant children. This requires "incorporating evidence-based information about migration in education curricula, and dedicating targeted resources to schools with a high concentration of migrant children for integration activities in order to promote respect for diversity and inclusion," and prevent discrimination.[23]

Objective 17 covers the elimination of all forms of discrimination and the promotion of evidence-based public discourse. Here states

> ... commit to eliminate all forms of discrimination, condemn and counter expressions, acts and manifestations of racism, racial discrimination, violence, xenophobia, and related intolerance against all migrants in conformity with international human rights law. We further commit to promote an open and evidence-based public discourse on migration and migrants in partnership with all parts of society, that generates a more realistic, humane and constructive perception in this regard. We also commit to protect freedom of expression in accordance with international law, recognizing that an open and free debate contributes to a comprehensive understanding of all aspects of migration.[24]

To realize these goals, they commit to enacting and implementing laws penalizing hate crimes targeting migrants, providing assistance for victims, empowering migrant communities, and informing them of mechanisms of redress.

---

[21] Ibid.   [22] Ibid., 24.   [23] Ibid.   [24] Ibid.

There are also important media obligations. These obligations include promoting independent, objective, and quality reporting in media outlets, through various actions including promoting ethical reporting standards and discontinuing public funding and support to media outlets that promote intolerance, racism, or discrimination toward migrants.

States also undertook to promote awareness concerning the positive contributions that flow from migration and end stigmatization and racism. States agreed to provide platforms to exchange experiences on implementation and share good practices on policies and cooperation, fostering multi-stakeholder partnerships around specific policy issues. They also committed to a seed fund for realizing project-oriented solutions and an online open data source that is globally available.[25] They noted that commitments to implement the Compact may well take account of "different national realities, capacities, and levels of development,"[26] and respect national policies and priorities, while also emphasizing a commitment to international law and implementation of the agreement consistent with such law.

States agreed to review progress made at local, national, regional, and global levels through a state-led approach with participation from all relevant stakeholders. States will hold an International Migration Review Forum about every four years, which constitutes the main intergovernmental platform for states and relevant stakeholders to share progress on implementing the Compact.[27] They also invited the Global Forum on Migration and Development to offer space for annual informal exchange on the implementation of the Compact, where states could report best practices and innovative approaches.[28]

The Compact is interesting for several reasons. The fact that 85 percent of states have adopted it is at least one kind of rather compelling answer to the worry that states will not be inclined to bring into being the kind of institutional architecture required. The Compact also describes numerous responsibilities in connection with managing people's beliefs and attitudes around migration. And it shows how to create the proper authority while allowing adequate scope for self-determination in a legitimate state system. I discuss all of these themes further in later sections.

Despite the Compact's making great strides in some areas, there are other deficiencies it seems to leave unaddressed. One very important area, to my mind, is that a legitimate state system must include the right to a fair process for determining migrants' rights, especially concerning the rights to

---

[25] Ibid., 32.   [26] Ibid.   [27] Ibid., 33.   [28] Ibid., 34.

admission and to remain. While I believe the main building blocks for this requirement can be located in core aspects of our human rights practice, this particular implication has not been drawn out in current prominent frameworks concerning migration justice, such as the Compact we have been discussing. The next section aims to focus on the requirements for such fair processes.

5   Fair Processes for Determining Migrants' Rights

A legitimate state system must include the right to a fair process for determining migrants' rights, especially concerning the rights to admission and to remain. After reviewing some key biases with current arrangements (5.1), I show why we have obligations to remedy these biases by implementing appropriate institutional mechanisms that can correct for them (5.2). I then discuss why migrants are entitled to a fair process for determining their rights, and what this entails (5.3). An important feature is that states must be held to account for the reasoning they use in determining migrants' rights, and that reasoning must be human rights compliant. I give examples of what this would entail, drawing on core elements of our human rights practice. I discuss the "sheer numbers" problem and whether denying migrants admission because of large application numbers does relevantly fall afoul of the requirement to give reasons that are human rights compliant. I argue that there are important human rights that can block large-scale admissions at one time (5.4). I also indicate how reasoning might fail (5.5) and pass (5.6) the test. These illustrative examples give us good insights about the test of being human rights compliant and show how there is still much space for self-determination to play a role.

5.1   Current Problems: Biases and Misinformation
Inform Our Admission Policies

Our current arrangements are improperly biased toward compatriots.[29] We need an even-handed, human rights compliant approach to determining admission policies. Let me explain why I think this.

---

[29] For another argument as to why our current arrangements are unacceptably biased, see Javier Hidalgo, "The Case for the International Governance of Immigration," *International Theory*, 8 (1) (2016): 140–170. His argument draws importantly on our procedural obligations whereas mine involves core obligations deriving from our human rights practice.

Most people hold some form of associative obligation view, according to which we owe more to those with whom we have relationships. So, consider how many people believe that we owe more to our family and friends than people with whom we do not share such associations. This view certainly has a place in our moral lives, but there are limits to what can plausibly be justified by this stance. For instance, we may not murder or steal from strangers in order to benefit our family or friends. These limitations apply as well to all kinds of other associative obligations. So, using parallel reasoning, there is a commonly held view that public officials owe more to citizens than foreigners. And, similarly, even if public officials have stronger obligations to benefit citizens than others, they may not treat others unjustly *in order to do so*.

However, when our interests are directly involved, we are not always well positioned to make good judgments about whether we are treating others unjustly. And we make institutional allowances in such cases. A judge may not adjudicate a case in which she has a predisposition to favor particular parties directly involved in a case, and the case is then assigned to someone who does not have similar conflicts of interest. Just as a judge cannot properly adjudicate cases where she is strongly inclined to favor one party over another, we may be similarly impaired when it comes to making fair judgments in migration matters.

This tendency toward bias is not just an interesting observation about human limitations. It strikes at the heart of what justice requires. An inability to give everyone their due is a hallmark feature of injustice, so we need to take measures to ensure we can protect against it. We need mechanisms that can offer protections against such biases. So far, I have highlighted that there is a structural bias toward compatriots baked into our state system. But there are several other important biases, and much misinformation in play as well.

In what ways are our views about migrants biased and misinformed? Let me count some of the ways and briefly summarize why this matters. Citizens have many biased views about migrants. For instance, they have a tendency to assume there are high costs associated with immigration. They also tend to underestimate benefits that immigration can bring. But citizens' views matter greatly since many officeholders' views track those of citizens. So, these false views matter to policies and laws that nations adopt. In fact, immigration policies in high-income democratic states are generally consistent with public opinion in those states.[30] In those

---

[30] See, for instance, Gary Freeman, Randall Hansen, and David Leal, "Introduction: Immigration and Public Opinion in Liberal Democracies" in Gary Freeman, Randall Hansen, and David Leal (eds.),

countries where the median voter is negatively disposed toward immigration, leaders tend to favor more restrictive immigration laws.

In what ways do citizens often hold biased beliefs concerning immigration? In many high-income democracies, many citizens believe these four, generally false, views:[31]

(1)   Immigration is harmful for citizens' economic prospects. One important way in which this is supposed to work is that immigrants compete with citizens for jobs, resulting in increases in unemployment and downward pressure on wages.[32]

(2)   Immigrants' presence has a negative effect on public finances. Immigrants contribute less in tax than they take from welfare benefits.

(3)   Immigrants' presence lowers service delivery and quality.[33]

(4)   Immigrants increase crime.[34]

Now it is important to note that the actual effects of immigration vary enormously from country to country and depend greatly on the policy environment in a particular state. There is no such thing as "the effects of immigration" that are invariable across place and time. The effects depend on who is migrating, factors in countries of origin and destination countries, policy choices that states have made, and the like. As we saw in the chapter on refugees (Chapter 6, Section 6.1), none of the feared effects concerning migration of refugees are inevitable. Much depends on various

Immigration and Public Opinion in Liberal Democracies (New York: Routledge, 2013), 2–3; and Giovanni Facchini and Anna Mayda, "From Individual Attitudes toward Migrants to Migration Policy Outcomes: Theory and Evidence," *Economic Policy*, 23 (56) (2008): 651–713.

[31] For generally negative views, along with specific negative views on service delivery and job competition, see "Global study shows many around the world increasingly uncomfortable with levels of immigration" available at: www.ipsos.com/en/global-study-shows-many-around-world-increasingly-uncomfortable-levels-immigration. For negative views on fiscal burdens, see, for instance, Laura Collins, "Pervasive Myths about Immigrants," blog post on *George W Bush Institute website*, Issue 09, Winter 2018, available at: www.bushcenter.org/catalyst/immigration/collins-immigration-myths.html. On the crime issue see, for instance, Anna Flagg, "The Myth of the Criminal Immigrant"; also Graham Ousey and Charis Kubrin, "Immigration and Crime."

[32] See, for instance, Giovanni Peri and Chad Sparber, "Task Specialization, Immigration, and Wages," *American Economic Journal: Applied Economics* 1 (3) (2009): 135–169; and Michael Clemens, Cindy Huang, Jimmy Graham, Kate Hough, *Migration Is What You Make It*.

[33] The idea is that citizens might need to wait in longer lines and, without further resources (including human resources), service providers will not be able to cope as well with their workload. They will be unable to offer the same level of service as when there were fewer demands on them.

[34] For more negative views see "Global study shows many around the world increasingly uncomfortable with levels of immigration" available at: www.ipsos.com/en/global-study-shows-many-around-world-increasingly-uncomfortable-levels-immigration. On the crime issue specifically, see for instance, Flagg, "The Myth of the Criminal Immigrant"; also, Ousey and Kubrin, "Immigration and Crime."

policy choices. Under the right complementary policy conditions, migrants can assist in increasing incomes and employment rates for natives, and generally contribute to more productive economies.[35] Complementary policies aimed at mitigating costs, especially those experienced by local workers, are critical.[36]

While there is much empirical evidence to sift through for each country, in the USA for instance, all four of the beliefs are mistaken. A dominant view in the literature is that immigration effects on wages and employment are unclear, but at any rate, small and sometimes positive.[37] Most studies of fiscal effects of immigration show that it has few net effects on public finances. Much depends on the policy environment.[38] And immigration is generally associated with lower levels of crime in the USA.[39]

More worryingly, underlying all these false beliefs may be a predisposition to forming views about migrants that are unfavorable. Some argue that this may be rooted in tendencies toward ethnocentrism, according to which in-group members are viewed more favorably than others based purely on the fact that they are in-group members. So, when this bias operates, there is a tendency to believe that in-group members are (for instance) more cooperative or trustworthy, compared with those who are not members of the group. When the bias operates, citizens would be disposed to believe that foreigners have less desirable characteristics than compatriots, based simply on their standing as not being members of their group. Various studies suggest that ethnocentrism is a significant factor in understanding American opposition to immigration.[40]

---

[35] Clemens, Huang, Graham, and Hough, *Migration Is What You Make It*; also Clemens, Huang, and Graham, *The Economic and Fiscal Effects of Granting Refugees Formal Labor Market Access* , 8.

[36] Clemens, Huang, and Graham, *The Economic and Fiscal Effects of Granting Refugees Formal Labor Market Access*, 8.

[37] See, for instance, Giovanni Peri and Chad Sparber, "Task Specialization, Immigration, and Wages," *American Economic Journal: Applied Economics,* 1 (3) (2009): 135–169.

[38] Clemens, Huang, Graham, and Hough, *Migration Is What You Make It.*

[39] Anna Flagg, "The myth of the criminal immigrant"; also Graham Ousey and Charis Kubrin, "Immigration and Crime,": 63–84.

[40] See, for instance, Donald Kinder and Cindy Kam, *Us against Them: Ethnocentric Foundations of American Opinion* (Chicago: University of Chicago Press, 2009). People also feel more threatened by non-white immigration, as discussed in Todd Hartman, Benjamin Newman, Scott Bell, "Decoding Prejudice toward Hispanics: Group Cues and Public Reactions to Threatening Immigrant Behavior," *Political Behavior,* 36 (1) (2014): 143–163.

5.2   Why Should Officeholders Care about Biases and Citizens' False Beliefs?

There are a few reasons. The biases may actually run counter to citizens' interests. For instance, the presence of immigrants may be hugely beneficial to promoting citizens' well-being.[41] But more importantly, as I argue in this section, there is an obligation to correct misinformation when holding beliefs that reflect this false information runs counter to core obligations of our human rights practice.

Within human rights practice there are several related obligations. There is a requirement to gather accurate information and disseminate it, as we saw from discussion of objective 17 of the Compact. Underlying this area of concern is the fact that people holding false beliefs about migrants are more likely to act in ethnocentric ways. But we have obligations to ensure ethnocentrism is managed better, including by correcting misinformation and promoting public dialogue based on accurate and constructive perceptions of migrants' real contributions. Failing to address beliefs that are wrongly held because they are based on false information is incompatible with commitment to human rights practice and responsibilities in relation to it. This is especially so when the falsehoods strike at the core tenets of the practice, and when there are obligations in connection with educating people about beliefs based on inaccurate facts.

There are many aspects of the human rights practice that are relevant here. Recall that objective 17 of the Compact commits states to eliminating all forms of discrimination, and promoting an open and evidence-based public discourse on migration that generates more realistic, humane, and constructive perceptions of migrants, while also committing to protect freedom of expression in accordance with international law. Committing to promote an open and evidence-based public discourse that is more realistic, humane, and constructive entails that we must take steps to correct misinformation when people have formed inaccurate views.

---

[41] For extended discussion of these themes see Clemens, Huang, Graham, and Hough, *Migration Is What You Make It*. For instance, they note that whatever the stage of development of a host country, potential benefits of hosting migrants include higher incomes and employment rates for natives, increased innovation, net positive fiscal effects, and more productive economies. Important studies include: Mette Foged and Giovanni Peri, "Immigrants' Effects on Native Workers: New Analysis on Longitudinal Data," *American Economic Journal: Applied Economics*, 8 (2) (2016): 1–34; Thomas Liebig and Jeffrey Mo, "The Fiscal Impact of Immigration in OECD Countries" in *International Migration Outlook 2013* (Paris, France: OECD Publishing, 2013), 125–189; and Giovanni Peri, "The Effect of Immigration on Productivity: Evidence from US States," *Review of Economics and Statistics*, 94 (1) (2012): 348–358.

In addition, consider also article 26 (2) of the Universal Declaration of Human Rights. It states that "education shall be directed to the full development of the human personality and to the strengthening of respect for human rights and fundamental freedoms. It shall promote understanding, tolerance and friendship among all nations, racial or religious groups, and shall further the activities of the United Nations for the maintenance of peace."[42] So we have very important obligations in virtue of this article to correct false beliefs when they run contrary to promoting understanding, tolerance, and possibilities for sustaining peace, security and the like.

And consider just one more core aspect of our human rights practice, namely the conventions on the elimination of all forms of discrimination.[43] According to these conventions, we have obligations to educate toward a spirit of "brotherhood" and toward societies in which people are inclined and oriented toward the key human rights elements. So, if citizens are prejudiced against certain groups and have false beliefs about them, believing them to be inferior, unworthy, or fitting objects of mistreatment, simply in virtue of such characteristics as their racial, religious, or national origin associations, there is an obligation to correct such views. Education that has an orientation toward understanding, tolerance, and respectful engagement is important for creating the kind of empathy needed to sustain a robust human rights practice. If we are seriously trying to bring about the kind of social and international order in which the rights and freedoms set forth in the Universal Declaration can be fully realized, as article 28 enjoins, we must nurture new generations to have well-informed and compassionate views toward others.

So, as we see then, there are strong elements of our human rights practice that entail duties to be concerned with challenging views based on ethnocentric, inaccurate, or biased beliefs and duties to facilitate better understanding.

5.3   *Migrants' Rights to a Fair Process and Accountability for Migration Decisions*

What rights do people have in connection with moving across borders? Do all who would like to join a state have a right to do so? As I argue in this section, there are some important rights in this area, but the content is not an unconditional right to move. Rather, the central right, I maintain, is to

---

[42] Available for instance here www.un.org/en/universal-declaration-human-rights/
[43] Available here for instance: www.ohchr.org/en/professionalinterest/pages/cerd.aspx

have one's case considered fairly. Contemporary processes do not achieve the minimal fairness bar. Today's processes fail in a number of respects. First, they fail to give proper consideration to people's human rights. Second, they lack even-handedness, are often based on false information, and are heavily biased towards trying to benefit compatriots. And third, the processes lack sufficient oversight: there is no requirement for states to be held accountable for their decisions.[44]

On my account, migrants have a right to a fair process for determining their rights concerning migration. This is grounded in core commitments of our human rights practice, such as those concerned with fair due process. As one core ground for what I take to be a rather uncontroversial claim (at least in the abstract), consider article 10 of the Universal Declaration of Human Rights, according to which, everyone is entitled to a fair and public hearing "by an independent and impartial tribunal, in the determination of his rights and obligations."[45]

What is the likelihood of transferring all admission decisions to a truly "independent and impartial tribunal"? I consider this option will not be entertained in the near future, given our state system and its commitment to recognition of a central role for national sovereignty, as strongly upheld by the human rights practice. Nevertheless, I think there are important options that we should entertain that might promote similar outcomes and can at the very least offer some much-needed correctives.

So, drawing on articles such as article 10, I believe migrants have the following right:

> Migrants have a right to a fair process governing the determination of their rights. This should include a clear statement from the state indicating how they reasoned towards their determinations, and that reasoning must be human rights compliant. There must be opportunities for states to be held to account for that reasoning.

Including the right to a justification for a decision that is compliant with a robust human rights practice, can operate in powerful ways, as I show in

---

[44] States do not currently have to give a justification for how they reasoned in making their exclusion decisions. For another author who finds this troubling, see Bas Schotel, *On the Right of Exclusion.* He makes an excellent case that the legal foundations of current immigration policies are not robust and our legal practice needs to change so that it is on firmer legal ground. Authorities must justify their decisions, particularly on exclusion, and it is up to those authorities to present the relevant data to substantiate their claims. For another excellent argument as to why there should be some international governance of immigration, see Javier Hidalgo, "The Case for the International Governance of Immigration": 140–170.

[45] It is not clear that all *migration* decisions need to be part of a public hearing if those directly involved would prefer relative privacy in sensitive cases.

later sections. Before we get there, it is worth noting that there are neglected aspects of our human rights practice that could do more normative work if made more visible. For instance, if we examine some core features of our current international law, there is more scope than many appreciate for human rights-based claims to be lodged against various states, and which they would have obligations to take more seriously than they apparently do. Under our human rights practice and our current international legal system, states have a right to exclude foreigners from their territory, *unless a treaty obligation requires admission*. This current norm can have more force than is acknowledged in contemporary practice.[46]

So, what are some of the relevant treaty obligations that might have this kind of force? The right to seek asylum is one. The right to family unification is another. But it also seems to me that there is considerable scope to argue for an even wider set. The right to health can be important in a number of special cases. So, consider that we have a right to health and consider further that treatment for a particular rare condition may be available only in a particular state that has developed treatment for that rare condition. In such cases we would have strong grounds to say that failure to admit the person in need of treatment constitutes a violation of her right to health. Where a basic human right can only be satisfied on a particular territory, then the state is effectively an "agent of last resort"[47] in being uniquely able to fulfill the human right. So, failure to admit in such cases would constitute a violation of a basic human right.

5.4 Toward an Account of Adequate Justification: The Sheer Numbers Problem

I have been arguing that migrants are entitled to a fair process governing the determination of their rights. The fair process should include human rights compliant reasoning for decisions. In addition, there must be fair processes for holding states to account for their migration decisions and performance on human rights.

---

[46] For others who argue that a more generous approach is consistent or required by current international law see, for instance, James Nafziger, "The General Admission of Aliens under International Law," *The American Journal of International Law*, 77 (4) (1983): 804–847; and also Bas Schotel, *On the Right of Exclusion*.

[47] This is terminology used in easy rescue cases. For a brief introduction, see Gillian Brock and Nicole Hassoun, "*Distance, Moral Relevance of*" in Hugh LaFollette (ed.), *The International Encyclopedia of Ethics* (Malden, MA: Blackwell, 2013), 1418–1426.

What might count as human rights compliant reasoning for decisions? Let us start off with an important challenge, one that we might call the "sheer numbers problem." Enormous numbers of people seem to want to move across borders, especially to middle- and high-income countries. Are such states obliged to take in all who apply? Would failure to do so constitute important violations of their human rights?

There is much that we can draw on in considering how to weigh the interests of citizens and foreigners that does not always tip the balance in favor of foreigners. Our human rights practice can offer many tools that I think can be assembled to powerful effect. Consider for instance article 29 of the UDHR:

(1)   Everyone has duties to the community in which alone the free and full development of his personality is possible.
(2)   In the exercise of his rights and freedoms, everyone shall be subject only to such limitations as are determined by law solely for the purpose of securing due recognition and respect for the rights and freedoms of others and of meeting the just requirements of morality, public order and the general welfare in a democratic society.

Article 29 actually places quite strong limits on enormous numbers of newcomers being admitted at one time. Article 29 (2) in particular can offer substantial resistance when large numbers of arrivals would undermine general welfare in a democratic society. How so? A large influx of migrants, without adequate advance warning and time to complete necessary planning, might significantly undermine delivery of essential goods and services, such as capacity to offer adequate education, health care, and law enforcement, all of which are necessary to secure fundamental human rights. Citizens might rightly feel aggrieved if such service delivery falls below what is needed to sustain their basic human rights. Any government wanting to argue that migrants would constitute a threat to public order have to cite specific compelling evidence that this would indeed be likely to occur. But, in principle, states can give a human rights compliant accounting for decisions to deny admission given sheer numbers within a particular time frame: too many demands can begin to threaten human rights fulfillment for citizens.

It is important to note that article 29 (2) can also set quite a high bar, because in many cases of attempts to offer justifications for admission decisions it will become quite clear that permitting entry of new members does *not* threaten general welfare. Consider, for instance, cases of labor migration. As one example, it is quite implausible that a migrant willing to do a job that no citizen wishes to do in an important sector in which employers cannot find enough people to do necessary jobs does indeed threaten general welfare.[48]

At any rate, let us now move on to the main part of this chapter, which shows how reasoning should be structured to be human rights compliant. The next two sections consider examples of reasoning that fails (Section 5.5) and passes (Section 5.6) the test of human rights compliance. One important lesson from Section 5.6 is that there is no single formula that dictates how justified reasoning *must* proceed in order to be human rights compliant. It seems to me there are many ways of structuring a justification that would count as adequate. But the two examples also give us a good sense of how human rights can play a powerful role in judging whether reasoning is compliant with core elements of our human rights practice. There are some bright lines between accounts that fail and can pass the test.

5.5   An Example of a Public Rationale That Would Not Pass the Test

Consider the following alleged public accounting aimed at justifying why a ban on Muslims entering the USA would be defensible.

> *We have vastly more applicants who would like to settle in the USA than we could possibly accept and we can therefore be highly selective. We have evidence that a large percentage of citizens from your country are hostile toward the USA. We would rather have people in our country who love America and its values. In addition, the recent election indicates that people are extremely concerned about their security and feel threatened by Muslims in their neighborhoods. So, we have a mandate to prioritize citizens' security and harmony in local neighborhoods in our admission decisions. Whether or not you personally intend to engage in behavior that is antagonistic towards citizens, your mere presence is likely to fuel tensions in communities that spill over into violence, which we would rather avoid. Furthermore, a majority of citizens support bans on further Muslim migration. Even if you personally would not commit terrorist acts, we must take account of citizens' fears that you or your associates might. We recognize that citizens' fears may not be well-grounded and may be based on misperceptions or inaccurate information. Nevertheless, we have a right to determine the shape and character of our future society and the people have spoken in support of a certain vision that does not include you. In fact, the people have spoken in favor of very restrictive immigration policies, so we are*

---

[48] Examination of such labor shortage cases would reveal that in many cases migrants would contribute greatly to general welfare rather than detract from it. See, for instance, Clemens, et al., *Migration Is What You Make It*.

drastically limiting the number of immigrants we admit more generally. Given this pressure, we must be convinced that any immigrants we admit will offer substantial advantages to our nation. In your case we do not judge this to be the case.

We understand that we are required to offer you reasons for our decision that can meet the test of being human rights compliant. We believe you should be able to appreciate the importance of easing tensions, civic harmony, felt security, and how protecting citizens from unnecessary violence are all likely to contribute to an environment in which human rights are well protected. Governments have responsibilities to respect, protect, and fulfill human rights. We judge that securing human rights through the means described are legitimate aims for governments to pursue. So, we believe our reasons are human rights compliant.

Would such an attempt at justification meet the criterion of being human rights compliant? From within the human rights framework I have been developing here, I believe there are several places where such reasoning can be challenged. One area that seems important concerns challenging reasoning that rests on false beliefs, which one has obligations to challenge when they run counter to core commitments of our human rights practice. Let me explain how this would work.

Recall that, on our human rights practice, we have important obligations to challenge views that are based on ethnocentric, inaccurate, biased, or prejudiced views. So, if citizens are afraid because they have false beliefs about Muslims, there is an obligation to correct misinformation and biases. We have important duties to manage ethnocentrism by correcting misperceptions. Even if it is true that some Muslims in some societies have hateful views, it is also true that there are many others who do not. And this is true of all major religious groups. We have obligations to ensure that citizens have well-informed views of other groups, which can take account of diversity within groups, inclines towards a spirit of tolerance, empathy, and understanding, and appreciates the multiplicity and complexity associated with any worldview that has hundreds of millions of committed followers. We also have obligations to ensure everyone is treated appropriately as an individual human being and that their case is given due consideration on the particular merits inherent in that person's case.

Recall that from within the human rights practice there is a requirement to ensure education includes elements that foster understanding and tolerance, which are important in creating the kind of empathy needed to sustain a robust human rights practice and to nurture the right kinds of dispositions in future generations. These responsibilities have been amply covered in Sections 4 and 5.2 so perhaps there is no need to labor the point any further.

Therefore, in citing as reasons for rejecting migrants, citizens' fears based on false beliefs, beliefs that the state has obligations to change, a government fails to offer a human rights compliant accounting for its decision. Not only are these false beliefs inadequate to count as appropriate grounds, but also in citing them as reasons and failing to correct the false beliefs, the state shows that it is not discharging its human rights obligations well. The whole attempt at accountability fails to show that the state's activities and reasoning are human rights compliant.

5.6 An Accounting That Would Pass the Human Rights Compliance Test

Consider the following justification offered by a state.

> *As a state that aims to be human rights compliant, we take seriously our obligations to give due consideration to all applications from those seeking permanent residence on our territory. Given the huge number of applications, we must rank them according to the strength and urgency with which applicants need to be admitted. Given these two overarching principles, we have prioritized claims in the following way:*
>
> *We must fulfill our international commitments first and, most urgently, we must admit all those seeking asylum, at least for the duration of time needed to assess their application.*
>
> *Second, we must take in our share of refugees who need to be resettled, while also contributing appropriately to other options we have obligations to offer refugees, such as subsidizing employment in the region where they would most like to remain.*
>
> *Third, we must admit all those who we are required to take in because of human rights to family unification or because we are the agent of last resort in being able to fulfill another fundamental human right, such as the right to health.*
>
> *In any given year the number of applicants that we admit from these first three categories totals about 200,000 people. By our calculation, given our commitments to a range of other important international initiatives and treaties, we can admit a further 200,000 people. These further international commitments include the contributions we must make to various sustainable development initiatives (such as those articulated in the Sustainable Development Goals) and to address climate change by committing to projects that would reduce emissions (as specified in our commitments under the Paris Climate Accord). Relevant to the last issue in particular is our current infrastructural capacity, concerning transportation, energy production, and distribution networks, availability of housing, places in schools, hospitals. and demands on other public facilities and services that we need to make available to ensure residents' human rights are met (while meeting our sustainable development and emissions targets and the like), which is why we can admit only a further 200,000*

people per year. Here is the way we have ranked other applications on our point system.

Applicants are awarded points for various categories. Having already resided on our territory for five or more years would typically mean that an application scores the threshold number of points required for consideration. Those who have already made important contributions to community functioning (such as by laboring in the community) or formed significant relationships with employers and other community members would also go a long way towards reaching the threshold number of points, and after five years would be eligible to apply for permanent residence. We also have labor shortages in certain areas, and applicants who can meet such shortages would also be eligible to apply for permanent residence.

We try to prioritize labor shortages required to fulfill human rights obligations. In our case, that means prioritizing skill shortages in the agricultural sector, since our agricultural sector would not be sustainable without this support and it would also undermine our food security thereby jeopardizing our citizens' human right to adequate subsistence, since we judge this would undermine the quality, diversity and affordability of food citizens need for a healthy diet.

While everyone in this fourth category deserves consideration, we need to prioritize those applications where granting permanent residency is more urgent. As everyone appreciates, individual cases can differ greatly in this area. We fill all the urgent claims in this fourth category first before attending to the others. Others are processed in the order in which they were received. If the case is not granted in a particular year, it can be held over to a subsequent year.

This is our process. We believe it meets our human rights obligations well, especially by giving due consideration to each individual case on its merits, balancing the human rights of non-compatriots along with those of compatriots in an even-handed fashion. We must also balance our responsibilities in the area of promoting migration justice with our responsibilities under other important justice initiatives, including contributing to global sustainable development and addressing climate change.

I believe this reasoning would pass the test I have imposed and is compliant with a robust human rights practice. One perhaps notable feature is that it offers a holistic accounting and shows how reasoning can balance concerns in multiple areas. Governments must typically make multiple justice-relevant decisions and those on migration are just a subset. Our migration decisions must also be consistent with other responsibilities we have. Another notable feature is that the reasoning shows the right kind of even-handedness that should be embodied in a fair process. When compatriots' interests are given weight, it is because of the connection to human rights obligations.

Another noteworthy point is that there is no single formula that dictates how justified reasoning must proceed.[49] Many ways of structuring a justification would count as adequate, so long as they meet the bar of being human rights compliant. The example cited in this section offers only one such case and there is scope to offer others.

6   Self-Determination

So far, I have argued that we should support a constellation of global arrangements conducive to migration justice, such as by committing to the Compact. I have also argued that commitment to the Compact should be supplemented by a fair process for determining migrants' rights and a process for holding states accountable for these determinations. Perhaps here is a good place to (1) add some content about how states can be held accountable, and (2) remind the reader about the conditions states must meet in order to have a defensible right to self-determination. These tasks seem important before we can analyze whether this cluster of arrangements allows appropriate scope for a legitimate state's rights to self-determination.

6.1   Some Ways to Hold States to Account for Their Migration Decisions

Mechanisms for holding states to account for the reasoning they offer in determining migrants' rights can take a variety of forms. The periodic follow-up and review process can serve as one such forum. However, I imagine that being called to account for reasoning concerning states' determinations of migrants' rights will have a huge volume of cases. Perhaps a special institution can be devoted to this purpose, or these requests for accountability can be channeled through some of the other existing bodies, such as the International Court of Justice[50] or through some of the regular Treaty bodies. The regional systems might also be effectively utilized, since many of them have some important enforcement power, such as the European Court of Justice.[51] In this area, there are important precedents and similarities with other courts in existence.

---

[49] For another excellent account of how reasoning might permissibly differ in different democratic communities, see Sarah Song, *Immigration and Democracy*, especially the concluding chapter.

[50] In the case of the International Court of Justice, currently only states may bring actions. But modifications might be made so that individuals can bring cases as well.

[51] Perhaps it would work through the court considering appeals or holding regular reviews of decisions.

Within the EU structure there is a supranational court that can issue judgment on, and therefore constrain, immigration policy of member states. And other regional governance bodies exist which can also perform similar functions, such as Mercosur within South America.

Perhaps, given the volume of additional work that I anticipate would be involved in holding states to account for the determination of migrants' rights, a new body might be created within the IOM especially for this purpose. Given that the IOM falls within the UN, this might also give the body effective channels for implementing sanctions if states' reasoning is found to fail tests of human rights compliance. There is much we should consider with all of these options, but we need not take a stand on which to support for the purposes of this work. For my purposes, it is enough to point out that there are several credible options worth further exploration.

It is anticipated that the mere existence of the institutions for holding states to account will have a normative effect over time. Whether or not these institutions are actually used they can have a highly positive effect on states' behavior, since they give states an incentive to perform some self-regulation and oversight over their own decisions. The mere presence of these institutions would encourage states to give more weight to the interests of foreigners and comply with expected court judgments. An analogy with other institutions might assist us to imagine better how these would operate. Consider how the ICC serves to operate for the 120-plus members that have signed up to it. The commitment to be part of the ICC has given states an incentive to ensure their own legal institutions can deal adequately with certain kinds of crimes. It operates on the principle of complementarity. The ICC is there to protect victims if domestic legal institutions are unable to do so. And, over time, it has led to improvements in domestic legal systems.[52]

6.2 Conditions That Must Be Met for Defensible Rights to Self-Determination

Core arguments from earlier chapters outlined important preconditions for states having a defensible right to self-determination. Recall that Chapter 3 sought a justification for states' claims to have rights to self-determination

---

[52] See, for instance, Jamie Meyerfeld, "The Democratic Legacy of the International Criminal Court," *The Fletcher Forum of World Affairs*, 28(2) (2004): 147–156. As Meyerfeld notes, "as Locke, Montesquieu, and Madison understood, unchecked power invites abuse, whereas the mere consciousness of institutional checks improves the behavior of government officials, and each check enhances the effectiveness of others," ibid., 155.

that entail the right to control admission to their territory. There we discovered that in order for states to have defensible rights to self-determination within the context of a state system, many responsibilities are generated, concerning meeting human rights commitments both within the state and beyond. Importantly, as we saw, states have obligations to cooperate in a host of international initiatives, agreements, institutions, and the like, that aim to secure arrangements capable of effective human rights protection. Meeting these contribution requirements satisfactorily affects both whether a particular state's right to self-determination is robust and whether we have a legitimate state system.

So, the right of a state to self-determination is conditional on a state's discharging its relevant responsibilities to contribute to conditions necessary for supporting self-determining, just communities. And since agreeing to the Compact is part of such an effort, it is a necessary condition for the defensible right to self-determination that a state commits to such endeavors. So, committing to the Compact does not get in the way of self-determination but rather is a prerequisite for having such a justified right at all.

6.3 Supporting a Legitimate State System and Self-Determination

An objector might still have this worry: Does supporting the cluster of arrangements I have indicated as necessary for meeting legitimacy requirements make adequate space for self-determination? Here I show why I think it can. First, let us deal with the issue of how joining up to the Compact affects self-determination. Second, I show how the kind of scope that remains for self-determination is consistent with meeting international obligations and so how all of this might work in practice.

Suppose a particular government is in the process of deciding whether or not to adopt the migration Compact. Signing up would commit the state to various actions aimed at reducing migration injustice in our world here and now. No other state will force this government to adopt the agreement and the state may withdraw in the future. Here we have a case of a self-determining state considering joining up with an important cooperative framework that represents a significant and credible attempt at collective action to solve a problem no individual state can solve alone. So, the state has strong moral reasons to sign up. I claim it has an obligation in such a case to join. But note that no state will force the government to do so. Binding itself to the terms of the Compact does not relevantly undermine the fact that the state remains a self-determining entity. Self-binding and self-determination are compatible.

That might be so, but someone might still wonder: Is there a non-trivial space left over for self-determination, given all the constraints that the Compact appears to bring in its wake? How would this work in practice? In answering these questions, we might consider how the EU works, as it is a reasonably good model for some aspects of models I favor. Countries can still determine quite a lot about their migration policies, even if EU law binds them in certain areas. So, under EU law, states have obligations to admit some migrants, such as fellow EU members. But they have much scope to decide on other aspects of their migration policy.

As an illustration, let us consider the case of Portugal and how free it is to set migration policy while being bound by EU laws. Faced with large labor shortages in the construction sector, Portugal has encouraged migration for those with relevant skills, and this opportunity has been taken up by sizable numbers of migrants from Brazil and former African colonies. Another aspect of Portuguese migration policy is that it offers citizenship to descendants of those who were expelled from Portugal in 1497. Many Turkish Jews have gained citizenship in this way. Portugal also offers citizenship to second generations of those who arrived illegally (so it has large populations from Russia, Moldova, and the Ukraine). So, we can see how a state within the EU that is bound to accept certain migrants from the EU is also free to determine significant aspects of migration policy in other areas. The fact that Portugal is bound by EU law has not undermined its ability to determine other migration policy that fits with its aims, ideals, and preferences.

Similarly, just because a state is obligated to take account of some cooperative agreement, this does not necessarily undermine self-determination. Complying with the Compact still allows plenty of space for states to engage in legitimate activities aimed at expressing their self-determination.

7 Citizens' Obligations

It is obligatory for citizens to support the kinds of institutions that would be needed for a legitimate state system, quite generally, and this will have more specific implications as well for obligations to support efforts that would promote just arrangements for people on the move. So, for instance, citizens have moral obligations to vote for candidates who would support reforms that take us in the direction of migration justice. They also have obligations to take steps in their local contexts that would give expression to their justice commitments, such as by showing hospitality to newcomers settled in their communities and making efforts to build local inclusive communities. There may not be a general obligation for any individual citizen to resist unjust immigration law, though such actions may be permissible and very often are commendable. Because resisting unjust immigration law can involve significant costs that we cannot always reasonably oblige particular citizens to absorb, we need to be careful about over-generalizing in this domain. However, if costs of resistance are fairly distributed among a set of citizens, such as in a particular city, citizens may have obligations to play a role in collective efforts.[53] All of this would take a great many pages to argue carefully.[54] Here I focus on an obligation that I think is somewhat neglected. There are many aspects of what citizens ought to do in support of migration justice. One key role they have is in helping to create the kinds of inclusive communities necessary to sustain migration justice. I concentrate on this issue as just one among several important kinds of responsibilities. I stress obligations to welcome new-comers in one's local environment as an important action in creating the kinds of inclusive communities we should endeavor to foster in seeking to promote justice on many levels.

7.1 Sanctuary Cities and the Sanctuary City Movement

Do citizens have obligations to resist unjust immigration law? Some cities have thought it important to resist unjust federal immigration and declared themselves to be sanctuary cities. What is involved in being a sanctuary city varies considerably and is worthy of some comment. Sanctuary cities can refer to some quite diverse practices, if we look at a range of states in

---

[53] Some maintain that citizens have a duty to obey the law. But citizens are not obliged to do so when laws violate basic rights or are issued from a body that does not exercise power legitimately. Any obligations we have to obey laws can be defeated by stronger obligations to avoid contributing importantly to injustice.

　　Also, perhaps it is worth noting that the duty to avoid participating in injustice is cost-sensitive. If the state will punish those who are asked to bear large costs, it may be morally permissible for people to comply rather than disobey. It is not always the case that citizens will incur large risks of punishment by disobeying. But even if there is some penalty, this can be equitably distributed. For instance, if Federal funding is to be withdrawn to sanctuary cities, costs associated with this policy can be fairly distributed among inhabitants and visitors through well targeted differential local rates and taxes.

[54] For some excellent treatment of duties to resist unjust immigration law see, for instance, Javier Hidalgo, "Resistance to Unjust Immigration Restrictions"; Javier Hidalgo, "The Duty to Disobey Immigration Law," *Moral Philosophy and Politics* 3 (2) (2016): 165–186; and Chris Bertram, *Do States Have the Right to Exclude Immigrants?* especially chapter 3.

Western Europe and North America.[55] In North America, the practices are largely confined to limits on cooperation with a national government aiming to enforce immigration law. Leaders of so-called sanctuary cities often argue that such cooperation limits make communities safer and protect basic rights better than policies of full cooperation. For instance, if residents fear deportation, they might be reluctant to report crimes. They will also be less willing to use health or social services when needed, and the rights of many, including citizens, may thereby be jeopardized. So, the arguments for a robust firewall between cooperation with immigration officials and access to services necessary to secure human rights are compelling.[56] Insofar as cities have taken steps to introduce such firewalls, such resistance is important and noble. And if the costs of resistance are born in equitable ways across the cities' members, taking such stands may well be obligatory.[57]

In Europe, the focus of sanctuary cities lies elsewhere. The emphasis is on creating a welcoming environment, especially for those seeking safety, and positive community relationships. A noteworthy local social movement in the United Kingdom encourages cities to take pride in their status as potential sanctuaries.[58] The City of Sanctuary Movement began in Sheffield in 2005. It aims to create a culture in which virtues of hospitality and welcome are valued and in which immigrants, especially asylum seekers and refugees, are able to engage positively with local communities and made to feel that they can make a full contribution to those communities.[59] A common goal is the creation of opportunities for migrants to meet local community members so that they can get to know one another in a positive environment. The precise activities each city engages in are different, reflecting the grassroots nature of the movement. Some cities have held exhibitions designed to show how refugees and asylum seekers have contributed to the city. Others have focused on improving understanding through sharing stories on blogs.

---

[55] See, for instance, Michael Kagan, "What We Talk about When We Talk about Sanctuary Cities," *UC Davis Law Review*, 52 (2018): 391–406; also, Hiroshi Motomura, "Arguing about Sanctuary," *UC Davis Law Review*, 52 (2018): 435–569.

[56] For compelling argument see, for instance, Joseph Carens, *Ethics of Immigration*, chapter 7.

[57] There can be further exceptions to this general view. We must take account of any costs that cities would incur in taking such stands. If the costs are extremely high and compromise other normatively salient considerations, cities can be excused from such general obligations.

[58] See, for instance, Jonathan Darling, Craig Barnett, and Sarah Eldridge, "City of Sanctuary – A UK Initiative for Hospitality," *Urban Displacement, Forced Migration Review*, 34, February 2010, available at: www.fmreview.org/sites/fmr/files/.../en/urban.../darling-barnet-eldridge.pdf

[59] See, for instance, the City of Sanctuary website at: https://cityofsanctuary.org/

And yet others have focused on more informal events, such as staging music concerts.[60]

In this section, my central claim is that the obligations citizens have include ones to support local organizations, such as those dedicated to creating a welcoming culture for everyone, especially newcomers. This obligation is already noted in the Compact, under objectives 16 and 17, and commits states to facilitating migrant participation in the receiving society through intercultural dialogue and activities that would promote mutual understanding and appreciation of migrant and destination country cultures. There are important organizations that are creating a helpful structure for such activities. So, as an example, consider the work of an organization like Welcoming America, which now has chapters or similar kinds of organizations all over the world. The motto of Welcoming America is "building a nation of neighbors." That defining idea is a good way to express a central ambition. The ideal of the good neighbor is worthwhile to have in mind in thinking through the kinds of local communities we might aspire to create.

Newcomers settle in specific communities so it makes sense to ensure local governments can assist in creating an inclusive environment. Local governments and communities are well placed to lead and implement welcoming community strategies. Welcoming America aims to build strong communities, but notes that in the 21st century this means intentionally aiming to connect and include people of all kinds of backgrounds. Welcoming America offers many resources for helping to create strong communities and here I highlight just a few. Creating truly inclusive policies requires broad community support.[61] We need to create opportunities for meaningful contact between diverse community members, to build opportunities for constructive relationships, that can include both newcomers and the long-settled. Local leaders can do much in promoting positive messaging that also helps highlight shared values. Building more unified and welcoming communities requires engagement from longer-term residents along with the newly settled. Citizens have a key role to play in building connections between newer immigrants and older residents, helping to reshape the boundaries of "us" and "them" in creating inclusive communities.[62]

---

[60] See the Welcoming America website at www.welcomingamerica.org/
[61] "Welcoming Standard," available from the Welcoming America website, p. 5. For more on these resources see: www.welcomingamerica.org/tags/welcoming-standard.
[62] There are many aspects to the welcoming standards on best practice, but importantly these include advice concerning communications. For instance, partnership programs prioritize positive

There is much more to say about citizens' obligations to bring about more just arrangements for people on the move. Citizens have general obligations to support institutions and organizations that have credible prospects for bringing about justice. Here I have focused on local obligations that give expression to some of our justice commitments, namely to build inclusive communities.

8   Addressing the Objections

Recall the objections that I introduced earlier, now briefly summarized again.

Objection 1: Ordinary people will not elect (and cannot be expected to elect) office holders who support and sustain policies necessary for a legitimate state system.

Objection 2: Over the last few decades, immigration has been bad for local (that is, state-level) justice.

Objection 3: There would be no scope for self-determination under my vision of what a legitimate state system requires.

Objection 4: No organization would have proper authority to enforce any requirements or policies that best align with a legitimate state system.

Objection 5: An account that gives a prominent place to human rights practice cannot be relied on to deliver migration justice, given that respect for human rights is waning.

What strategies are available to disarm these objections? There are several. The first involves challenging the so-called evidence. Has immigration been bad for justice in communities? Does it undermine democracy by increasing intolerance, civic tensions, polarization, and so forth? It is hard to deny that politicians have been whipping up a frenzy of animosity toward immigrants for their own political advantage, as we saw in previous chapters. Politicians have been keen to blur fact and fiction. But, as we note from studying the Compact, states and their leaders have obligations to promote evidence-based dialogue, so in fact obligations to ensure a well-informed, evidence-based, public discourse can transpire.[63] We have also seen that citizens often hold many inaccurate and biased views about migrants and that, again, there

---

messaging, communicating community-wide benefits for all residents from immigrant inclusion and a welcoming culture.

[63] It is hard to separate the ways in which manipulation of popular sentiment has been harnessed for political advantage from the facts. Also, not insignificant is the role of companies such as Cambridge Analytica, not to mention the interests of other states that have their own reasons to spread discord.

are important responsibilities to correct this misinformation and manage people's ethnocentric tendencies.

So, when objectors make claims about how migration has been bad for local justice, we need to examine the context in which the so-called empirical support for such views has arisen. We should also look at any contrary evidence that can be brought to bear that raises doubts about such views as well. So, for instance, many assumptions are made in the cluster of objections that bad effects are attributable to increased migration. When we reflect on salient histories and empirical evidence, we realize some of these assumptions must be false. For instance, while some of the ethnocentric dynamics concerning migrants triggering perceived threat levels may exist,[64] these tendencies can be, and have been successfully managed through innovative programs and positive messaging.[65] All nations contain citizens who migrated from some other place but whose credentials as a citizen are now beyond reproach. We should be skeptical about arguments that suggest migrants are necessarily a threat to justice within communities, since who we consider part of our community is malleable. Indeed, the work of many NGOs that aim to create inclusive communities deserves more prominence and I highlighted the work of Welcoming America and the Sanctuary City Social Movement in this regard. And we have obligations to participate in the welcoming process to create the kinds of inclusive communities that create space for newcomers, and recognition of everyone's valuable contributions. Citizens operating in local contexts have important obligations to help governments manage people's ethnocentric inclinations in ways that create communities conducive to harmonious living.

So much for objection 2. What about some of the others? Now that we understand core features of the Compact, it can also help address several other challenges, such as objection 4. The Compact shows how the proper authority for implementing the framework can be generated. Recall that the authority rests on "its consensual nature, credibility, collective ownership, joint implementation, follow-up and review."[66] This seems to me an

---

[64] As Jonathan Haidt maintains in "When and Why Nationalism Beats Globalism," *The American Interest*, 12 (1), 2016, available at: www.the-american-interest.com/2016/07/10/when-and-why-nationalism-beats-globalism/

[65] For the important role communication strategies can play in motivating a widening sense of citizenship, see for instance, John David Cameron "Communicating Cosmopolitanism and Motivating Global Citizenship" *Political Studies*, 66 (3) (2018): 718–734. See also material from the Welcoming America website for more resources.

[66] IOM, "The Global Compact," 4.

excellent way of locating and describing the source of the authority the framework enjoys. The fact that we have agreed to implement, follow up, and hold each other to account for delivering on the terms of the agreement, constitutes a clear explanation of the source of the authority. It also grounds the very good reasons we have to follow through on our promises. There is no great mystery where the authority can come from then: it can arise from our own promise making and the fact that justice generally requires us to keep our promises.

The Compact, suitably supplemented with mechanisms for requiring accountability on the determination of migrants' rights, can form the main elements for a constellation of international arrangements aimed at securing justice for people on the move. Given this constellation, we can also clarify how there is adequate scope for self-determination, and so address objection 3, as I explained in Section 6, showing just how a state can commit to an international initiative and retain ample space for meaningful self-determination.

In addition, the fact that 85 percent of states have adopted the Compact is at least one kind of rather compelling answer to the worry that states will not be inclined to bring into being the kind of institutional architecture required for a legitimate state system. One powerful answer to objection 1 is that in the height of all these so-called new rampant anti-immigrant sentiments, 85 percent of nations have adopted a convention that makes significant progress toward arrangements that would reduce migration injustice. We have huge support from the world's peoples to make progress in the direction of migration justice.

What are we to make of the fifth objection? We can respond to it in several ways. First, we can acknowledge that today there are important threats to human rights. There are threats that arise because of weakened democratic institutions, the rise of authoritarian leaders, increased economic and social inequality, climate change, shifting geopolitical forces, and the like. However, threats to human rights are ever-present, and even when human rights seem secure, things can change quite quickly. Poverty and disadvantage can place many rights at risk, and given that we live in a changing world where the threat of natural and human-induced disasters always exists, human rights are always potentially at risk.

Furthermore, even if there has been some backsliding on human rights in recent years, the general trajectory over the last seventy years has been positive.[67] The main way in which human rights principles are

---

[67] For some evidence substantiating that claim, see Ann Marie Clark and Kathryn Sikkink, "Informative Effects and Human Rights Data: Is the Good News about Increased Human Rights

implemented in practice is via UN treaties. There have also been some important international conferences that have given rise to impressive international guidelines and plans for actions on issues such as women's rights, reproductive rights, and sustainable development.[68] And as we saw in Section 4 on the Compact, conferences in New York and Marrakech, which paved the way for the Compact, have produced some important commitments and plans of action on migration.

Of course, there is much room for improvement. States are selective in the parts they wish to focus on. Progress may well be slow. However, "one need only look back to see that there is indeed a path being forged."[69] And important steps are being taken all the time, even in a context where some backsliding is happening. For instance, European Union foreign ministers recently unanimously supported the idea of introducing sanctions on human rights violators, such as asset freezes and travel bans on those guilty of such violations.[70]

Furthermore, as Kathryn Sikkink notes, to assess progress we need to examine human rights on an issue-by-issue basis. Trying to make accurate general statements about all human rights is impossible.[71] Within each issue area, she envisions a spectrum of progress ranging from none to complete.[72] There can be both forward and backward movement on this continuum. Like all human creations, human rights institutions need care and attention. So, pretty much all of what we might consider to be progress on human rights exists "in a context where further improvements need to be made ... Human rights progress is always a process and never an endpoint. Moreover, it is a process that can be reversed, that has often

---

Information Bad News for Human Rights Measures?" *Human Rights Quarterly*, 35 (3) (2013): 539–568. It is worth noting that the effectiveness of human rights treaties can also vary greatly depending on the strength of civil society. See, for instance, Oona Hathaway, "Do Human Rights Treaties Make a Difference?," *Yale Law Journal*, 111 8(2) (2002): 1935–2042; and Emilie M. Hafner-Burton and Kiyotery Tsutsui, "Human Rights in a Globalizing World: The Paradox of Empty Promises," *American Journal of Sociology*, 110 (5) (2005): 1373–1411.

[68] See, for instance, Elisabeth Jay Friedman, Kathryn Hochstetler, and Ann Marie Clark, *Sovereignty, Democracy, and Global Civil Society: State-Society Relations at UN World Conferences* (Albany, NY: SUNY Press, 2005).

[69] S. Ilgu Ozler, "The Universal Declaration of Human Rights at Seventy: Progress and Challenges" *Ethics and International Affairs*, December 7, 2018, 10.

[70] "Fighting back: EU sanctions for human rights violations and corruption" *Transparency International*. December 3, 2018 available at: https://voices.transparency.org/fighting-back-eu-sanctions-for-human-rights-violations-and-corruption-f945548o0fe5e

[71] Kathryn Sikkink, *Evidence for Hope: Making Human Rights Work in the 21st Century* (Princeton University Press, 2017), 227–228.

[72] Ibid.

been reversed. Vigilance is necessary to sustain human rights progress and prevent retrogression."[73]

Interestingly, as much research shows, progress on human rights is most impressive in places where there are both strong regional human rights institutions and robust social movements.[74] Domestic human rights advocates continue to be indispensable in the struggle to progress the human rights agenda. However, "international and regional human rights institutions, transnational human rights networks, and the foreign policies of democratic states, both in the North and in the South"[75] can support domestic human rights advocates at many points.

Like Sikkink, I believe that human rights will remain a discourse that can effectively mobilize "domestic and international publics."[76] Human rights movements are at least among the most effective and legitimate emancipatory practices capable of promoting human well-being. We have learned that progress on human rights takes time. In evaluating progress, we need to look back over decades rather than any shorter time frame. And therefore, we should not be discouraged by some apparent recent setbacks.

9   Conclusions

As I argued in this chapter, while the Compact is an important beginning, it fails to offer sufficient progressive guidance on the issue of whether states should be more generous in their admissions policies. I argued that a legitimate state system must include rights to a fair process for determining migrants' rights and states must be held accountable for the reasoning they deploy in determining migrants' rights. I argued that these arrangements would result in more open and transparent processes for admission and are expected to lead to an opening of borders, though there would still be important ways in which states could plausibly restrict the numbers of new members and have reasonable control over the selection process. My position might be characterized as a human rights oriented middle ground between the positions of those who advocate for open borders and their critics.

I also argued that citizens are all too often biased against immigrants and that the state has many obligations to correct for this bias and the false beliefs on which the bias often rests. They also have important responsibilities to manage ethnocentrism in more constructive ways. In all of these responsibilities, the work of international bodies can play a useful role.

---

[73] Sikkink, *Evidence for Hope,* 228.
[74] Ibid., 233; Also, Hathaway, "Do Human Rights Treaties Make a Difference?"; and Hafner-Burton and Tsutsui, "Human Rights in a Globalizing World."
[75] Sikkink, *Evidence for Hope,* 235.   [76] Ibid., 244.

Such bodies can help collect and disseminate reliable information on migration matters necessary to making evidence-based policy decisions. They can also gather examples of innovation and share models of good migration practice in how to meet key migration-related objectives. They can offer technical assistance and advice on how to implement core guidelines and frameworks in challenging settings. They can also provide a framework for states to be able to follow up and review performance and to be held to account for their migration decisions. More generally, they can provide spaces for states to be held accountable for their compliance with migration-related guidelines and requirements.

Also important is how we communicate about migration success and failure, in our attempts to disseminate accurate information. For instance, in an era thoroughly dominated by social media, we need to consider strategies for communicating about migrants in ways that are accurate and compassionate. Perhaps in partnership with communications researchers and professionals, we need to understand the communications landscape better so that citizens are well informed about migration-related matters and are helped to adopt the attitudes necessary to sustain robust human rights practice. International bodies can help facilitate such goals, helping to contribute the expertise and data needed for these tasks. This communication can be an important element in how well we are able to discharge our responsibilities.

No country can address all the migration challenges it faces alone. International cooperation is essential. Fortunately, many states have come to this realization themselves and have taken essential steps in committing to a global framework and key objectives that aim to facilitate safe, orderly, and regular migration. They have acknowledged their shared responsibilities and formally adopted a cooperative approach in seeking to promote the security and prosperity of all states.

With these ground-breaking moves, states have already taken important steps toward a credibly legitimate state system. Recall that in order for states to exercise power defensibly, they must adequately fulfill their human rights commitments, both within the state and beyond. Importantly, this entailed that states have obligations to cooperate in a host of international activities, initiatives, institutions (and so forth) that aim to secure arrangements capable of effective human rights protection. The Compact is an excellent example of such an initiative that states are obligated to support.

As I argued in Chapter 3, we have a contender for a legitimate state system when there is sufficiently good performance on human rights, so that they are respected, protected and fulfilled to a reasonably robust level. When compliance falls sufficiently below internal requirements, there are adequate international measures available to remedy the situation. As well, states make sufficient positive contributions such that the state system functions reasonably effectively in delivering on human rights, with measures in place to deal well with non-compliance.

Over the course of this book, I have argued that our current state system cannot pass a basic legitimacy test yet. I take it that this conclusion is reasonably obvious given the arguments over different chapters (especially Chapter 6 on refugees), so here I remind the reader of just a few points in support of this conclusion starting with some from this chapter. We have not yet begun to follow up on how states are performing in relation to the Compact's objectives, let alone follow up on how well we are managing non-compliance. Also, we do not yet have in place arrangements for securing migrants' rights to a fair process for determining their rights, nor arrangements for states to be held accountable for their reasoning in determining those rights. So, much will depend on states' follow through on the commitments they have made in the Compact and whether they will add procedures relevant to ensuring robust rights to fair processes for determining rights and for being held to account for those determinations. In addition, as we saw in Chapter 6, we currently have large forced migrations with inadequate protective measures for refugees, largely because the original arrangements were not designed to deal with our current scale of displacement (in 2019 evaluated to be over 70 million) and its many causes. As we also saw in Chapter 7, while we have recently forged some agreements that might point us in the direction of fairness for temporary labor migrants, there has not yet been sufficient effort aimed at compliance with the agreements' terms. So, while there are important corrective measures in view, I do not believe that these have yet been implemented to a satisfactory level. All of this might well change in a matter of decades, but we are not there yet.

So, all things considered, the conclusion we must reach is that we do not yet have a legitimate state system, even though we do have in place credible procedures for holding states to account in some areas and some good channels for managing non-compliance.[77] I have also given a clear indication of the direction we must take to make our states and our state system legitimate and capable of supporting justice for people on the move.

---

[77] To remind the reader, our human rights practice provides many channels for raising issues of non-compliance with relevant states and many of these channels have inbuilt sanctions mechanisms. While some of them amount only to the publication of poor performance, naming and shaming, and international condemnation, such sanctions can have remarkable effects over time. At any rate, the periodic review system allied with the Compact provides good opportunities for constructive engagement concerning how to improve performance. This process also affords opportunities for appropriate offers of assistance (technical, financial, capacity-building, and the like). Over time, this process therefore offers considerable potential for progress.

Bibliography

Abizadeh, Arash, "Democratic Theory and Border Coercion: No Right to Unilaterally Control Your Own Borders," *Political Theory*, 36 (1) (2008): 37–65.

The African Union Convention Governing Specific Aspects of Refugee Problems in Africa, available at: www.achpr.org/instruments/refugee-convention/

Alizadeh, Sima, "The 'Waiver' Camouflage, a Closed Door Policy for Travel Ban Countries" blog post, *Think immigration* website, available at: https://slate.com/news-and-politics/2018/06/trump-travel-ban-waiver-process-is-a-sham-two-consular-officers-say.html

Allen, Mike, "Ten biggest national security threats facing U.S.," *Axios AM*, available at: https://fortunascorner.com/2018/08/05/ten-biggest-national-security-threats-facing-u-s/

Altman, Andrew and Christopher Wellman, *A Liberal Theory of International Justice* (Oxford: Oxford University Press, 2009).

Anderson, Benedict, *Imagined Communities: Reflections on the Origin and Spread of Nationalism* (London: Verso, 1991).

Banting, Keith and Will Kymlicka, "Introduction: The Political Sources of Solidarity in Diverse Societies" in Keith Banting and Will Kymlicka (eds.), *The Strains of Commitment: The Political Sources of Solidarity in Diverse Societies* (Oxford: Oxford University Press, 2017): 1–58.

Banting, Keith and Will Kymlicka (eds.), *The Strains of Commitment: The Political Sources of Solidarity in Diverse Societies* (Oxford: Oxford University Press, 2017).

Barnett, Corey, "Hate Groups Targeting Religious Minorities on the Rise in the US," February 24. Based on research done by the Southern Poverty Law Center.

Baron, Amanda and Jose Magana-Salgado with Tom K. Wong, "Economic Contributions by Salvadorean, Honduran and Haitian TPS Holders," *Policy Report*, April 2017.

Barry, Christian and Luara Ferracioli, "On the Rights of Temporary Migrants," *Journal of Legal Studies*, 47 (2018): 149–168.

BBC, "FBI: Spike in US hate crimes for third year in a row," *BBC*, November 13, 2018, available at: www.bbc.com/news/world-us-canada-38781973

"Trump executive order banning refugees," *BBC* January 29, 2017, available at: www.bbc.com/news/world-us-canada-38781973

BBC News, "Calls to stop President's state visit to the UK," *BBC News* January 29, 2017, available at: www.bbc.com/news/world-us-canada-38781973

"Trump's refugee and travel suspension: World reacts," *BBC News*, January 28, 2017, available at: www.bbc.com/news/world-us-canada-38781973

"Windrush: Sixty-three people may have been wrongly removed," *BBC News*, May 15, 2018, available at: www.bbc.com/news/uk-politics-44131136

Begum, Rothna and Human Rights Watch, "I Already Bought You: Abuse and Exploitation of Female Migrant Domestic Workers in the United Arab Emirates" October 22, 2014, available from the *Human Rights Watch* website at www.hrw.org

Beitz, Charles, *The Idea of Human Rights* (Oxford: Oxford University Press, 2009).

Bell, Daniel and N. Piper "Justice for Migrant Workers? The Case of Foreign Domestic Workers in Hong Kong and Singapore" in Will Kymlicka and H Baogang (eds.), *Multiculturalism in Asia* (Oxford: Oxford University Press, 2005): 196–222.

Bergen, Peter, *United States of Jihad: Investigating America's Homegrown Terrorists* (Crown Publishing Group, 2016).

Bertram, Christopher, *Do States Have the Right to Exclude Immigrants?* (Cambridge: Polity, 2018).

Betts, Alex, *Survival Migration: Failed Governance and the Crisis of Displacement* (Ithaca, NY: Cornell University Press, 2013).

Betts, Alex and Paul Collier, "Help Refugees Help Themselves: Let Displaced Syrians Join the Labor Market," *Foreign Affairs*, September 11, 2015.

Refuge: Rethinking Refugee Policy in a Changing World (New York: Oxford University Press, 2017).

Bhagavan, Manu, "Minority Report: Illiberalism, Intolerance, and the Threat to International Society," *Raisina Files*, January 2018, 42–43.

Bocquet-Appel, Jean-Pierre, "When the World's Population Took Off: The Springboard of the Neolithic Demographic Transition," *Science*, 333 (July 29, 2011): 560–561.

Bradley, Megan, "Unresolved and Unresolvable? Tensions in the Refugee Regime," *Ethics and International Affairs*, 33 (1) (2019): 45–56.

Brill, Steven, "Is America any safer?" *The Atlantic*, September 2016.

Brinkhurt-Cuff, Charlie, Martin Chulov, and Saeed Kamali Dehhan, "Muslim-majority countries show anger at Trump travel ban," *The Guardian*, January 30, 2017.

Brock, Gillian, "Liberal Nationalism versus Cosmopolitanism: Locating the Disputes," *Public Affairs Quarterly, 16*, 307–327, 2002.

"Needs and Global Justice" in Soran Reader (ed.), *The Philosophy of Need* (Cambridge: Cambridge University Press, 2005), pp. 51–72.

Global Justice: A Cosmopolitan Account (Oxford: Oxford University Press, 2009).

(ed.), *Cosmopolitanism versus Non-cosmopolitanism: Critiques, Defenses, Reconceptualizations* (Oxford: Oxford University Press, 2013).

"Global Poverty, Decent Work, and Remedial Responsibilities: What the Developed World Owes to the Developing World and Why" in Diana Meyers (ed.), *Poverty, Coercion and Human Rights* (New York: Oxford University Press, 2014), pp. 119–145.

"Addressing the refugee crisis in Europe," talk presented at the *American Philosophical Association, Pacific Division Meetings* (2017).

Brock, Gillian and Michael Blake, *Debating Brain Drain: May Governments Restrict Emigration?* (Oxford: Oxford University Press, 2015).

Brock, Gillian and Nicole Hassoun, "Distance, Moral Relevance of" in Hugh LaFollette (ed.), *The International Encyclopedia of Ethics* (Malden, MA: Blackwell, 2013), 1418–1426.

Brown, D. E., *Hierarchy, History, and Human Nature: The Social Origins of Historical Consciousness* (Tucson, AZ: University of Arizona Press, 1988).

Buchanan, Allen, *Justice, Legitimacy, and Self-Determination: Moral Foundations for International Law* (Oxford: Oxford University Press, 2004).

Buchanan, Allen and Robert Keohane, "The Legitimacy of Global Governance Institutions," *Ethics and International Affairs*, 20(4) (2006): 405–437.

Cadwalladr, Carole, "Cambridge Analytica has gone. But what has it left in its wake?" *The Guardian*, May 6, 2018.

Cameron, John David, "Communicating Cosmopolitanism and Motivating Global Citizenship," *Political Studies*, 66 (3) (2018): 718–734.

Campbell, David, *Writing Security: United States Foreign Policy and the Politics of Identity* (Minneapolis, MN: University of Minnesota Press, 1998).

Carens, Joseph, *The Ethics of Immigration* (Oxford: Oxford University Press, 2013).

The Cartagena Declaration on Refugees, available at: www.unhcr.org/about-us/background/45dc19084/cartagena-declaration-refugees-adopted-colloquium-international-protection.html

Center for American Progress website, "The Facts on Immigration Today: 2017 Edition," *Center for American Progress website*, available at: www.american progress.org/issues/immigration/reports/2017/04/20/430736/facts-immigra tion-today-2017-edition/

Center for American Progress and Michael Nicholson, "Some Facts on Immigration Today: 2017 Edition from the Center for American Progress," available at: www.americanprogress.org/issues/immigration/reports/2017/04/20/430736/facts-immigration-today-2017-edition/

Chalabi, Mona, "How bad is US gun violence? These charts show the scale of the problem," *The Guardian*, October 5, 2017, available at: www.theguardian.com/us-news/2017/oct/05/us-gun-violence-charts-data

Chamberlain, Muriel E., *The Scramble for Africa* (London: Longman, 1999).

Chang, Howard, "Liberal Ideals and Political Feasibility: Guest-Worker Programs as Second-Best Policies," *North Carolina Journal of International Law and Commercial Regulation* 27 (2002): 465–481.

Chemerinsky, Erwin, *Constitutional Law: 2018 Case Supplement* (New York: Wolters Kluwer Law and Business, 2018).

Chen, Michelle, "Donald Trump's rise has coincided with an explosion of hate groups," *The Nation*, March 24, 2017.

Choksi, Niraj, "Trump voters driven by fear of losing status, not economic anxiety, study finds," *New York Times*, April 24, 2018.

Chua, Amy, *Political Tribes: Group Instinct and the Fate of Nations* (London: Bloomsbury, 2018).

   Invited talk at the Carnegie Centre on "Political Tribes: Group Instinct and the Fate of Nations," available from the Carnegie Centre website at: www.youtube.com/watch?v=6FSMoqJ5mNM

City of Sanctuary, available at: https://cityofsanctuary.org/

Clack, T., *Ancestral Roots: Modern Living and Human Evolution* (New York: Macmillan, 2009).

Clark, Ann Marie and Kathryn Sikkink, "Informative Effects and Human Rights Data: Is the Good News about Increased Human Rights Information Bad News for Human Rights Measures?" *Human Rights Quarterly*, 35 (3) (2013): 539–568.

Clemens, Michael, Global Skill Partnerships: A Proposal for Technical Training in a Mobile World," *IZA Journal of Labor Policy*, 4 (2) (2015), 1–18.

Clemens, Michael, Cindy Huang, and Jimmy Graham, *The Economic and Fiscal Effects of Granting Refugees Formal Labor Market Access* (Washington, DC: Center for Global Development, October 2018).

Clemens, Michael, Cindy Huang, Jimmy Graham, and K. Gough, *Migration Is What You Make It: Seven Policy Decisions That Turned Challenges into Opportunities* (Washington, DC: Center for Global Development, 2018).

Cohen, Robin and Nicholas Van Hear, "Visions of Refugia: Territorial and Transnational Solutions to Mass Displacement," *Planning Theory and Practice*, 18:3 (2017): 494–504.

Cohn, D' Vera and Jeffrey Passel, "More than 100 000 Haitian and Central American immigrants face decision on their status in the U.S.," *Pew Research Center* (November 8, 2017), available at: www.pewresearch.org/fact-tank/2017/11/08/more-than-100000-haitian-and-central-american-immigrants-face-decision-on-their-status-in-the-u-s/

Cole, Phillip, *Philosophies of Exclusion: Liberal Political Theory and Immigration* (Edinburgh: Edinburgh University Press, 2000).

Collins, Laura, "Pervasive Myths about Immigrants," blog post on *George W Bush Institute website*, Issue 09, Winter 2018, available at: www.bushcenter.org/catalyst/immigration/collins-immigration-myths.html

Cranston, Maurice, *What Are Human Rights?* (London: Bodley Head, 1973).

Crawley, Heaven, "Migration: Refugee Economics," *Nature*, 544, 26–27, 6 April 2017.

Crawley, Heaven, et al., Are Jobs the Answer? (video) available at: www.odi.org/events/4467-refugees-are-jobs-answer

Darling, Jonathan, Craig Barnett, and Sarah Eldridge, "City of Sanctuary – a UK initiative for hospitality," *Urban Displacement, Forced Migration Review*, 34,

February 2010, available at: www.fmreview.org/sites/fmr/files/.../en/urban.../darling-barnet-eldridge.pdf

Davies, Stephen, "The Social Conditions for Sustainable Technological Innovation" in Berys Gaut and Mathew Kieran (eds.), *Creativity and Philosophy* (London: Routledge, 2018), pp. 251–269.

Devereaux, Ryan, "Ignoring violence in El Salvador, Trump ends years of special protective status for immigrants" *The Intercept*, available at: https://theintercept.com/2018/01/08/el-salvador-immigration-tps-trump/

Dunbar, Robin, *The Human Story* (London: Faber and Faber, 2004).

The Economist, "A fearful welcome: How will El Salvador cope with deportees from America?" *The Economist*, January 2018.

Elimination of All Forms of Intolerance and Discrimination Based on Religion, Resolution 1997/18, and the accompanying declaration of the same name, Article (3(c)), available at: http://hrlibrary.umn.edu/UN/1997/Res018.html

Ellis, Ralph, Sara Mazloumsaki, and Artemis Moshtaghian, "Iran to take 'reciprocal measures' after Trump's immigration order," *CNN*, January 29, 2017.

Erickson, Amanda, "Here's how the world is responding to Trump's ban on refugees, travelers from 7 Muslim nations," *The Washington Post*, January 29, 2017.

Facchini, Giovanni and Anna Mayda, "From Individual Attitudes toward Migrants to Migration Policy Outcomes: Theory and Evidence," *Economic Policy*, 23 (56) (2008): 651–713.

Farbenblum, Bassina, "Governance of Migrant Worker Recruitment: A Rights-Based Framework for Countries of Origin," *Asian Journal of International Law*, 7 (2017): 152–184.

Ferracioli, Luara, "Family Migration Schemes and Liberal Neutrality," *Journal of Moral Philosophy*, 13 (2016): 553–575.

"International Migration and Human Rights" in Chris Brown and Robyn Eckersley (eds.), *The Oxford Handbook of International Political Theory* (Oxford: Oxford University Press, 2018), 520–532.

Fiddian-Qasmiyeh, Elena, Gil Loescher, Katy Long, and Nando Sigona, "Introduction: Refugee and Forced Migration Studies in Transition" in Elena Fiddian-Qasmiyeh, Gil Loescher, Katy Long, and Nando Sigona (eds.), *The Oxford Handbook of Refugee and Forced Migration Studies* (Oxford: Oxford University Press, 2014, 2014): 1–19.

Fine, Sarah and Lea Ypi (eds.), *Migration in Political Theory* (Oxford: Oxford University Press, 2016).

Fisher, Michael, *Migration: A World History* (Oxford University Press, 2014).

Flagg, Anna, "The myth of the criminal immigrant" *New York Times*, March 30, 2018.

Foged, Mette and Giovanni Peri, "Immigrants' Effects on Native Workers: New Analysis on Longitudinal Data," *American Economic Journal: Applied Economics*, 8 (2) (2016): 1–34.

Freeman, Gary, Randall Hansen, and David Leal, "Introduction: Immigration and Public Opinion in Liberal Democracies" in Gary Freeman, Randall Hansen, and David Leal (eds.), *Immigration and Public Opinion in Liberal Democracies* (New York: Routledge, 2013): 1–18.

Friedman, Elisabeth Jay, Kathryn Hochstetler, and Ann Marie Clark, *Sovereignty, Democracy, and Global Civil Society: State-Society Relations at UN World Conferences* (Albany, NY: SUNY Press, 2005).

Friedman, Uri, "Where America's terrorists actually come from," *The Atlantic*, January 30, 2017, Available at: www.theatlantic.com/international/archive/2017/01/trump-immigration-ban-terrorism/514361/

Frost, D., "Islamophobia: Examining Causal Links between the Media and 'Race Hate' from 'Below'," *International Journal of Sociology and Social Policy*, 28 (11/12) (2008): 564–578.

Gibney, Matthew, "Refugees and Justice between States," *European Journal of Political Theory*, 14 (2015): 448–463.

The Ethics and Politics of Asylum: Liberal Democracy and the Response to Refugees (Cambridge: Cambridge University Press, 2004).

"The Global Compact for Safe, Orderly and Regular Migration," available at: www.iom.int/global-compact-migration

Griffin, James, *On Human Rights* (Oxford: Oxford University Press, 2008).

Hafner-Burton, Emilie M. and Kiyotery Tsutsui, "Human Rights in a Globalizing World: The Paradox of Empty Promises," *American Journal of Sociology*, 110 (5) (2005): 1373–1411.

Haidt, Jonathan, "When and why nationalism beats globalism," *The American Interest*, 12 (1), (2016): available at: www.the-american-interest.com/2016/07/10/when-and-why-nationalism-beats-globalism/

Hansen, Randall, *Citizenship and Immigration in Postwar Britain* (Oxford: Oxford University Press, 2000).

Harroff-Tavel, Helene and Alix Nasri, "*Trapped and tricked*" (Geneva: International Labour Organization, 2013).

Hartman, Todd, Benjamin Newman, and Scott Bell, "Decoding Prejudice toward Hispanics: Group Cues and Public Reactions to Threatening Immigrant Behavior," *Political Behavior*, 36 (1) (2014): 143–163.

Hassoun, Nicole, *Globalization and Global Justice* (Cambridge: Cambridge University Press, 2012).

"Human Rights and the Minimally Good Life," *Res Philosophica*, 90 (3) (2013): 413–438.

Extending Access to Essential Medicine: The Global Health Impact Project (Oxford: Oxford University Press, forthcoming in 2020).

Hathaway, Oona, "Do Human Rights Treaties Make a Difference?," *Yale Law Journal*, 111 8(2) (2002): 1935–2042.

Henley, Jon, "Videos tweeted by Trump: Where are they from and what do they show?" *The Guardian*, November 30, 2017.

Hersh, M. A., "Terrorism, Human Rights and Ethics: A Modelling Approach," *Journal of Socialomics*, 5 (2) (2016) 148.

Heuer, Richard, *Psychology of Intelligence Analysis* (Washington, DC: Center for the Study of Intelligence Analysis, 1999).

Hidalgo, Javier, "Resistance to Unjust Immigration Restrictions," *The Journal of Political Philosophy*, 23 (4) (2015): 450–470.

"The Duty to Disobey Immigration Law," *Moral Philosophy and Politics*, 3 (2) (2016): 165–186.

"The Case for the International Governance of Immigration," *International Theory*, 8 (1) (2016): 140–170.

Hochschild, Arlie, *Strangers in Their Own Land: Anger and Mourning on the American Right* (New York: The New Press, 2016).

Hoffman, Paul, "Human Rights and Terrorism," *Human Rights Quarterly*, 26 (4) (2004): 932–955.

Huang, Cindy, *Global Business and Refugee Crises: A Framework for Sustainable Engagement*. The Tent Foundation and the Center for Global Development, 2017.

Huang, Cindy and Jimmy Graham, "Are Refugees Located Near Urban Job Opportunities?" Center for Global Development, Policy Brief, June 18, 2018.

Huang, Cindy, S. Charles, L. Post, K. Gough, *Tackling the Realities of Protracted Displacement: Case Studies on What's Working and Where We Can Do Better* (Washington, DC: The Center for Global Development and the International Rescue Committee, 2018).

Hublin, J. J., A. Ben-Ncer, et al., "New Fossils from Jebel Irhoud, Morocco and the Pan-African Origin of Homo Sapiens," *Nature*, 546 (2017): 289–292.

Heuer, Richard, *Psychology of Intelligence Analysis* (Washington, DC: Center for the Study of Intelligence Analysis, 1999).

Hughes, Roland, "Trump's America: Are things as bad as he says?," *BBC News*, 9 February, 2017, available at: www.bbc.com/news/world-us-canada-38911708

Human Rights Watch, World Reports, especially "United States: Events of 2017" available at the Human Rights Watch website: www.hrw.org/world-report/2018/country-chapters/united-states

Ignatieff, Michael, *Human Rights as Politics and Idolatry* (Princeton, NJ: Princeton University Press, 2001).

The Independent, "Theresa May finally passes judgment on Donald Trump's immigration ban," *The Independent*, January 29, 2107.

International Labour Organization, "Labour Migration (Arab States)," www.ilo.org

ILO, *Global Employment Trends* (Geneva: ILO, 2012).

Migration and International Human Rights Law: A Practitioners' Guide. (Geneva: ICJ, 2014).

"General Principles and Operational Guidelines for Fair Recruitment" (Geneva: ILO, 2016), 1, available at: www.ilo.org/global/about-the-ilo/multimedia/maps-and-charts/enhanced/WCMS_626548/lang–en/index.htm

World Employment and Social Outlook – Trends 2018, ILO website.

IOM, "International Organisation for Migration, International Recruitment Integrity System" (Geneva: IOM, 2018), 2, available at: https://iris.iom.int/ *Global Compact for Migration* (GENEVA, IOM, 2018), 2, available at: www.iom.int/global-compact-migration

Iran Ministry of Foreign Affairs, "Statement of the Ministry of Foreign Affairs of the Islamic Republic of Iran," January 28, 2017. 436947.

IRIS, "International Organization for Migration, International Recruitment Integrity System" (Geneva: IOM, 2018), 2, available at: https://iris.iom.int/

Jacobsen, Karen, "Can Refugees Benefit the State? Refugee Resources and African Statebuilding," *Journal of Modern African Studies*, 40 (4) (2002): 577–596.

"*Livelihoods and Forced Migration*" in Elena Fiddian-Qasmiyeh, Gil Loescher, Katy Long, and Nando Sigona, *The Oxford Handbook of Refugee and Forced Migration Studies* (Oxford: Oxford University Press, 2014), 99–110.

Jenkins, Brian Michael, "Why a travel restriction won't stop terrorism at Home," The RAND blog, Rand Corporation, 2017, available at: www.rand.org/blog/2017/02/why-a-travel-restriction-wont-stop-terrorism-at-home.html

Johnson, Jenna, "Trump calls for 'total and complete shutdown of Muslims entering the United States'," *Washington Post*, December 7, 2015.

"Donald Trump is expanding his Muslim ban, not rolling it back" *Washington Post*, July 24, 2016, available at: www.washingtonpost.com/news/post-politics/wp/2016/07/24/donald-trump-is-expanding-his-muslim-ban-not-rolling-it-back/?noredirect=on&utm_term=.29f2c77512f3

Johnson, Jenna and Abigail Hauslohner, "'I think Islam hates us': A timeline of Trump's comments about Islam and Muslims," *Washington Post*, May 20, 2017.

Jones, Robert, Daniel Cox, and Rachel Lienesch, "Beyond economic: Fears of cultural displacement pushed the white working class to Trump," *Public Religion Research Institute/The Atlantic Report*. PRRI, 2017.

Kagan, Michael "What We Talk about When We Talk about Sanctuary Cities," *UC Davis Law Review*, 52 (2018): 391–406.

Khan, Yasmin, *The Great Partition: The Making of India and Pakistan* (New Haven, CT: Yale University Press, 2007).

Kinder, Donald and Cindy Kam, *Us against Them: Ethnocentric Foundations of American Opinion* (Chicago: University of Chicago Press, 2009).

Klein, R. G., *The Human Career* (Chicago: University of Chicago Press, 2009).

Koppel, Ted, *Lights Out: A Cyberattack, a Nation Unprepared, Surviving the Aftermath* (New York: Penguin Random House, 2015).

Koser, Khalid, *International Migration: A Very Short Introduction* (Oxford: Oxford University Press, 2007).

Kymlicka, Will, "Solidarity in Diverse Societies: Beyond Neoliberal Multiculturalism and Welfare Chauvinism," *Comparative Migration Studies*, 3 (17) (2015): 1–19.

Landman, Todd, *Studying Human Rights* (London: Routledge, 2006).

Langlois, S., "Traditions: Social" in Neil J. Smelser and Paul B. Baltes (eds.), *International Encyclopedia of the Social & Behavioral Sciences* (Oxford: Pergamon, 2001), 15829–15833.

Lean, Nathan, *The Islamophobia Industry: How the Right Manufactures Fear of Muslims* (Pluto, 2012).

Lenard, Patti Tamara, "Why Temporary Labour Migration Is Not a Satisfactory Alternative to Permanent Migration," *Journal of International Political Theory*, 8 (1–2) (2012): 172–183.

Lenard, Patti Tamara and Christine Straehle, "Temporary Labour Migration: Exploitation, Tool of Development, or Both?" *Policy and Society*, 29 (2010): 283–294.

Levin, Sam, "Legitimized in their hatred: A weekend of violence in Trump's America," *The Guardian*, May 31, 2017.

Liebig, Thomas and Jeffrey Mo, "*The Fiscal Impact of Immigration in OECD Countries*" in *International Migration Outlook 2013*, (Paris, France: OECD Publishing, 2013), 125–189.

Lipka, Michael, "Muslims and Islam: Key findings in the US and around the world," *Pew Research Center*, August 9, 2017, available at: www/pewresearch .org/author/mlipka/

Lister, Matthew, "Immigration, Association, and the Family," *Law and Philosophy*, 29 (2010): 717–745.

"Justice and Temporary Labor Migration," *Georgetown Immigration Law Journal*, 29 (2014): 95–123.

"*The Rights of Families and Children at the Border*" in Elizabeth Brake and Lucinda Ferguson (eds.), *Philosophical Foundations of Children's and Family Law* (Oxford: Oxford University Press, 2018), 153–170.

Mangla, Ismat Sarah, "Islam is a 'malignant cancer': The hateful rhetoric of Trump's new national security adviser," *Quartz*, November 19, 2016.

Margalit, Avishai and Joseph Raz, "National Self-Determination," *Journal of Philosophy*, 87 (9) (1990): 439–461.

Martin, Rex *A System of Rights* (Oxford: Clarendon Press, 1993).

The Maytree Foundation, *Practice to Policy: Lessons from Local Leadership on Immigrant Integration* (Toronto: The Maytree Foundation, 2012), available from the *Cities of Migration* website at: http://citiesofmigration.ca/

Mayer, Robert, "Guestworkers and Exploitation," *Review of Politics*, 67 (2005): 311–334.

Mencken, H.L., *In Defense of Women* (London: J. Cape, 1929).

Merry, Sally Engle, *The Seductions of Quantification: Measuring Human Rights, Gender Violence, and Sex Trafficking* (Chicago: University of Chicago, 2016).

Meyerfeld, Jamie, "The Democratic Legacy of the International Criminal Court," *The Fletcher Forum of World Affairs*, 28:2 (2004): 147–156.

Miller, David, *National Responsibility and Global Justice* (Oxford: Oxford University Press, 2007).

Mindock, Clark, "Number of hate crimes surges in year of Trump's election," *The Independent*, November 14, 2017.

Miller, David, *Strangers in Our Midst: The Political Philosophy of Immigration* (Cambridge, MA: Harvard University Press, 2016).

Mithen, Steven, *The Prehistory of the Mind: A Search for the Origins of Art, Religion, and Science* (London: Thames and Hudson, 1996).

After the Ice (Cambridge: Harvard University Press, 2004); N. Roberts, *The Holocene: An Environmental History*, 2nd edition, (Oxford, Blackwell, 1998).

Moore, Margaret, *A Political Theory of Territory* (Oxford: Oxford University Press, 2015).

Motomura, Hiroshi, "Arguing about Sanctuary," *UC Davis Law Review*, 52 (2018): 435–569.

Moyo, Dambisa, *Dead Aid* (New York: Farrar, Strauss and Ciroux, 2009).

Mueller, John, *Overblown: How Politicians and the Terrorism Industry Inflate National Security Threats, and Why We Believe Them* (New York: Free Press, 2006).

Are We Safe Enough? Measuring and Assessing Aviation Security (Elsevier, 2018).

Mueller, John and Mark Stewart, *Chasing Ghosts: The Policing of Terrorism* (Oxford: Oxford University Press, 2015).

Murrow, Edward R., "No one can terrorize a whole nation, unless we are all his accomplices." CBS television broadcast, March 7, 1954.

Mutz, Diana, "Status Threat, Not Economic Hardship, Explains the 2016 Presidential Vote," *PNAS* May 8, 2018 115 (18), E4330–E4339.

Nafziger, James, "The General Admission of Aliens under International Law," *The American Journal of International Law*, 77 (4) (1983): 804–847.

Nakache, Delphine, "Migrant workers and the right to family accompaniment: A case for family rights in international law and in Canada," *International Migration*, March 2018.

Nakamura, David, "Study: White House plan slashes legal immigration rates by 44 percent – 22 million fewer immigrants over a half-century," *Washington Post*, January 29, 2018, available at: www.washingtonpost.com/news/post-politics/wp/2018/01/29/study-white-house-plan-slashes-legal-immigration-rates-by-44-percent-22-million-fewer-immigrants-over-a-half-century/?noredirect=on&utm_term=.7f737410dc06

Napolitano, Janet, *How Safe Are We? Homeland Security since 9/11* (New York: Hachette Book Group, 2019).

New York Declaration. Retrieved from https://refugeesmigrants.un.org/declaration

Newby, Tom, "Refuge: Transforming a broken refugee system – but into what?" *Care Insights*, Development Blog, May 30, 2017, available at: https://insights.careinternational.org.uk/development-blog?start=98

Nickel, James, *Making Sense of Human Rights* (Oxford: Oxford University Press, 2006).

Nixon, Ron, "People from 7 travel-ban nations pose no increased terror risk, report says," *New York Times*, February 25, 2017.

Nowrasteh, Alex, "Post 9/11 America is remarkably safe," *Cato at Liberty* website, available at: www.cato.org/blog/post-911-america-is-remarkably-safe-0

Oberman, Kieran, "Immigration as a Human Right" in Sara Fine and Lea Ypi (eds.), *Migration in Political Theory: The Ethics of Movement and Membership* (Oxford: Oxford University Press, 2016), pp. 32–56.

OHCHR," International Convention on the Elimination of All Forms of Racial Discrimination," available at: www.ohchr.org/en/professionalinterest/pages/cerd.aspx

O'Keefe, J. H. and L. Cordain, "Cardiovascular Disease Resulting from a Diet and Lifestyle at Odds with Our Paleolithic Genome: How to Become a 21st Century Hunter-Gatherer," *Mayo Clinic Proceedings (Review)*, 79 (1) (2004): 101–108.

Ousey, Graham and Charis Kubrin, "Immigration and Crime: Assessing a Contentious Issue," *Annual Review of Criminology* 1(2018): 63–84.

Owen, David, "In Loco Civitatis: On the Normative Basis of the Institution of Refugeehood and Responsibilities for Refugees" in Sarah Fine and Lea Ypi (eds.), *Migration in Political Theory* (Oxford: Oxford University Press, 2016), pp. 269–289.

"Refugees, Fairness and Taking up the Slack," *Moral Philosophy and Politics*, 3 (2) (2016): 141–164.

Ozler, S. Ilgu, "The Universal Declaration of Human Rights at seventy: Progress and challenges," *Ethics and International Affairs*, December 7, 2018, 10.

Pattisson, Pete, "Death toll among Qatar's 2022 World Cup workers revealed," *The Guardian*, December 23, 2014.

"Migrants claim recruiters lured them into forced labour at top Qatar hotel," *The Guardian*, October 29, 2018.

"Revealed: Qatar's World Cup 'slaves'," *The Guardian*, September 25, 2013.

Peri, Giovanni, "The Effect of Immigration on Productivity: Evidence from US States," *Review of Economics and Statistics*, 94 (1) (2012): 348–358.

Peri, Giovanni and Chad Sparber, "Task Specialization, Immigration, and Wages," *American Economic Journal: Applied Economics* 1 (3) (2009): 135–169.

Peter, Fabienne, "Political Legitimacy" in Ed Zalta (ed.), *Stanford Encyclopedia of Philosophy*, (Palo Alto: Stanford, 2016), available at: http://plato.stanford.edu/

Pew Research Center, December 10, 2018, available at: www.pewresearch.org/fact-tank/2018/12/10/many-worldwide-oppose-more-migration-both-into-and-out-of-their-countries/

Poynting, S. and V. Mason, "The Resistible Rise of Islamophobia: Anti-Muslim Racism in the UK and Australia Before 11 September 2001," *Journal of Sociology*, 43 (2007): 61–86.

Reilly, Katie, "Donald Trump on proposed Muslim ban: 'You know my plans'," *Time*, December 21, 2016.

Reuters, "Assad says Trump travel ban targets terrorists, not Syrian people," *Reuters*, February 19, 2017.

"UAE says Trump travel ban an internal affair, most Muslims unaffected," *Reuters*, February 1, 2017.

Revesz, Rachael, "US Islamophobia: Threats and acts of vandalism against mosques double so far in 2017," *The Independent*, March 15, 2017.

Riaz, Maleeha, "A Culture of Slavery: Domestic Workers in the United Arab Emirates," 30 November 2016, *Human Rights Brief,* available at: http://hrbrief.org/2016/11/culture-slavery-domestic-workers-united-arab-emirates/

Risse, Thomas, Stephen Ropp and Kathryn Sikkink (eds.), *The Power of Human Rights: International Norms and Domestic Change* (Cambridge: Cambridge University Press, 2009).

Roberts, Chief Justice John, Supreme Court Syllabus No. 17-965, "Trump, President of the United States, et al.," Argued April 5, 2018 – Decided June 26, 2018.

Ross, David, *Ireland: History of a Nation* (New Lanark: Geddes & Grosset, 2002).

Ruhs, Martin, *The Price of Rights* (Princeton, NJ: Princeton University Press, 2015).

Ruhs, Martin and Philip Martin, "Numbers vs. Rights: Trade-Offs and Guest Worker Programs" *International Migration Review*, 42 (1) (2008): 249–265.

Rumsfeld, Donald, "A new kind of war," *New York Times*, 27 September 2001.

Sands, D. C., C. E. Morris, E. A. Dratz, A. Pilgeram, "Elevating Optimal Human Nutrition to a Central Goal of Plant Breeding and Production of Plant-based Foods," *Plant Science (Review)*, 177 (2009): 377–389.

Scarre, Chris (ed.), *The Human Past: World Prehistory and the Development of Human Societies* (London: Thames and Hudson, 2013), 3rd edition.

"The World Transformed: From Foragers and Farmers to States and Empires" in Chris Scarre (ed.), *The Human Past*, pp. 176–199.

Schotel, Bas, *On the Right of Exclusion: Law, Ethics and Immigration Policy* (Abingdon: Routledge, 2012).

Shacknove, Andrew, "Who Is a Refugee?" *Ethics* 95 (1995): 274–284.

Sikkink, Kathryn, *Evidence for Hope: Making Human Rights Work in the 21st Century* (Princeton, NJ: Princeton University Press, 2017).

Skinner, G., J.-M. Lebrun, and D. Bijwaard, "Global Study Shows Many around the World Increasingly Uncomfortable with Levels of Immigration," available at: www.ipsos.com/en/global-study-shows-many-around-world-increasingly-uncomfortable-levels-immigration

Smith-Spark, Laura, "Report: 600 000 forced labor victims in Middle East," *CNN*, April 9, 2013.

Song, Sarah, *Immigration and Democracy* (New York: Oxford University Press, 2018).

Sotomayor, J., dissenting on *Trump versus Hawaii*, 585 U.S. (2018), No. 17-965, decided June 26, 2018.

Stahl, Jeremy, "The Waiver Process Is Fraud," *Slate*, June 15, 2018, available at: https://slate.com/news-and-politics/2018/06/trump-travel-ban-waiver-process-is-a-sham-two-consular-officers-say.html

Stilz, Anna, "Why Do States Have Territorial Rights?" *International Theory*, 1 (2) (2009): 185–213.

"Occupancy Rights and the Wrong of Removal," *Philosophy and Public Affairs* 41 (4) (2013): 324–356.

"Territorial Rights and National Defense" in Cecile Fabre and Seth Lazar (eds.), *The Morality of Defense in War* (Oxford: Oxford University Press, 2014), 203–228.

"Settlement, Expulsion and Return," *Politics, Philosophy and Economics*, 16(4) (2017): 351–374.

Stringer, Chris, "The Origin and Dispersal of Homo sapiens: Our Current State of Knowledge" in P. Mellars, K. Boyle, O. Bar Yosef, and C. Stringer (eds.), *Rethinking the Human Revolution* (Cambridge: McDonald Institute for Archaeological Research, 2007), 15–20.

Sunstein, Cass, "Terrorism and Probability Neglect," *Journal of Risk and Uncertainty*, 26 (2/3) (2003): 121–136.

Talbot, William, *Which Rights Should Be Universal?* (Oxford: Oxford University Press, 2005).

Timmons, Heather, "Questions US officials couldn't answer about ending 'temporary protected status' for 200 000 people," *Quartz*, January 9, 2018, available at: https://qz.com/1174581/tps-trump-and-dhss-decision-on-el-salvador-immigrants/

"Trump's obsession with immigration is making the US more vulnerable to terrorism," *Quartz*, December 18, 2017.

Trilling, Daniel, "Should we build a wall around North Wales?" *London Review of Books*, 39 (14) (July 13, 2017): 15–18.

Trump versus Hawaii, 585 U.S. (2018), No. 17-965, decided June 26, 2018, 37.

Tuck, Richard, *Natural Rights Theories* (Cambridge: Cambridge University Press, 1978).

Ucak, S., J. Holt, and K. Raman *Another Side to the Story: A Market Assessment of Syrian SMEs in Turkey* (New York, NY: Building Markets, 2017).

United Nations Committee on Migrant Workers, *General Comment No. 1 on Migrant Domestic Workers*, UN Doc CMW/C/GC/1 (2011).

Walsh, James and James Piazza, "Why Respecting Physical Integrity Rights Reduces Terrorism," *Comparative Political Studies*, 43 (5) (2010): 551–577.

Walter, Christian, "Religion or Belief, Freedom of, International Protection," *Oxford Public International Law*, Max Planck Encyclopedia of International Law, 2008.

Walzer, Michael, *Spheres of Justice* (New York: Basic Books, 1983).

Welcoming America, available at: www.welcomingamerica.org/

Wellman, Christopher Heath and Phillip Cole, *Debating the Ethics of Immigration: Is there a Right to Exclude?* (New York: Oxford University Press, 2011).

Wells, S., *The Journey of Man: A Genetic Odyssey* (New York: Random House, 2002).

World Bank, *World Development Report: Jobs.* (Washington, DC: World Bank, 2019).

Yaghmanian, Behzad, "How not to fix the refugee crisis – A response to 'refuge,'" *Refugees Deeply*, April 20, 2017, available at: www.newsdeeply.com/refugees/community/2017/04/20/how-not-to-fix-the-refugee-crisis-a-response-to-refuge

York, Chris, "Britain First denounced by every major Christian denomination in the UK," *The Huffington Post*, January 30, 2016.

Ypi, Lea, "*Cosmopolitanism without if and without but*" in Gillian Brock (ed.)., *Cosmopolitanism versus Non-cosmopolitanism: Critiques, Defenses, Reconceptualizations* (Oxford, Oxford University Press, 2013), 75–91.

Zurcher, Anthony, "What Trump team has said about Islam," *BBC*, February 7, 2017.

Index

243